An Immigrant Neighborhood

An Immigrant Neighborhood

*Interethnic and Interracial Encounters
in New York before 1930*

Shirley J. Yee

TEMPLE UNIVERSITY PRESS
PHILADELPHIA

TEMPLE UNIVERSITY PRESS
Philadelphia, Pennsylvania 19122
www.temple.edu/tempress

Library of Congress Cataloging-in-Publication Data

Yee, Shirley J., 1959–
    An immigrant neighborhood : interethnic and interracial encounters in New York
before 1930 / Shirley J. Yee.
        p. cm.
    Includes bibliographical references and index.
    ISBN 978-1-59213-127-3 (cloth : alk. paper) — ISBN 978-1-59213-128-0 (pbk. :
alk. paper) — ISBN 978-1-59213-129-7 (e-book)   1. Immigrants—New York (State)—
New York—History—20th century.   2. Ethnic neighborhoods—New York (State)—New
York—History—20th century.   3. New York (N.Y.)—Race relations—History—20th
century.   4. New York (N.Y.)—Social conditions—20th century.   I. Title.
    F128.9.A1.Y44 2011
    305.8009747—dc22

                                                                    2011002610

∞ The paper used in this publication meets the requirements of the American National
Standard for Information Sciences—Permanence of Paper for Printed Library Materials,
ANSI Z39.48-1992

Printed in the United States of America

2   4   6   8   9   7   5   3   1

In memory of Kathryn Moy
and James and Barbara Wong

Contents

Acknowledgments   ix

Introduction   1

1   Forming Households, Families, and Communities   29

2   Building Commercial Relations   54

3   Sustaining Life and Caring for the Dead   77

4   Mixing with the Sinners: *The Anti-vice Movement*   104

5   On (Un)Common Ground: *Religious Politics in Settlements and Missions*   138

Conclusion   173

Notes   179

Bibliography   215

Index   239

Illustrations follow page 122

Acknowledgments

It has always amazed me how so many people from so many different places can contribute to a research project. I have had the good fortune to have a number of excellent research assistants over the years: Zakiya Adair, José Díaz, Ileana Howard, Holly Johnson, Sarah Palmer, Karen Rosenberg, and Tania Zapata-García. I thank the wonderful librarians and archivists on both U.S. coasts who have contributed their expertise to the various threads of research that went into this project: Cass Hartnett, government documents librarian at the University of Washington; Robert Fleming, research librarian at Emerson College; the archivists at the National Archives and Records Administration (NARA) in New York City, Columbia University Rare Books Division; and the Chinatown History Museum have been of invaluable assistance. Loring Eutemey and William Sadlier Dinger shared fascinating information about the Eutemey and Naughton families. June Hopkins clarified important details of her grandmother's life. The Royalty Research Fund and the Institute for Ethnic Studies in the United States (IESUS) at the University of Washington provided financial support. Carol Langdon, Virginia Lore, and Elaine Haig-Widner provided good humor and vital staff assistance throughout the long process.

The following colleagues at the University of Washington and elsewhere provided both encouragement and critical review on various aspects of the project: Becky Aanerud, Carolyn Allen, David Allen, Gerald Baldasty, Eileen Boris, Rachel Chapman, Tom Dicke, Gail Dubrow, Kathie Friedman, Angela B. Ginorio, Susan A. Glenn, Michelle Habell-Pallan, Judy Howard, Sue-Ellen Jacobs, Moon-Ho Jung, Joycelyn K. Moody, Sonnet Retman, Caroline Chung Simpson, Kathryn Kish Sklar, and Priscilla Wald. For their support and patience, I offer my heartfelt thanks to Janet Francendese and the Board of Review at Temple University Press.

Friends and family have provided me with love, laughter, and friendship: Carolyn Allen, Peter Arvanitas, Cathana Butler, Diane Eileen, Kathie Friedman, Rachel Hodges, Carla Johnston, Machelle Jones, Reşat Kasaba, Joanie La Russa, J. D. LaSalle, Margaret Lawrence, Jan Penta, Louise Pitell, Eileen Surdez, and the late Vince Surdez. I especially thank Mary P. Travers, who made a special trip to the Queens Public Library to retrieve materials about Chinese truck farmers; Linda Yedlin, who helped me find citations at the last minute; my colleague across the hall, Sasha Welland, for helping me scan materials; and Roberta Gold and Alice Church Cheseborough for their photographic assistance.

I would not have completed this book without the continued support of family members, who have provided constant nurturance and logistical assistance. During my many summer visits to the East Coast, my mother, Audrey W. Yee, drove me to the bus stop so I could commute into Manhattan to conduct my research. After my long day in the city, she picked me up and chatted with me during the short ride home—about family, the city, my work, and, near the end of her life, her health. Our last visit was in July 1998, shortly before she died—before I could fully thank her for her love and unbounded support.

I am especially grateful to Lily and Steven Yee. Not only did they provide excellent company, transportation, and shelter, but they also sustained me with Italian sweet sausage and ribs from Esposito's Meats and Deli in East Hanover, New Jersey. Carrie Ferenchiak and Nancy Peters Dolan have always welcomed me home and have kept me connected to my New Jersey roots.

As children often do, Melis, Alexander, Audrey, Matthew, Rebecca, and Dylan remind me of what is important in life just by being themselves. I hope that together they will contribute much to their generation.

Finally, I thank Diane Eileen, who put up with this project for longer than I want to admit and whose unwavering love and support inspire me every day.

An Immigrant Neighborhood

Introduction

In the winter of 1877, a group of mourners gathered in a dimly lit funeral parlor on Pearl Street in lower Manhattan to pay their last respects to Ah Fung (sometimes referred to as Ah Lung), a Chinese man who had been brutally murdered in his Lower East Side apartment. He had died of "ghastly wounds" at Bellevue Hospital after living for eighty hours with his brain exposed.[1] Both Irish and Chinese people attended the funeral, including Mrs. Ah Fung, a woman of Irish ancestry. The *New York World* described the mixed gathering as "something unprecedented . . . [that gave] a good idea of the cosmopolitan character of the city."[2] Given the well-publicized history of anti-Chinese hostility among the Irish working class, it is not surprising that the editors viewed the Ah Fung funeral as an anomaly.[3]

The details of Ah Fung's life are murky. The *World* described him as a laundry worker, while the *New York Times* reported that he had eked out a living making cigars and cigarettes with a Chinese man, Tung Ha, also known as "Peter Johnson," and his white wife, Theresa.[4] The three lived at 17 Forsyth Street, located in an ethnically mixed neighborhood across from the future site of the Manhattan Bridge. For unknown reasons, the household had not included Ah Fung's wife; the two apparently had been living apart for several months before the attack.[5]

Like other working-class immigrant communities, the Chinese called on their local mutual aid societies to help cover the funeral costs.[6]

Members of the Ene E. Jong, a Chinese burial society, raised $200 for the funeral and burial expenses. But the dead man's friends and relatives had to look outside the Chinese community for an undertaker, for it would not be until the 1930s that the Chinese could hire a licensed Chinese funeral director. They hired William H. Kennedy, who placed Ah Fung's coffin in his carriage house "amidst numerous hacks, coffins of several sorts, and a dreary looking hearse." The forty-five-year-old Irish immigrant was a former carpenter and stable and livery keeper known for having "buried all the Chinese that [had] died in the down-town settlement for a number of years past." Readers of the *World* caught a glimpse of Chinese customs from Kennedy, who provided a lengthy description of Chinese funeral and burial rituals, information he had acquired after many years of serving the local Chinese community.[7] He also provided details of the Ah Fung funeral, noting that Mrs. Ah Fung, whom he described as "bright and intelligent," was apparently unmoved by her husband's violent death. In the undertaker's view, the young woman was "not in the least crushed by affliction, for having left a tidy sum to his widow, she [was] not left in poverty by the demise of her husband."[8] Kennedy's perception that Mrs. Ah Fung was not aggrieved but satisfied at her newly acquired financial state reinscribed popular racial stereotypes of the time—that she could never have entered the marriage out of love, but only for economic gain.

The newspaper reports of Ah Fung's murder and the funeral that followed were no different from other tales of interracial love, sex, and violence that had become standard fodder in an increasingly sensationalist press by the late nineteenth century. But once we sift through the lurid details of the crime and the "colorful" descriptions Kennedy provides, a layer of interracial/interethnic social and economic relations that operated beneath the radar of popular depictions of urban life begins to surface. Ah Fung's community in 1877 consisted of both Chinese and non-Chinese people who in various ways provided friendship, kinship ties, social services, and financial as well as emotional support.

Ah Fung's situation was not unusual. Interrracial/interethnic relations were a common feature of daily life among working-class New Yorkers even as the ethnic composition of working-class neighborhoods in lower Manhattan changed over time. Nearly fifty years after Ah Fung's funeral, a few blocks north of Forsyth Street, Johanna Hurley sat with Ching

Yeng and her four-year-old daughter, Lung Som Moy, as Ching's husband, Lung Lin, lay dying. Hurley, a widowed German immigrant, lived in the same apartment building and had summoned the ambulance. The building on Division Street, where Hurley's and Ching's families resided, housed an ethnically mixed population of old and new immigrants, the latter being mostly Russian and Polish Jews who worked in the city's garment factories, ran small shops, or peddled wares in the densely populated neighborhoods of lower Manhattan.[9] Moy's father worked as a store manager several blocks over on Pell Street in the area popularly known as "Chinatown."

Shortly after her husband died, Ching made plans to return to China. But she hoped that one day her daughter would return to the United States, her country of birth. Thus, in accordance with the Chinese exclusion laws, she applied for a return certificate for Lung Som Moy before leaving the country. The friendship between Hurley and Ching Yeng continued over time and space, as the two women kept in touch for several years after Ching and her daughter moved to China.

In 1935, thirteen years after Moy had left the United States, she applied for readmission. Chinese friends of her family who still lived in New York City called on Hurley, now living on Chrystie Street, to testify on the young woman's behalf. Despite ill health, she accompanied two Chinese men to Ellis Island. Hurley stated that she had been friendly with a number of Chinese people in her old neighborhood, who had even given her a Chinese name, "Wah Moo." For instance, she recalled the Lum family who lived on Mott Street and had visited Moy's family frequently. So many years later, she still remembered the names of some of the Lum children: "The oldest girl is May—there's George—there's one I used to call 'cowboy.'" The Chinese immigration inspectors evidently found Hurley's testimony convincing, for they admitted Moy into the country as a U.S. citizen. Then, like so many working-class people, Hurley, Moy, and the Lums disappeared from the public record.[10]

I begin with the stories of Ah Fung and Johanna Hurley not because they exemplify every aspect of interracial/interethnic social relationships, but precisely because they are fragments of a larger, more complicated story of urban life. Their stories serve as temporal bookends within which we can piece together the social connections that helped working-class people cope with life and death, create families, and sustain liveli-hoods. Both stories involve Chinese people but take place on the edges of "Chinatown." They illustrate how working-class immigrant people often crossed paths at the interstices of designated community bound-aries, signifying sets of social and economic relations that often defied popular notions of neighborhood borders.

The purpose of this project is to explore the social and economic conditions under which people participated in the simultaneous devel-opment of co-ethnic and interracial/interethnic relations in their daily lives. My main argument is that between the end of Reconstruction and the 1930s, national and local efforts to reify racial boundaries through Jim Crow segregation, immigration exclusion laws, and urban reform movements often facilitated interracial/interethnic social and economic relations. An examination of lived experiences and everyday practices—sexual relationships, marriage, the formation of families and friendships, work, play, and political activities—can provide meaning, motion, and specificity to the analytic categories of race, class, gender, and nation. Studying the conditions under which people crossed the lines of dif-ference as they negotiated systems of power at the national, state, and local levels also allows historians to chart both changes and continuities in conceptions of race, ethnicity, gender, and sexuality and, in the pro-cess, revisit ethnic and racial "isolation" as both a lived experience and a concept.

Social and economic networks across ethnic lines evolved out of necessity as much as personal desire and ranged from loving intimate relationships to outright hostility. They also varied according to circum-stances and residential patterns. In New York City, the ethnic compo-sition of neighborhoods, blocks, apartment buildings, and households varied greatly. Between the time of Ah Fung's murder and the 1920s, much had changed in the neighborhoods of lower Manhattan. Many of the Irish inhabitants of southern Manhattan had dispersed throughout the city in search of cheap housing and better employment. This region by 1900 now housed the "new" immigrants from Southern and Eastern Europe. Large clusters of European Jews settled in the southeastern part of lower Manhattan on Orchard, Allen, Cherry, and Ludlow streets.[11] First- and second-generation Italian immigrant families came to domi-nate Elizabeth and Mulberry streets and part of Mott Street. But much of lower Manhattan was still ethnically diverse. According to the 1900 federal census, residents of Mott Street, the so-called "heart" of Chinatown, listed their countries of origin as Algeria, Africa, Canada, China, Cuba, England, Germany, Hungary, Ireland, Italy, and Russia. Italian immigrants made up the largest group, followed by Chinese and Russians.[12] Other streets, such as Bayard, the Bowery, and Park Row, also housed a mix of ethnic groups and household configurations.

Despite the reality of ethnically mixed neighborhoods, the popular images of urban ethnic communities as isolated from one another and from the rest of the "modern" world have persisted in the popular imagination since the nineteenth century. Groups that had immigrated to the United States from Asia and from Southern and Eastern Europe bore the brunt of mostly negative images perpetuated by lawmakers, journalists, reformers, the clergy, scholars, and popular writers. As a result, ethnic neighborhood designations such as "Chinatown," "Little Italy," and the "Lower East Side" remain in the public imaginary as unchangeable.

Such images underscore the presumed strength of ethnic isolation as a social and psychological process of community and identity formation that overrode ethnically mixed residential demographic patterns. During the early 1950s, the author and critic Lloyd R. Morris described the Lower East Side, for example, as a "fusion of nationalities" that was "less obvious than their persistently maintained identity, their continuing separateness."[13] In a humorous reference to European Jewish cuisine, Edwin Burrows and Mike Wallace, in their 1999 Pulitzer Prize-winning history of New York City, likened Jewish immigrants from Hungary and Russia to "herrings in a barrel," suggesting that these groups not only were crowded into streets and tenements but also were unmovable.[14] A tourist guide to New York City's "Chinatown" adhered to similar images: "It's almost as though the entire community has been plucked from the Far East and laid to rest in Manhattan, its inhabitants unaware of the transition."[15] Such images have outweighed the competing idea of the "melting pot," that immigrants discarded all vestiges of their original culture to become "a new, composite American." Both interpretations contradicted the uneven processes of acculturation and the persistence of racism and xenophobia at the local and national levels.[16]

Federal and state policies and local segregationist practices explicitly intended to isolate those groups deemed "undesirable" and "unassimilable" or even a danger to U.S. society and culture. Such measures took the form of antimiscegenation laws, the Indian Removal Acts, immigration restriction and citizenship laws, and discrimination in housing, education, and employment.[17]

The new immigrant groups who entered the United States during the late nineteenth century were perceived as different kinds of "problems" and, hence, experienced discrimination in particular ways. Exclusion laws barred the immigration of Chinese laborers and women suspected of entering the United States for "immoral purposes" (i.e., prostitution) and deemed all Chinese immigrants ineligible for naturalization and citizenship. Even some who opposed exclusion rejected the notion that Chinese immigrants even wanted to integrate themselves into American culture. U.S. Supreme Court Justice David Josiah Brewer ridiculed efforts to exclude the Chinese, arguing in 1904 that "no Chinaman comes to this country or goes to any other with the intention of casting his lot with it. . . . So far from meaning to be naturalized, he intends to remain alien."[18]

Other ethnic groups also came under scrutiny. Questions over whether Jewish and Italian immigrants could successfully assimilate emerged in both religious and secular realms. In New York City, Catholic parish priests, most of whom were of Irish ancestry, consistently expressed frustration at what many of them viewed as the backwardness of Italian co-religionists. For Lillian W. Betts, a social worker and urban reformer, the Italians in New York were clearly not a part of the city's larger identity: "A year's residence in an Italian tenement in New York taught me first of all the isolation of a foreign quarter; how completely cut off one may be from everything that makes New York, New York." According to the attorney and writer Madison Grant, Jews threatened to degrade the Anglo-Saxon population. In his *The Passing of the Great Race* (1916), Grant asserted that "the result of the mixture of two races, in the long run, gives us a race reverting to the more ancient, generalized and lower type. The cross between a white man and a negro is a negro; the cross between a white man and a Hindu is a Hindu; and the cross between any of the three European races and a Jew is a Jew."[19] During World War I, ethnic stereotypes bore the additional associations with political unrest—Italians with anarchism and Jews with bolshevism.

Academic scholarship forwarded the concept of ethnic isolation between the 1920s and the 1950s as a central framework for analyzing race and ethnic relations in the United States. The sociologist Robert E. Park maintained that Asians in particular were isolated from American society and slower to assimilate than other groups, a phenomenon he called the "Oriental Problem." In an effort to find out why, he initiated his "Survey of Race Relations" in the 1920s as a means of gathering data on whites' attitudes toward Asian American people. Park's student Louis Wirth, a German Jewish immigrant, and Wirth's student Paul Siu, a Chinese immigrant, continued the study of social isolation by analyzing the immigrant experiences of their own ethnic groups. Wirth's book, *The Ghetto* (1928), examined the adjustment strategies among European Jews to U.S. cities. Like his mentor, Wirth argued that the experience of ghettoization as a form of physical and cultural isolation applied to other ethnic/racial groups.[20]

Siu's study, aptly titled *The Chinese Laundryman: A Study of Social Isolation* (1953), departed significantly from both Park and Wirth. Siu lived among Chinese laundry workers in Chicago as a participant observer during the 1930s. As the historian John Kuo Wei Tchen has pointed out, the significance of Siu's study lies in its portrayal of the Chinese immigrant experience as unique. Siu countered Park's and Wirth's contention that the "ghetto" experience was uniformly applicable to all ethnic groups. The strength of anti-Chinese prejudice, as exemplified in the exclusion movement and the immigration restriction laws that specifically targeted Chinese immigration, set the Chinese apart from other immigrant groups. According to Siu, Chinese immigrants were not "marginal men" who straddled two cultural worlds, as Park had posited, but were continual strangers in a hostile country, "sojourners" who clung to their ways of life in a new land rather than actively seeking to assimilate. In the process, they developed "immigrant economies" or occupational niches that did not compete with those of whites. The latter concept in particular is a place to further explore the degree to which such occupations functioned separately from one another.[21] For Wirth and Siu, life imitated art. Both men experienced institutional isolation within and outside academia. Although widely popular among Jewish readers, Wirth's book was virtually ignored in academic circles. Siu found a similar lack of interest and recognition for his scholarship on the Chinese.

The Civil Rights Movement facilitated a resurgence of scholarship in urban, immigration, and ethnic studies on ethnic identity politics and community formation by the 1970s and 1980s.[22] Ethnic isolation remains a central mode of understanding race and ethnic community formation in U.S. society in scholarly and popular works. In Asian American history, for example, the Chinese have been portrayed as "exotics," ardent nationalists positioned as outsiders of the body politic, or as contagions whose very presence threatened the health of the nation.[23]

The continued engagement with the concept of isolation is an important phenomenon not only for Asian American history but also for urban history in general. The debates allow historians to probe further into the various ways isolation functioned in the lives of marginalized groups. Thus, my intention is not to argue that immigrants either were or were not isolated in U.S. society or that some groups were more isolated than others. Rather, I argue that "isolation" or "segregation" and their presumed antonym, "integration," were rarely totalizing or uniform experiences and that the degree of "isolation" or "integration" was contingent on particular social and economic conditions. The stories of a diverse ethnic population raise the inevitable questions, such as isolation from what and from whom? How do we define "isolation"? Did all ethnic groups experience isolation in the same ways? The 1989 edition of the *Oxford English Dictionary* lists several definitions of "isolation," the primary of which refers to "the fact or condition of being isolated or standing alone; separation from other things or persons; solitariness." One of the primary definitions of "integration" stems from antiracist social movements, "the bringing into equal membership of a common society those groups or persons previously discriminated against on racial or cultural grounds."[24]

Southern Manhattan during the late nineteenth century and the early decades of the twentieth century offers a good locale to examine the degree to which isolation and integration functioned, for it is in this geographic space where narratives of ethnic isolation have emerged the most strongly in American urban history. Comparative studies of ethnic/racial groups, as well as studies of interracial sex and marriage, have facilitated the process of thinking beyond the experiences of any one particular group and encouraging an examination of the differential effects of systems of oppression and the historical specificity of relations between ethnic/racial groups and the state.[25] As Susan Glenn has pointed out, immigrants from different ethnic groups may have developed friendly relations in the workplace, but they often kept a "comfortable social distance" from each other.[26]

Interactions across ethnic and racial lines have been an integral part of the history of New York City since the settlement by the Dutch in Manhattan during the seventeenth century. Between the nineteenth century and the twentieth century, the city's rapid growth as a major seaport and industrial center increased such possibilities. New immigrants from Southern and Eastern Europe and smaller numbers of East Asians increased the city's population. Joining them were rural, working-class, and college-educated men and women within the United States in search of employment, leisure, and education.[27]

Cultural shifts accompanied these large-scale demographic changes. Middle- and working-class white women enjoyed increased physical mobility, regularly traversing the city streets to and from shops, missions, jobs, amusement parks, and "exotic" offerings in shops and restaurants. While many educated middle-class women moved into working-class and poor neighborhoods to participate in the settlement house and missionary movements, immigrant working-class "ghetto girls" crafted identities and social practices that more accurately reflected their lives as wage-earning, immigrant women. They dressed in less expensive versions of the latest fashions, wore makeup, and socialized in public spaces with young working-class men.[28]

The potential for mixing across lines of difference, however, raised concerns about sexual behavior both within and outside the heterosexual norm, especially in densely populated urban areas. Writers expressed anxieties over the transgression of racial and ethnic boundaries at the same time that they reinforced normative white heterosexuality. In New York City, as in San Francisco and Chicago, homosexual men came under periodic surveillance by reformers, municipal leaders, the police, and the clergy, who were determined to shore up heterosexual, middle-class, Protestant normativity among the poor, immigrants, and those deemed sexually deviant.[29]

By the late nineteenth century and early twentieth century, concerns about interracial sex and marriage found expression in short stories, plays, and songs that capitalized on popular anxieties. William Norr's *Stories of Chinatown*, published in 1892, and Anne Nichols's play *Abie's*

Irish Rose, which opened on Broadway thirty years later, exemplify works that revealed popular understandings of race and ethnic differences as much as they sought to entertain.[30] Both writers situated their stories in New York City, a contested site of race, ethnic, and sexual politics, as expressed in the tension between the so-called old and new immigrants and between "whites" and "non-whites."

Norr, a former sports writer, turned to writing "true-to-life" fiction that perpetuated popular representations of working-class lower Manhattan as a center of both ethnic isolation and interracial mixing. Like many local newspapermen, Norr socialized with urban working-class people at bars and opium houses in the "Chinatown" neighborhood. He gained notoriety especially for his "discovery" of the "Mayor of Chinatown," the infamous former pugilist and self-promoter "Chuck" Connors.[31] Popular stereotypes and his own experiences formed the basis of his stories, which highlighted the supposed dangers of interracial love between young working-class white women and Chinese immigrant men who "kept" their women by plying them with alcohol and opium. The message was clear: Such liaisons could never succeed, for all of the tales in Norr's collection ended in tragedy, with the death of white women who took up with the "repulsive Chinese."[32] The weakness of the women lured to Chinatown also affected Irish men, who sought to rescue "their" women. In the stories, a number of which feature Connors, working-class Irish men ultimately lost out to the lure of the exotic, as these liaisons fragmented and destroyed the possibility of intraethnic Irish relationships.

Nichols took a comedic approach to interracial/interethnic tensions. *Abie's Irish Rose* was set in the Bronx, well north of lower Manhattan, where a large concentration of European Jews still resided when the play opened at the Fulton Theater in New York. The play ran until 1923 and then appeared as a Hollywood film in 1928. The story focused on the marriage between a young Jewish man and a woman of Irish ancestry. Although billed as a comedy, the main characters' struggle to hide their marriage from their parents exemplified the generational conflict within immigrant communities over assimilation and the potential loss of religious and cultural practices as a result of intermarriage. In a case of life imitating art, one of the play's lead male actors was Bernard Gorcey, an immigrant of Swiss and Russian ancestry who had married an Irish

Catholic woman. Other plays and films about Jewish–Irish romances followed during the 1920s, including "Kosher Kitty Kelly" and "The Cohens and the Kellys." As these plays suggest, ethnic differences signaled the uneven process of "whitening" among groups of European ancestry and the degree to which cultural differences resulted in social distances between groups.

Humorous songs, such as "Moysha Machree" (1906) and "If It Wasn't for the Irish and the Jews (1912)," highlighted different aspects of assimilation, as well as Jewish–Irish relations. Each group at different historical moments had achieved relative upward social, economic, and political mobility, despite the continued existence of anti-Catholicism and anti-Semitism. What the songs do not reveal, however, is that the Irish and European Jews still occupied distinct positions on the black–white continuum in American society precisely because of the new immigration. Unlike the Irish by this time, Jews and other newly arrived immigrant groups remained on the margins of whiteness.[33]

The comic portrayals of parental hysteria over Jewish–Irish romances disguised the tensions that persisted throughout the 1920s as the rise of white supremacy groups and racial violence throughout the nation attested, especially when it involved crossing the color line. Public furor over the murder of a nineteen-year-old white missionary, Elsie Sigel, in the summer of 1909 illustrated the ways in which the investigation of a homicide quickly gave way to municipal action that focused on interracial sex and marriage, especially between white women and non-white men. At the height of the Sigel case that summer, members of the New York City police determined to rid "Chinatown" of white women who did not possess marriage certificates in an effort to curtail contact with Chinese men. It did not matter that Sigel's body was found on Eighth Avenue, well outside of southern Manhattan. The association of the Chinese in New York and of all new immigrant groups to this region persisted, regardless of demographic realities.[34]

The Sigel case underscores the power of memory, popular representations, and the development of co-ethnic communities. Together, they have contributed to the dominant view of these communities as distinct and separate from each other and the rest of society. The "Chinatown" case serves as one example. The association between European Jews and the Lower East Side is another. The turn-of-the-century writers Abraham Cahan, political activist, journalist, novelist, and editor of the *Jewish Daily Forward*, and Israel Zangwill, were instrumental in making the connection between the Lower East Side and American Jewish history.[35] Michael Gold's autobiographical novel *Jews without Money* (1935) captured much of the romanticized, sometimes satirical memories of Lower East Side life, as well as its tensions: "The East Side never forgot Europe. We children heard endless tales of the pogroms." Memories also included a wariness of other ethnic groups in America. Gold's mother figure expresses these anxieties: "My mother was opposed to the Italians, Irish, Germans, and every other variety of Christian with whom we were surrounded." There was also the "memory" of the Chinese, as represented by a Chinese laundryman who engaged in sex with a young neighborhood Jewish woman, whom they nicknamed "Sweetheart of the Yellow Cholera."[36]

Local understandings of "difference" to a large extent contributed to a social distancing between groups. For Rose Cohen, a young Russian immigrant woman, "difference" turned on expressions of gender identity. For Cohen, being a "civilized" woman in America meant adopting the working-class codes of "new womanhood," a fashionable "ghetto girl." In her memoir, she recalled thinking that her fellow Italian workers were not civilized because they were willing to work for low pay and forego accessories like hats, gloves, and umbrellas. For many young immigrant women like Cohen, demanding higher pay and purchasing accessories with their own wages was part of an assimilating process that the writer Anzia Yezierska described as becoming "a person," an independent, assertive, and, hence, "American" woman who embraced early-twentieth-century consumerism. In Cohen's view, an *Italian* characteristic was to refrain from acculturation to American consumerism. Whether Cohen ever would have used the term "race" as a way to understand and describe the distance between herself and her Italian co-workers is unclear; nonetheless, she perceived differences between Jewish and Italian women in terms that were relevant to her life as a young working-class immigrant woman.

Overt hostilities were also not uncommon. According to Cohen, the harassment of Jewish pushcart peddlers by local Irish youths happened frequently. The disruption of the funeral of a prominent rabbi provides another example. In the summer of 1902, a large group of non-Jewish factory workers attacked the passing funeral cortege of Jacob Joseph, the chief rabbi of the U.S. Jewish Congregation and head of the Congregation Beth Hamedrash Hagodai on Norfolk Street. The assailants threw objects out of the upper factory windows at the passing mourners, whose numbers reached several hundred. A riot ensued when the mourners fought back. The story made the front page of the *New York Times*, which pointed out that conflicts such as this were not uncommon in the heavily Jewish neighborhood where the incident occurred.[37] John Eng recalled being harassed by Irish and Italian boys when he was a youth in the 1930s: "I had a lot of trouble. . . . The problem was the Irish and Italian kids. You know, 'Hey, Chinky, go back to Chinatown!' You think Mulberry Street was Chinatown back then? It was all Italian. I fought back. I had to."[38]

Amid such tensions, however, ethnic groups could also influence and benefit from each other, as in the case of the Irish and Italians in Greenwich Village. Their physical proximity to one another and a shared religious faith helped bridge differences and facilitate the process of assimilation. Conflict and avoidance between the two groups had been the norm since Italians began immigrating into the area in the late nineteenth century. But by the 1920s, the Irish, now "white" and hence "American," served as models for Italians as they strove for assimilation and acculturation into white American society. The "Irish ways" of Americanization operated through the structure and culture of machine politics and ethnic institutions, such as the local Catholic churches.[39] As individuals and as members of larger social networks, the people in this book were both products of and agents in a changing urban environment in which they carved out social, economic, and physical spaces by choice *and* as a result of racism and poverty.

As I discuss in greater depth in Chapter 3, the reclassification of the Irish and other European groups as Caucasian or white by the early twentieth century signaled a number of shifts in systems of inclusion and exclusion that affected the ethnic composition of urban occupations between the nineteenth century and the early twentieth century. Such changes created a system of dependency that brought people of different races and ethnicities into contact with one another out of necessity. With the growth of New York City as an industrial and mercantile center, many occupations also expanded to serve the needs of businesses and the public, such as hauling and livery. Irish men were already numerous in many of these occupations, to the exclusion of other groups, who then came to rely on their services. A stratified and segmented urban occupational labor force, then, created a social and economic context that brought people of different races together out of mutual necessity.

Although one could explore interracial/interethnic social relations in any number of geographic locations, I want to revisit this region of New York City precisely because it has long been considered, in popular and academic texts, a cluster of ethnic enclaves isolated from the rest of the modern city. My goal is to sift through the memories and assumptions about urban communities, to unearth the history of complex social relations across and within ethnic and racial groups and, in so doing, make sense of the sometimes fragmented stories behind those such as Ah Fung, Mrs. Ah Fung, their friends, William Kennedy, Johanna Hurley, and Lung Som Moy. The larger forces of transnational migration flows, settlement patterns among immigrants and U.S.-born transplants to the city, and the development of a segmented and stratified occupational labor structure and new perspectives on gender relations—the "new masculinity" and the new woman—provided the social, economic, and political context within which to view daily relations among a diverse population who lived and labored in lower Manhattan.

How do we comprehend the different contexts within which interracial and interethnic interactions occurred? Kevin Mumford's conceptual model of *interzones* is particularly valuable because it locates specific spacial environments within which urban working-class people worked and socialized. Mumford conceptualizes black–white sex districts as sets of concentric circles, with the most stigmatized vice, interracial sex, occupying the center.[40] Such a model helps readers visualize the structure of urban vice districts simultaneously as marginalized social spaces and as sites for the possibility of resistance and transgression of sexual and racial norms. However, the model of concentricity alone cannot encompass a broader range of social relations. I propose intersecting and overlapping spheres as another way to visualize urban interracial/interethnic relations that includes, but is not limited to, sexual interactions. What we are left with is a vision of an extraordinarily complex system of social relations that defies any one particular model and that takes into account the simultaneity of different types of social relations. Such relations are shaped by particular conditions in the workplace, home, streets, and so forth. People's interactions across lines of difference in a variety of social, political, and economic contexts suggests that intersecting, overlapping, and concentric spheres of contact could co-exist at any given moment. At the core of such interactions was power: the power of the state to regulate the social, political, and economic status of people at the local level, based on presumptive notions of race, class, gender, and sexuality, as well as the power of individuals to carve out opportunities out of oppressive systems.

To conceptualize long-term and short-term interactions across lines of ethnic and racial difference as intersecting and overlapping applies the social-science paradigm of intersectionality, which posits that forms of oppression act in conjunction and are mutually constitutive. The legal scholar Kimberlé Crenshaw developed the concept of intersectionality to more fully comprehend systems of oppression and identity formation. In urban studies, such an approach allows us to see the city as a set of geographic and social sites in which inhabitants could develop relations simultaneously across and within lines of race, ethnicity, class, and gender as part of a complex process of urban community formation.[41]

Where, exactly, can we locate these interactions? The urban built environment provides historians with clues. Interior and exterior spaces then, as now, were at a premium and often functioned as sites of multiple, overlapping activities. Shops, tenement and apartment dwellings, schools, saloons, missions and settlement houses, the streets, wharves, alleyways, and beneath the bridges provided physical and cultural space where particular kinds of social and economic relationships took place between urban working-class women, men, and children and between the middle classes and the poor, working-class, and immigrant populations. The crowded, noisy tenements concerned social reformers but evoked mixed responses from the residents. Some complained to social reformers about drunken, dirty, noisy neighbors, while others enjoyed the cacophony of voices and the tunes played out by local musicians in the streets and apartments.[42]

In these locations, people crossed paths with one another in particular contexts and under conditions produced by a combination of factors, including the racialized and gendered urban paid labor force, Progressive-era social reform movements, and the emergence of new forms of urban masculinity and femininity. In some circumstances, however, these same factors could also work to drive a wedge between groups. For example, as Chapter 5 demonstrates, much as the workers at Christodora House, a settlement on Avenue B and 9th Street, wanted to create a "common ground" on which men and women of different ethnicities and class positions could base their interactions, gender, class, and ethnic divisions nevertheless manifested themselves in settlement house activities. Interactions between middle-class Protestant social workers and working-class immigrants underscored exactly how *uncommon* that ground actually was when one looked carefully at the power structure that guided the settlement.

This book takes the reader to different geographic locations of southern Manhattan to examine the ways in which race, ethnicity, class, and gender shaped daily interactions. This area was not a homogeneous region; nor was it simply a set of isolated ethnic clusters, as suggested by the "ethnic enclave" model. Within these neighborhoods, people regularly transgressed social categories as much as they assisted in hardening the lines between them. Moreover, these neighborhoods functioned as nodes of social, economic, and political connection to other areas of the city, especially with the growth of the boroughs of Brooklyn, Queens, and Staten Island. Thus, one can conceptualize New York City as a system of interconnected boroughs, based on kinship and community ties, paid labor, and social relationships, at the same time that the people in each neighborhood within a borough maintained a distinctive identity.

In part, this book grew out of my own competing memories of the area. Conventional images have never resonated with my memories and experiences. I grew up in northern New Jersey, but my familial roots lie in Manhattan's "Chinatown." The maternal side of my family began in New York City, when my great-grandmother left Portland, Oregon, where she had immigrated as a child, and moved to New York to marry an older Chinese merchant. My memories of ordinary life focus not on the supposed isolation of this community nor on the lurid or the criminal. Rather, my strongest recollections focus on other aspects of daily life: the interactions between neighbors in my great-aunt Kate's apartment building on Mott Street, where Naughton's funeral home and stables were once located; the elderly Italian couple who lived down the hall and assisted her in her old age; a biracial uncle who grew up on

Doyers Street in the 1920s and 1930s and had both white and Chinese playmates; a great-aunt who came of age in the 1920s and performed in the theater and married a Chinese man but also maintained intimate relationships with white women. Guests at family banquets during the 1970s always included Chinese and non-Chinese family and friends.

Interracial marriages have been a common occurrence on both sides of my family. My paternal grandfather, George Yee, was born in San Francisco, the son of a Tong hit man. In the early 1930s, the entire family, including George's Chinese wife and two sons, fled first to Pittsburgh, where my grandmother, a young woman in her twenties, died of unknown causes. After finally settling in Boston's working-class Chinatown neighborhood, George Yee remarried. His second wife, Marie Ouellette, was a white woman of French Canadian ancestry from Salem, Massachusetts. George's parents, my father's grandparents, so disapproved of the marriage that they raised my father and uncle themselves, while my grandfather raised a bi-racial family on the outskirts of Boston's Chinatown. In New York City's Chinatown, my mother's cousin married a man whose mother was third-generation Irish and whose father was a Chinese restaurant manager. When Wong Jung Que and Margaret Hart married around 1920, unions between women of Irish ancestry and Chinese men, while not typical, also were not uncommon.

My family's experiences as working-class urbanites, while unique in some ways, were at the same time familiar in the complex history of urban family and community formation in New York City. The chapters that follow explore the various dimensions of race and ethnic relations, beginning in the late nineteenth century and ending in the early 1930s. This study is organized thematically. Each chapter explores the ways in which gender, race, ethnicity, and class, not simply as categories of identity but as systems of power relations, opened up or limited opportunities. Within these categories, factors such as family backgrounds and friendship networks also played integral roles in people's lives and their modes of interactions. This study does not purport to cover all possible venues for cross-cultural relations. There are, for example, further possibilities for examining the social implications of cross-ethnic and cross-racial alliances in factories and sites of labor organizing.[43]

The book begins in the semi-private realm of urban residential households. Chapter 1 explores the ways in which immigration patterns and policies shaped the demographics of working-class households, a small percentage of which were interethnic/interracial. Chapters 2 and 3 examine the ways in which an urban paid labor force, which was stratified along the lines of gender, race, and ethnicity, brought working-class people into contact with one another. Chapter 2 focuses on commercial relations that took place in retail establishments, restaurants, and laundries. Chapter 3 demonstrates how caring for people in urban communities, which involved physicians, nurses, midwives, undertakers, and certain urban trades, mainly related to the building industry, were vital to maintaining the health of urban people and the physical infrastructures that sustained residences and workplaces. As these chapters demonstrate, immigration, occupational patterns, public policies, and local practices resulted in systems of inclusion and exclusion, creating an economic and social necessity that often brought different groups of people into one another's lives.

The discussion then moves outside of the domain of small business enterprises and family economies to working-class people's interactions with anti-vice activists, settlement house workers, and missionaries in their neighborhoods. While people across race, gender, and ethnicity worked to sustain life and build a healthy economic and social infrastructure, the presence of increased numbers of poor and working-class people raised concerns among Progressive reformers about poverty, crime, and the ability of the new immigrants to acculturate into American society. Residential dwellings, shops, restaurants, saloons, and the streets, places that fostered economic and social networks, together with settlement houses, also served as physical sites of social reform and surveillance.

Chapters 4 and 5 analyze the ways in which urban reform institutions and organizations served as a locus for interactions across lines of race, ethnicity, gender, and class. Most scholars have focused primarily on the settlement and anti-vice movements from the vantage points of middle-class reformers, due in large part to the availability of sources such as organizational records, correspondence, and speeches. Non-elite people were not completely absent, however, from these documents. The city-wide private anti-vice organization the Committee of Fifteen, for example, received numerous memos and letters from men and women inquiring about employment or volunteer opportunities as agents or clerical staff or reporting instances of prostitution and gambling in their neighborhoods. The committee, in fact, did hire men from the neighborhood as agents posing as "johns." Chapter 4 focuses specifically on the anti-vice movement in New York City, led by organizations such as the Committee of Fifteen and the Committee of Fourteen. Within a relatively short period, reformers shifted their organizing tactics to incorporate new social-science methods and practices in an effort to gather information within brothels, pool halls, hotels, saloons, and gambling parlors. It was the reliance on social science that intensified and systematized interactions and encounters between undercover agents and prostitutes and other purveyors of illicit activities.

The composition of anti-vice committees and the methods they used to gather information from local businessmen and residents changed dramatically between 1900 and 1905. By the time the Committee of Fourteen organized in 1905, social-science methodology, which experimented with surveys and interviews and employed "objective" analysis and the systematic gathering of "facts," had taken hold. Moreover, educated women, the new women of the Progressive era, were important players in the quest for tenement house, hotel, and saloon reform; improvements in industrial labor conditions; and the prosecution of procurers, "white slave" traffickers, and corrupt police—all factors that, the committee's experts argued, supported prostitution, rape, and child abduction.

Such interactions were framed partly by the movement to control the masses, as well as the desire by social reformers themselves to mix with immigrants and the working classes in what by then were considered the less desirable, yet alluring, areas of the city. Saloons, houses of prostitution, opium dens, and gambling joints were simultaneously sites of conflict and conviviality across lines of gender, class, ethnicity, and race. The national shift in gender roles played itself out in the neighborhoods as male and female social reformers attempted to eliminate urban vices. Chapter 5 extends the discussion on reform by focusing on the ways in which the politics of religion in settlement houses and Christian missions shaped race, gender, and ethnic relations.

This book includes a diverse population of racial and ethnic groups but highlights first and subsequent generations of Irish, Chinese, Jews, and Italians. These groups figure prominently in the chapters that follow for two main reasons. First, their experiences illuminate the ways that systems of power affected groups that at some point in their history as urban immigrants had hovered within the black–white paradigm that for so long has defined race relations in U.S. history. The comparative experiences of these groups also illustrate the process of "whitening"— how Asians, as exemplified by the Chinese experience in the United States, never shed the possibility of representing a "yellow peril," while European groups by the 1930s had been deemed "white ethnics." Even in the "great metropolis" of cosmopolitan New York City, the collective experiences of the Chinese and their representations in the popular imagination have been pivotal in the juxtaposition of white and non-white in U.S. society. One of the most haunting aspects of the history of southern Manhattan is that by the late nineteenth century the black population had begun its migration to other parts of the city, particularly Harlem and the borough of Brooklyn. Yet the black–white model was firmly in place as a national ideological anchor that shaped economic opportunities for many residents.

Ultimately, this is a story of the lives of non-elite people—men, women, and children of diverse ethnic, racial, and class backgrounds who negotiated the cosmopolitanism of southern Manhattan as much through their interactions with people of different cultural backgrounds as through their participation in the creation and sustenance of distinct urban ethnic communities. The challenge for historians is to determine the extent to which such interactions were meaningful at any level. The distinction between "relationship" and "interaction" is often difficult to assess. The following chapters aim to reveal something about the conditions of people's lives that not only made cross-cultural relationships possible but also at times prevented them from developing, as well as the motives of individuals for initiating and sustaining social and economic relations across lines of gender, race, ethnicity, and class.

Historians have written extensively about the artificiality of racial definitions and classifications. By the 1920s, the classification of whiteness as a race included all European immigrants, but at the same time, the distinction between "white" and "non-white" had solidified. Although anti-Catholic sentiment would also pervade American society into the early 1960s, Irish and German Catholics (as well as Protestants) could claim a white identity that was not yet available to European Jews. Anti-Semitism was a constant reminder of the "not quite whiteness" of Jews until after World War II, even though, like the Irish and, later, the Italians, European Jews had been designated "white" in the census since the 1880s.[44]

The language and politics of difference have undergone significant changes over the past two centuries, encoded in the categories "nationality," "race," "ethnicity," "gender," "culture," and "class." Such terms can denote group identities as well as official designations for enumeration and the development of public policy. Popular, legal and social-science definitions of race and ethnicity have been fluid and often inconsistent. In 1911, the Immigration Commission, headed by William P. Dillingham, departed from the practice of classifying people according to country of origin, opting instead to categorize people according to race.[45] The commission defined race broadly rather than adopting the accepted notion that five distinct races existed—Caucasian, Mongolian, African, Malay, and Indian—which, its report argued, confined itself to only physical characteristics and color. According to the report, widening the definition of race to include what social scientists of the time would have referred to as "culture" was, the commission believed, more statistically accurate and practical in its effort to identify diverse groups coming from particular countries of origin. Thus, the commission retained the desire to classify, coming up with forty categories that it believed more accurately represented the identity of immigrant groups.[46]

The terminology of race remained inconsistent in "objective" government documents, as well as in the courts. The social construction of race as an official classification shaped the ways in which government documents, such as the census, have categorized immigrants and their descendants into specific "racial" groups and reported their country of origin, or nationality. Even though federal census reports added more detail in terms of the numbers of categories, race remained an ambiguous category. Once classified as simply "colored" along with African Americans, the Chinese, for example, were classified as "Ch" for Chinese by 1890, but their children could be classified as either "Chinese" or "white," especially if they had been born of marriages between Chinese and women of European ancestry. People of African descent were categorized alternatively as "colored," "Negro," "Black," or "mulatto." Such inconsistencies reflected the continued confusion among census takers about what race "really" was. At the root of the race problem were shifting meanings of whiteness.

Between the late nineteenth century and the 1930s, popular understandings of "race" had undergone important changes. As the nation moved steadily toward the narrow "one-drop" rule that signified "blackness," the meaning of "whiteness" expanded to include the Irish and, later, all Europeans of Caucasian ancestry. By 1920, concerns about how to define "white" and, hence, "non-white" made its way into the U.S. Census guidelines. For the first time, the introduction to the census articulated the notion of racial purity as a way to resolve the problem of classifying mixed-race people and provided guidelines for census takers (who, as it turned out, used their own discretion when classifying people anyway). While previous census reports had simply declared "whiteness" to mean people of European ancestry, in the 1920 guidelines, the government added the terms "purity" and "blood" to further specify the meanings of "white," "non-white," and mixed-white: "The term 'white' as used in the census reports refers to persons understood to be pure-blooded whites. A person of mixed blood is classified according to the nonwhite racial strain or, if the nonwhite blood itself is mixed, according to his racial status as adjudged by the community in which he resides."[47]

Although racial classification was one of several components of the census enumeration process, its inclusion was a consequence of a larger national discourse about maintaining white racial purity and the dangers of interracial marriage, which fulfilled the promise of the myth of the melting pot and assimilation but also fed fears about the future of the nation. For eugenicists, race mixing between whites and non-whites threatened to pollute white purity.

Whiteness as an expression of racialism has had a powerful impact on the everyday lives of people. Those who historically have been categorized by immigration law and the popular imagination as "non-white" have been denied access to citizenship rights, full employment opportunities, and education. Cohen's commentary underscores Matthew Jacobson's point that "one can be both white *and* racially distinct from other whites."[48] Both Italians and Jews at the time Cohen was a young woman were "not quite white" Europeans, yet they were officially categorized as "white" in government documents such as the census.

Official classifications and census takers' observations, however, did not always coincide with how people identified themselves. During the early decades of the new immigration, people tended to identify themselves according to the village or region from which they had emigrated. For example, many of those who had migrated from Italy often referred to themselves as "Sicilian" and "Calabrian" and created communities of people from these areas, particularly around Elizabeth, Mulberry, and Mott streets. Immigrants from Germany often identified themselves according to principalities such as Hesse-Cassal.[49] Moreover, the categories as listed by the "Report of the U.S. Immigration Commission" did not always mean non-white. For example, by 1911, the Irish had indeed "become" white, although they were listed as a distinct race.

It is tempting to use the term "ethnicity" to encompass a range of characteristics, ranging from the biological and phenotypical to language and religion. In the twenty-first century, race and ethnicity have come to mean different things. Race, as Jacobson illustrates, is a fabrication, creating artificial markers of difference to sort out groups. Since the 1920s, "ethnicity" has become synonymous with "culture," also a fluid category of identity that includes such attributes as language, religious practices, and social customs. During the period under consideration, however, "race" held much more purchase than the concept of "ethnicity," despite the fact that some encyclopedias and dictionaries used both terms in their definition of "race." Take, for example, the *Century Dictionary and Cyclopedia with a New Atlas of the World* in 1913, which defined "race" as "an Ethnical stock; a great division of mankind having in common certain distinguishing physical peculiarities, and thus a comprehensive class appearing to be derived from a distinct primitive source: as, the Caucasian *race;* the Mongolian *race;* the Negro *race.*"[50]

But in many ways, "race" remains an ambiguous and contradictory way to define difference. As Peggy Pascoe has shown, the indeterminacy of race has emerged in local and federal courts as judges, lawyers, and juries have struggled to define it within the intimate venue of marriage.[51] For this study, I use the term "race" as it was commonly used during the late nineteenth century and early twentieth century, the report by Dillingham's Immigration Commission notwithstanding—a fluid yet identifiable distinction among people of European, Asian, and African ancestry. I use "ethnicity" as a way to distinguish among groups that came under common racial categories, especially in regard to European immigrants who, for a relatively short time, stood on the cusp of whiteness and eventually came under the state rubric "Caucasian."[52]

Madison Grant and his patrician contemporaries who opposed the new immigration lived a world apart from the new immigrants and races about which they wrote; little did Grant realize that the immigration-restriction policies that he had so ardently supported actually facilitated many different kinds of interactions between the very racial groups he and others sought to separate. This is the story about how institutionalized power operated in people's everyday lives: Grant took power for granted; Ah Fung, his wife, and their Irish and Chinese friends never could. It is the obvious and stark contrast between Grant's ideas about race and the daily lives of urban working-class people that ultimately frames this book.

An analysis of interracial/interethnic families, households, and friendship networks necessitates a discussion of the meaning(s) of "family" and "community" in an urban setting. I use "family" in the broadest sense to include those who are related by blood and marriage, as well as others who maintain close personal ties over time within residential spaces and workplaces. In this sense, "community" and "family" potentially overlap. Broad interpretations of "family" and "community" are useful because they allow for the possibility of understanding urban social relations as fluid and changing rather than as rooted in traditional conceptions of kinship.

Finally, I place quotation marks around popular neighborhood designations to signal the semi-accuracy of these labels. "Ethnic" clustering was a reality of urban settlement patterns in U.S. cities. At the same time, however, as this study shows, such clustering was as much psychological as it was physical. "Little Italy," "Chinatown," and the European Jewish "Lower East Side" housed large clusters of Italians, Chinese, and Jews. But, as Donna Gabaccia has pointed out, "Italians" emigrated from villages within distinct regions with which people identified, such as Calabria and Sicily. Eastern European Jews hailed from Russia, Poland, Rumania, and Lithuania, bringing with them distinct cultural practices. Although most Chinese immigrants had come from rural communities in Guandong Province of southern China, they identified with specific villages. Moreover, many came to the United States via the Caribbean, Mexico, Central America, and Canada, often bringing with them fragments of cultural practices and languages from these "stop-over" places.

Moreover, within "ethnic" neighborhoods in New York City, a fair amount of ethnic diversity existed. As the following chapters demonstrate, "Chinatown," "Little Italy," and the "Lower East Side" housed individuals and families from a range of European ethnic backgrounds, as well as whites who claimed to be native New Yorkers over several generations and whites and a small population of blacks who had migrated from other parts of the United States.

The logical places to begin the search for interracial/interethnic households are the state and federal manuscript census reports, but one must be mindful of the limitations of these documents. Beyond locating and enumerating households and the people within them during a given census period, they reveal nothing about the social dynamics and levels of intimacy between people in families and households. But it is through this albeit imperfect method of counting people and households that the manuscript census provides a glimpse into the organization and structure of households and family and, beginning in the late nineteenth century, a detailed picture of the ethnic composition of a geographic area, from the macro- to the micro-levels—that is, by state, county, enumeration district, street, and building. They permit us to look into people's households and know their names (or approximates thereof), what their occupations might have been, their ages, whether or not they attended school, and approximately when they had immigrated. At the macro-level, census documents also allow historians to analyze the national discourses on race, gender, and ethnicity, which include the invisibility of married women's lineages. That designers of the census also understood the changes in configurations of household units during the industrial period is clear in the changing definitions of "family" for enumeration. For example, by the early twentieth century, to accommodate the reality that many urban working-class families lived in one flat, the census redefined "family" as a unit that shared a "common roof and table" with other families in the household. Census enumerators assumed that each family would rotate usage of a dining table with other families in the household.[53]

These documents, however, hide as much as they reveal. What seems to be clear from census lists might actually muddy our understanding of how families and households functioned on a daily basis. For example, the patriarchal and heteronormative assumptions of both family and household structures prevailed; household members were named in relation to the head of household, usually male. Although the head of the household might indeed have been the primary breadwinner in a family or household, this was not always the case, as shown by working-class people's reliance on the wages of children, boarders, and other relatives who might have resided in the same apartment dwelling. Second, and particularly vexing to genealogists and historians, was the erasure of married women's birth surnames, another reflection of patriarchal social norms. But as that erasure suggests, absences or silences can also reveal certain assumptions about cultural norms. Moreover, heterosexuality historically has been both an invisible and dominant feature of census reports. Thus, all of the households listed in manuscript censuses belie the social reality of gay and lesbian identities and communities, which flourished throughout New York City during the period under consideration.

Third, the census assumes "family" as constructed on the basis of blood ties, thus hiding the ways in which many groups, including African Americans, Chinese, and American Indians, in the United States also have included non-blood kinship ties as part of familial bonds. The fragmentation of blood kin as a result of slavery and the phenomenon of Chinese "paper" sons and daughters have rendered the concept of family a more flexible and fluid configuration of people who live together.

Reconstructing interracial/interethnic social relations in daily life is like chasing ghosts. Not only were most people in this book not famous; in many ways, they lived in the shadows of history, from the thousands of unnamed people who were crammed into photographs of street life to the long lists of households recorded by census takers. I have attempted to integrate as many types of printed primary documents available on social and economic life in New York City in general, and in southern Manhattan in particular. All of these sources embed their own inherent biases and limitations. Although rare, the voices of working-class people who lived and worked in the area emerge, albeit mediated, through interviews and letters. Although none of these sources together or alone can give us the full picture of personal and group dynamics, they provide a glimpse into the joys and struggles of people living in an ethnically diverse region of Manhattan. From their own positions within the structure of urban society, working-class people, reformers, police, and tourists enacted in their own ways and on their own terms the constructions of race, class, and gender that prevailed during their lifetimes. The task of *An Immigrant Neighborhood* ultimately is to illuminate how they negotiated their understandings of "difference" (and similarities) in everyday life. The extent to which the story of interethnic/interracial relations in southern Manhattan applies to other cities, or even to other parts of New York City, remains an open and intriguing question.

1

Forming Households, Families, and Communities

ert Val Eutemey and Louise Holmes were married in New York City in the 1920s. Holmes was an African American who had come from a long line of New Yorkers on her mother's side. Her father was originally from Virginia, one of many African Americans who had migrated from the South to Northern cities after the Civil War. Her husband had been born in Jamaica in 1878 of mixed Chinese, English, and African ancestry and had immigrated to the United States around 1910. After their marriage, Bert and Louise lived in compartmentalized worlds. They made their home in Brooklyn, which enabled them to maintain ties to their extended families, as well as to the African American and Afro-Caribbean communities. There they raised two sons, Edward and Loring. In the meantime, Bert established himself in the Chinese community in Manhattan, where he built a successful undertaking business on Mulberry Street and, in the process, created important social and political networks.[1]

The story of Bert Eutemey and Louise Holmes introduces a narrative of interracial family and community formation in New York City within the larger themes of migration and race politics during the early decades of the twentieth century. In some ways, the Eutemeys were no different from most other urban working-class families who struggled to earn a livelihood. At the same time, as a racially as well as ethnically mixed family, they encountered specific kinds of obstacles to survival and success during a period in which shifting definitions of race and citizenship created both opportunities and limitations within the urban economy.

Historians have written extensively about interracial marriage in U.S. history: their implications for race, gender, and sexual relations and the public discourses that surrounded them at specific historical moments. Although all marriages face the challenge of crossing boundaries, unions across lines of race, class, and gender present particular challenges. As Henry Yu writes, interracial/interethnic marriages lie at "the most intimate point" along lines of deeply held popular understandings of difference.[2] The purpose of this chapter is to explore the ways in which working-class people who married across lines of class, race, or ethnicity struggled to create and sustain families and communities in the face of a legally and socially restrictive environment. Interracial/interethnic marriages reveal much about how class, as a gendered and racialized signifier of both identity and layers of power and privilege, has operated in public and private life. Such marriages illustrate the uneven effects of discrimination and assimilation, as well as the instability of racial classifications during the early twentieth century. Depending on their individual positioning as "white," "non-white," or "in-between," urban working women and men encountered and negotiated systems of oppression in particular ways

Interracial/interethnic households among working-class and impoverished men and women in New York City were not unusual and date at least as far back as the early nineteenth century.[3] Unlike many states, New York had never passed an antimiscegenation law. On the face of it, the absence of laws banning interracial marriage was liberating—freeing heterosexual couples to marry whomever they chose without interference from the state. The lack of such laws, however, did not mean the absence of anxiety over interracial sex and marriage, especially between white women and men who were classified as non-white.

Each person shouldered a particular legacy of race relations in U.S. history and, hence, a specific historical relationship to race law. Such policies, combined with other factors, such as migration, urban residential patterns, and a racialized and gendered occupational structure, shaped the choices interracial married couples could make at specific historical moments. Thus, even within heterosexual and legal boundaries, interracial/interethnic marriages were "outlaw" unions in that they often resulted in the marginalization of the individuals in these marriages from family and communities.

In New York State, two of the most public cases occurred within a year of each other and involved working-class people of color, each of whom married a white upper-class person. In both cases, wealthy white male plaintiffs sought to dissolve marriages with black women. Leonard (Kip) Rhinelander sought to annul his marriage to Alice Beatrice Jones within months of their secret marriage in November 1924. About a year later, the father of Sarah Mildred Ziegler successfully annulled his daughter's marriage to a black bricklayer, Charles Edgar Smith.[4] Both cases illustrate how new and old narratives of race and sexuality shaped public discourses of class and gender in a state that had never barred interracial marriage. While Kip accused Alice of fraud, arguing that she had lied to him about her racial identity, Calvin Ziegler brought charges of abduction and rape against Smith, who later fled the state rather than face either a lynch mob or a trial in which, as a black man, his chances of winning were slim. In both cases, the power of money and legal arguments that resurrected conventional understandings of race, gender, and class ultimately prevented two young couples from forming families across race and class differences.

Not surprisingly, the power of the wealthy was unmistakable as the plaintiffs pushed for the observance of Jim Crow segregation during a period in which cultural shifts in gender roles and race boundaries were being challenged, especially in metropolitan areas such as New York City. In the absence of an antimiscegenation law, efforts to dissolve these marriages relied on other arguments, such as fraud, rape, and seduction, all three of which were highly racialized and gendered. In both cases, narratives of race, gender, and class found expression in the courtroom and in the local and national press. Major black publications such as the *Chicago Defender* and *Opportunity*, the official publication of the interracial civil-rights organization the National Urban League, also covered the stories. The rise of the black press and social movements that sought to end segregation and lynching assured the wide reportage of racially charged incidents and offered a competing antiracist narrative.

Had Alice Jones and Charles Smith married other working-class people, their stories likely would not have made headline news, although they might not have escaped entirely the attention of local journalists, who saw interracial sex and marriage as intriguing material in New York City's poor and immigrant neighborhoods. Interracial marriage among the working classes was much more common than among the elite but still constituted a relatively small percentage of the total working-class population by the early 1920s.[5] Despite their relatively small numbers, interracial marriages and the creation of mixed households among the urban working classes had caught the attention of the press since the late nineteenth century and focused particularly on unions between Chinese men and white women. Representations of these marriages reproduced the popular negative images of Chinese men as seducers of white women, who then turned to prostitution and drugs.

Social scientists began exploring the phenomenon of interracial marriages in the 1920s. In Chicago during the 1930s, most of the women with whom Chinese men interacted were working-class black or "white ethnic" women who had come from the city's large Slavic community and had worked in Chinese hand laundries. It was not uncommon for sexual relations to develop within the workplace.[6] New York City followed a similar pattern.[7]

The political economy and physical structure of urban working-class neighborhoods created opportunities for the simultaneous development of co-ethnic enclaves and interethnic/interracial interactions. In the narrow streets, outdoor peddlers, youths, shoppers, and workers competed for the use of sidewalks and alleyways as spaces for leisure, commerce, or laboring. Three- and four-story brick buildings accommodated retail shops, restaurants, and other small businesses, as well as Christian missions and charity organizations. These establishments typically occupied the basements and first floor levels in addition to apartment flats. Most of the urban dwellings were poorly heated cold-water flats with no indoor plumbing and scant lighting. By the early twentieth century, some were fortunate enough to reside in the so-called New Law apartments that had resulted from the tenement reform movement begun in the late nineteenth century.[8] Little had changed for many buildings, though, as the twentieth century progressed. In the early 1970s, one observer noted that 74 Mott Street had changed "imperceptibly" since its construction earlier in the century and cautioned visitors to proceed carefully through an "unlocked dingy entranceway," into a "dark, narrow, uninviting hallway" and entering an apartment that lacked "essential plumbing."[9]

Within this semi-private environment, interracial couples carved out a niche for themselves and their families.

Interracial households in southern Manhattan included a range of racial and ethnic configurations. Chinese men who married non-Chinese women were one of the more common interracial couples in lower Manhattan. The Chinese were no strangers to this area of New York City. In the early nineteenth century, a small, predominantly male Chinese population first settled among the working class and poor along the docks on the southern part of the island. The first generation of Chinese New Yorkers consisted of sailors, street vendors, and manufacturers of cigars, a number of whom married or cohabitated with working-class women of northern European ancestry.[10] Over the course of the nineteenth century, the Chinese began to settle several blocks north of the docks into what would become known as the "Chinatown" neighborhood, which included Pell, Mott, Mulberry, and Doyers streets. The tendency for Chinese–non-Chinese couples to cluster in certain buildings increased as the relative numbers of this configuration of mixed couples grew between 1880 and 1930.

In the late nineteenth century, only a few Chinese–Caucasian households could be found scattered in apartment buildings and tenements in the emerging "Chinatown" neighborhood. According to the 1880 census, most of Mott Street housed second-generation Irish and other European groups and Chinese men. Ah Nie and his wife, Jane, an Irish immigrant, were the only interracial couple at 17 Mott Street. Down the street, at number 45, lived Sak Ging, a worker in a candy factory; his white wife, Allis; their two young daughters, Malia and Elizabeth; their infant son, John; and a fifty-four-year-old laundress, Bridget Murphy. Two mixed couples also resided in the building next door at number 47 and one at number 49.[11]

By the early twentieth century, communities of Chinese–non-Chinese households concentrated within certain buildings. Although the number of such marriages remained relatively small, the clustering of these couples likely heightened their visibility in the eyes of social reformers, journalists, and the police. In 1900, thirty-one interracial households resided in the Chinatown neighborhood. Most were composed of Chinese immigrant men and white women; three Japanese immigrant men and their white wives also resided there. For example, an apartment building at 11 Pell Street housed a total of eleven Asian–Caucasian households in 1900, which consisted of nine Chinese–Caucasian and two Japanese–Caucasian households. Nearby, at number 15, Kino Takahashi, a restaurant worker, lived with his Caucasian wife, Marie.[12]

Among Asian immigrant men in the city, the Chinese predominated, despite a decline in Chinese immigration as a result of the exclusion laws. Most Japanese people had immigrated after the passage of the Chinese Exclusion Act under the careful supervision of the Japanese government. After witnessing the discrimination against the Chinese, the government had sought to prepare its citizens for potentially hostile treatment the United States. The majority of Japanese immigrants settled in Hawaii and the western region of the U.S. mainland. Kino Takahashi was one of a small number of Japanese immigrants who settled in East Coast cities. Between 1880 and 1900, the Japanese population in the United States had grown from 148 to 86,000, most of whom (61,000) worked on the sugar and pineapple plantations in Hawaii. The total number of Japanese in the Northeast, however, remained small.[13] As a result, the Japanese people in this area did not attract the same degree of invective as did the Chinese. In New York State, the number of Japanese residents had increased from 17 to 354 between 1880 and 1900. In 1900, 175 of New York City's 286 Japanese residents lived in Manhattan. Despite the Gentlemen's Agreement of 1907, which had intended to curb the influx of Japanese labor into the United States, the number of Japanese steadily increased, even in the Northeast. By 1910, the Japanese population living in New York City numbered 1,037, with 787 residing in Manhattan, compared with 4,686 Chinese who lived in the borough. Approximately a third of Japanese men living on the East Coast married non-Japanese women and performed menial labor.[14]

Several buildings continued to rent to interracial couples over time. For example, the building at 11 Mott Street housed five such couples in 1900. Ten years later, five different couples resided at this address: four Chinese men and a Japanese man and their white wives. The white women in this building may have been prostitutes. In 1901, an investigator for the private anti-vice organization in New York City the Committee of Fifteen reported that, when questioning one Annie Gilroy at

Callahan's Bar on Chatham Square one evening, Gilroy allegedly told the investigator to visit "the girls" at 11 Mott Street for a "good time."[15]

At 17 Mott Street, the composition of the resident population changed from mostly Chinese male lodgers and two white households in 1900 to one that included ten Chinese–white couples in 1910 out of a total of twelve households. In 1920, interracial households dominated the building. Out of twenty-one households, nineteen were composed of Chinese men and non-Chinese women. One household revealed multiple ethnic/racial identities. Edith Lee, a woman of mixed Irish and African ancestry, resided with her laundryman husband, Young. Roy Lee, a carpenter, constituted the only single Chinese household in the building. Within ten years, Roy Lee had married a woman named Mary. They lived in the building with their four young children and Mary's fourteen-year-old daughter from a previous marriage. The only other non-Chinese resident in the building in 1920 was the janitor, fifty-five-year-old Henry Pelz, a German immigrant, who also remained in the building for at least another ten years.[16]

By 1910, a greater number of apartment buildings housed mixed households but with fewer large clusters. Numbers 11, 13, and 19 Pell Street contained two mixed households in 1910. Each household was configured differently. Young Wing lived with his wife, Theresa, and Hop Chu headed a household that contained himself and a white couple, John and Helen Baptiste, both of whom were recent immigrants from Germany. Chu was a salesman in a general store, and Baptiste was a bookkeeper. Another Chinese man named Chu lived with his white wife, Alice, and three boarders—two Chinese men and one white man. Chu Suey's large household included his wife, Anna, and five boarders: Anna Armstrong, who had her own income; Bow Kee and Bow Sing, both of whom worked as salesmen in a store; and Charlie Chu and his white wife, Annie. One of their neighbors in the building was the infamous Mock Duck and his family. Mock Duck later rose to the leading ranks of the Chinese gang the Hip Sings during the 1930s.[17]

Doyers Street was the smallest of the main streets in Chinatown and housed a few interracial households between 1900 and 1930. In 1900, two Chinese men and their Caucasian wives resided at number 19. By 1930, the only non-Chinese residents at this address were two African American men: Edward Emerson, the superintendent of the building, and his son Joseph, a plumber. Two interracial households resided at 15 Doyers Street in 1910. Ung and Sallie Chu shared their apartment with four Chinese men; Chung Wing resided with his Cuban immigrant wife, Marie Fernando Wing, one white male boarder, and four Chinese male boarders. All of the boarders were restaurant workers.[18]

The stability of residency varied. In 1910, William Hook, a cook, and his wife, Jenny, a second-generation Irish woman, resided at 57 Bayard Street, a building that contained only one other mixed couple: Walter Otachi, a Japanese immigrant merchant, and his wife, a white woman who had migrated to New York from Texas. By 1920, the Hooks had moved further south to Cherry Street, the only mixed-race couple in a building that housed one other family, John and Lillie Gizzi, Italian immigrants, and their two U.S.-born children. By this time, the Hooks had also taken in a boarder, James Wing, a Chinese sailor.

Some households remained in the neighborhood for at least a decade. The Goon family, which consisted of Annie and Li Goon, a laundryman, and their five children, resided on Mott Street between 1900 and 1910. A number of the white wives who had lived at 17 Mott Street in 1920 were living by themselves in individual households in the same building ten years later. Some reported their status as widowed, while others reported that they were either married or single. Unlike in the previous census, a number of these women, reportedly in their late thirties and forties, now reported an occupation, which included working in restaurants, movie theaters, and shops. Dora Wing, a daughter of either German or Russian immigrants, had been married to Hae Wing, a cook. Widowed by 1930, she worked as a waitress. Jessie Suey, also a widow, worked as a waitress, as well, and Florence Lee worked as a salesperson in a dress shop.[19] The census is silent about the lives of these women, but their long-term residence in the "Chinatown" neighborhood suggests that over the years they had carved a niche that probably helped sustain them socially and financially.

With the exception of the famous gang leader Mock Duck, little is known about the lives of the people who appear in census reports. Manuscript censuses provide historians with only tantalizing fragments of the experiences of working-class and poor people. In some cases, however, historians can piece together shards of evidence into a kind of jigsaw puzzle, using government documents, newspapers, oral histories, and personal correspondence to illuminate the opportunities, barriers, and tensions people faced in daily life. The stories of Bert Eutemey and Louise Holmes, Margaret Hart and Wong Jung Que, and Ethel Gross and Harry Hopkins illustrate the diverse experiences of interracial/inter-ethnic couples. Their stories illustrate the ways in which race politics at the national, state, and local levels shaped their migration experiences to and within the city, their establishment of family and community ties, and their participation in the paid and unpaid urban workforce. Their individual racial and ethnic identities resulted in specific kinds of inter-actions with family, workers, community, and the state within the larger process of racial and ethnic formation in U.S. society.

Migration and settlement patterns among the working classes, struc-tured simultaneously by immigration law and the promise of economic opportunities, played a crucial role in the lives of these couples, who traced their family lineages to Africa, the British Isles, the Caribbean, China, and Southern and Eastern Europe. The Wongs followed a long legacy of Chinese and Irish working-class immigration and marriage patterns that date back to the early nineteenth century. In part, a com-mon class status brought Chinese men and Irish women into close prox-imity to one another. Both groups had resided in the poorest sections of the area, often making their homes in shacks, attics, and basements near the docks. By the mid-nineteenth century, complementary gender migration patterns contributed to the frequency of marriages between the two groups. While the majority of Chinese immigrants were male, the numbers of Irish immigrant women either equaled or, in some years, outnumbered Irish male immigrants. The dearth of Chinese women and Irish men and the absence of state antimiscegenation laws help explain why Chinese men and Irish women married.

At the same time that such marriages and cohabitation between Chinese men and women of Irish ancestry took place, anti-Chinese pro-tests among the Irish working class were also on the rise. In the western states, anti-Chinese sentiment among predominantly Irish male workers eventually resulted in the passage of federal laws to restrict the immigra-tion of Chinese laborers. In the Northeast, Irish working-class men and women struggled to distance themselves from blacks and other "non-whites," as demonstrated by the Draft Riots in July 1863.

By the late nineteenth century, local writers, many of whom had begun their careers as newspapermen, took up the subject of Irish–Chinese marriages and sexual liaisons and the tensions that often emerged between Irish working-class men and Chinese men. Their fictional and nonfictional stories of urban life, typically set in lower Manhattan, reproduced popular ethnic and gender stereotypes. Here the concern focused on the migratory character of city life and the dangers it presented to otherwise innocent and impressionable young white women. The relatively small neighborhood where Chinese immigrant men such as Wong Jung Que lived and worked functioned simultaneously as a site of danger and corruption, as well as of continued consumption of things Oriental, a pattern that began with the extension of the China trade to the United States in the early nineteenth century.[20] Over the course of the century, Chinese business owners offered white middle-class "slummers" and white working-class locals inexpensive Chinese food, trinkets, herbs, and other items from restaurants, shops, and apothecaries.

Crossing racial boundaries alarmed city officials and reformers and provided fodder for beat journalists who published their lurid stories in local newspapers and racy magazines such as the *Police Gazette*. Many published true-to-life fiction based on prevailing images of Chinese and white women and the realities of social mixing in working-class urban neighborhoods. In his introduction to *Stories of Chinatown*, William Norr wondered "how young and comely women can cast their lot with the repulsive Chinese."[21] Sexual relationships and marriages between Chinese and white women were striking to observers and raised questions about the "purity" of white women's sexuality. In *How the Other Half Lives*, Jacob Riis noted that "the 'wives' of Chinatown are of a different stock that comes closer to home."[22]

Few writers blamed white women for inveigling Chinese men. One exception was a former New York City police chief who wrote, "The moon-faced gentle Chinaman who plies his iron all day and slips through the streets fearful of contact with the rude American is an easy victim to the wiles of the immoral white woman."[23]

Some stories portrayed young Irish women as both victims and offenders. In these stories, if young women did not meet a tragic demise, they ended up as brutal and uncouth middle-age working-class wives who railed at their gambling husbands, as depicted in the character of "Mrs. Gin-Seng" in Alfred Trumble's *The Mott Street Poker Club*

(1889).[24] In *Stories of Chinatown*, published several years after Trumble's story, Norr deploys classic stereotypes of Irish and Chinese men and of "fallen women" and rearticulates mounting concerns among reformers, journalists, and the police about the increased ability of young women to traverse the city streets unsupervised. Thus, Norr does not portray Mamie Cavanaugh as completely blameless when she runs off with a Chinese man. Rather, he sees her as the cause of her father's drift toward alcoholism and the demise of the family's financial and emotional resources. Mamie's waywardness contributes to an already fragile but respectable working-class immigrant family's sinking even further into poverty and moral profligacy.

As Mary Liu has demonstrated, the "Chinatown Trunk" murder case of 1909 concretized all of the fears and anxiety about the social interactions between Chinese men and white women. In June 1909, the body of nineteen-year-old Elsie Sigel, the granddaughter of the distinguished Civil War General Franz Sigel, was found in a trunk in an apartment on Eighth Avenue in Manhattan. Prior to her murder, Elsie and her mother had been missionaries among the mostly male Chinese population in New York City. Public furor over the case illuminated racialized sexual politics at both the local and the national level.

Although the killing had occurred outside the Chinese neighborhood well south of Eighth Avenue, the press nevertheless dubbed the incident the "Chinatown" murder case. The "Chinatown" neighborhood became the focus of a widespread police crusade to rid the area of its white female population. Captain Michael Galvin of the Elizabeth Street police station declared his intent to "purge" the area of its white female population by requiring white women who lived there to produce marriage certificates. Galvin's vigilance was apparently so great that, just two months after the murder and after driving two hundred white women from the neighborhood, he suffered a physical breakdown and went on an indefinite leave of absence.[25]

Margaret Hart grew up amid the proliferation of popular images of Chinatown and the Chinese and the daily realities of immigrant and working-class life. Her childhood was not unlike that of most working-class women in New York City. Margaret was the eldest of three daughters born to Dominick and Elizabeth Madden Hart at her family's apartment at 149 Cherry Street.[26] Located a few blocks from the

East River, Cherry Street was home to a working-class population where co-ethnic households clustered. Like many neighborhoods, the ethnic and racial composition of Cherry Street had changed over time. Heavily populated by people of Irish ancestry during the nineteenth century, many of the Irish, including the Harts, had moved out of Cherry Street by 1910, when Italian and Russian Jewish households heavily populated the area.[27]

Undaunted or perhaps even intrigued by such horrific stories as the Sigel case and the myriad fiction that focused on the dangers of interracial relationships, young working-class women like Hart continued to venture into Chinatown and other "forbidden" spaces in the city. Although we do not know exactly how she met her future husband, it is quite possible that Margaret had visited Wong's restaurant at 11 Pell Street with friends who sought to partake of its "exotic" and inexpensive fare.

Once married, the Wongs not only lived amid the local discourses of Chinese–white marriages; they also confronted the anti-Chinese foundations of federal immigration laws when they decided to travel to China to visit Jung Que's family. Fortunately, they married before the passage of the Cable Act in 1922, which stripped American women of their citizenship if they married an alien deemed legally ineligible for citizenship. Unlike Chinese American women, however, non-Chinese women could regain their citizenship through naturalization unless they lived in their husbands' country for more than two years.[28]

The couple still had to face the Chinese Exclusion Act, which remained in effect until 1943. Under the exclusion laws, any Chinese person who wished to leave the United States with the intention of returning first had to obtain a return certificate from the Immigration and Naturalization Service (INS).[29] As in all cases, the administration of the exclusion laws was left to the discretion of the immigration inspector. Applicants had to provide the inspectors with written documents verifying their original admission into the United States and produce both white and Chinese witnesses to confirm their identity and occupation. These documents provide a glimpse into a wider social world that extended beyond co-ethnic relations and reveal the kinds of daily networks that were critical to the survival of urban working-class immigrants. As Kitty Calavita reminds us, in the end the actual administration of the law by local immigration inspectors typically made the ultimate difference in the decision.[30]

Wong did not have the necessary papers to confirm his right to be in the United States when he and his wife sat down before Chinese Inspector Albert B. Wiley. Wong claimed that his father had made all of the arrangements for their admission when he was just sixteen years old. He was in luck, though, for two reasons. First, he produced reliable white witnesses. Although remuneration for testifying was typical, incentives other than cash payments also factored into the willingness of whites to testify on behalf of Chinese people. White witnesses were not strangers to the applicants; many had developed some kind of social or economic relationship with Chinese individuals and, in some cases, with the larger Chinese community. Wong's witnesses included George F. Randles, a grocery store wholesaler, and Harry D. Gilbert, a restaurant supplier. Both men served as witnesses for Chinese applicants in a number of cases.[31] Second, and perhaps more important, Wong sat before an official with whom he had grown familiar over years of travel back and forth to China and who viewed Wong's marriage to a white woman not as a liability but as a positive attribute. Wiley recommended approval despite the absence of "any proof substantiating his admission." The inspector wrote in his report to the commissioner of immigration that "as he [Wong] is married to a white woman and has been known to the writer for at least fifteen years, it is believed that this office is not justified in claiming that he is unlawfully within the United States." In the end, it was the immigration inspector himself whose "testimony" via memo would clinch the approval of Wong's application.[32]

That Wong's marriage to a white woman turned out to be somewhat of an advantage (or, at least, not an obstacle) is striking, given proposals at the national level to penalize white female citizens if they married Chinese men. The Wong case illustrates the power of administering law at the local level to determine an applicant's entrance into or exclusion from the country. Most interrogations were lengthy and often grueling experiences. In this instance, the power of whiteness and positive personal relations with individual immigration inspectors together eased the application and interrogation processes.[33]

The Hart–Wong marriage followed a long history of marriages between Chinese men and Irish women in New York City. The marriage of

Bert Eutemey and Louise Holmes was part of an equally long legacy of intermarriage in Jamaica, the country of Eutemey's birth. In both cases, an association with whiteness proved advantageous. Wong Jung Que's marriage to a white woman, in the eyes of a friendly immigration inspector, led to a positive outcome. For Eutemey, his claim to British citizenry helped him circumvent the exclusion laws and gain entrance into the country despite his Chinese heritage. The story of Louise Holmes and Bert Eutemey also illustrates other important demographic changes that resulted from new migration patterns, including the changing role of the Caribbean in transnational flows of capital and people during the early twentieth century and the impact of black migration from the U.S. South into Northern cities on the creation of families and communities.

A British passport made it possible for Bert Eutemey and his brother, Enos, to leave the British colony of Jamaica and settle in New York City with little difficulty. Little is known about their lives before they immigrated to the United States. They had been part of a relatively small Chinese community, compared with the black and white populations, in Jamaica. By the time Bert left Jamaica, just over 2,000 people of Chinese ancestry resided on the island, which constituted about 0.3 percent of the total population.[34] The Eutemeys migrated as part of a typical chain migration process in which family and other members of one's village or community migrated after the initial group had settled. They likely departed on one of the many "banana boats" that transported bananas and emigrants out of the Caribbean. These ships then brought return migrants back to the islands, as well as vacationers as part of an emerging tourist industry. Bert immigrated to the United States in 1910; Enos arrived five years later.[35]

Most people of Chinese ancestry in Jamaica were descendants of a predominantly male population that had been recruited or kidnapped or had voluntarily left China to work as "coolie" labor on the sugar plantations after the British government abolished slavery in 1834.[36] Between the 1850s and the 1880s, the sources of the Chinese male labor force in Jamaica expanded to include Panama and laborers directly from Hong Kong.[37]

The Jamaican class/race hierarchy created the social and economic conditions under which blacks and Chinese could come into regular contact with one another. The long history of importing African slaves, and later Chinese coolie labor, to the island resulted in a black and Chinese agricultural workforce that shared a similar class status. Even after many Chinese entered the grocery and retail trade after their indenture contracts had been fulfilled, the social and political status of Jamaican Chinese remained below that of whites. As a result, blacks and Chinese often resided in close physical proximity to one another in the poor sections of the island. Moreover, as in the United States, the uneven sex ratio among the Chinese also led Chinese men to seek out non-Chinese women. In 1891, for example, there were 345 Chinese men for every 100 Chinese women. Not surprisingly, marriages between Chinese women and non-Chinese men on the island were uncommon.[38] The children of Chinese and black Jamaicans were categorized as "Chinese coloureds" in the Jamaican census reports.[39]

Despite the frequency of intermarriage between Chinese and blacks on the island, relations in Jamaica between the two groups were often strained.[40] By the time the Eutemey brothers left Jamaica, anti-Chinese sentiment was on the rise, resulting in large part from the system of racial classification that had facilitated the move by some Chinese out of low-paying, low-status agricultural work and into shopkeeping, retail, and some trades and professions. Unlike darker-skinned Jamaicans, light-skinned people of mixed Caucasian or Chinese ancestry were considered closer to whites and typically enjoyed better treatment and greater economic opportunities. Mutual suspicion between the two groups emerged, as many poor black Jamaicans resented the upward mobility of the Chinese. Likewise, Chinese attitudes toward blacks were not always positive. Lee Tom Yin, a Chinese Jamaican writer who published and edited a book on the history of the Chinese on the island in the 1950s, attributed the absence of blacks in the grocery store business to their "carefree nature," which supposedly precluded them from working the long hours necessary for running a store.[41]

Internal political problems within the Chinese community in Jamaica also may have motivated the Eutemey brothers to leave the island when they did. Increased factionalism within the 400-member Chinese Benevolent Society (CBS) between 1903 and 1916 that resulted from the "tyranny" of the new leader, Lin Biang, according to Lee Tom Yin, was the "darkest period in the history of Chinese settlement in Jamaica." Under Lin's leadership the Chinese Tong controlled gambling and the funds of the CBS, which led to the emergence of a splinter organization. Street fighting between members of the rival organization was a common occurrence until Lin's death.[42]

Avoiding the Chinese exclusion laws was paramount to Bert Eutemey's entrance into the United States. His Chinese ancestry would work against him, especially if he could not prove merchant status. Bert Eutemey probably circumvented the laws by obtaining a British passport that contained no reference to his Chinese ancestry. Thus, he did not have to face interrogation by immigration agents and risk being denied admission. Once in the United States, Eutemey used his Chinese name, Leung Lai Tin.

For people of mixed ancestry, racial categories fluctuated according to the perceptions of census takers or the individuals themselves. The racial identity of the Eutemeys illustrated the inconsistencies of racial classification in government documents.[43] Chinese could be classified as "Chinese" or "colored." The classification of mixed children of Chinese heritage varied among "Chinese," "colored," and "white." The U.S. census reports for 1920 and 1930 list the Eutemey brothers as "Negro," although Enos's draft registration card lists him as "white" and Bert's card lists him as "Chinese/Other."[44]

That Bert and Louise Eutemey would decide to maintain their home in Brooklyn rather than in Manhattan is not surprising. By the 1920s, Afro-Caribbean immigrants from throughout the West Indies made up a small but growing component of New York City's black population. In and around Dean Street, where Enos's family lived, resided a number of black West Indians. Relations between the two groups were sometimes strained. Although white supremacy had subordinated all people of African ancestry since the seventeenth century, over time cultural and class differences created different understandings of "blackness" within the ethnically diverse black population. Well-established elite black families sometimes looked down on the new immigrants and maintained a distinct social distance from the black Caribbean population.[45]

Bert and Louise Eutemey moved at least once within Brooklyn between 1920 and the outbreak of World War II, but they always lived near both Enos Eutemey and Louise's parents. During the 1920s, they resided on Bergen Street (three blocks south of Atlantic Avenue) amid Italian immigrants and blacks who had migrated from the West Indies and Jamaica. Sometime during the 1930s, the Eutemeys moved around the corner to 9 Revere Place.[46] Both streets were located near Kingston Street, perhaps named for the concentration of Jamaican immigrants who lived in the area.

Thus, although lower Manhattan provided opportunities for forming interracial households for some people, it was also an isolating space for mixed Chinese–black families like the Eutemeys. By the time Louise and Bert married, most black New Yorkers had moved out of southern Manhattan to the Harlem neighborhood north of Central Park. The black community in Brooklyn was also growing. According to the federal census of 1930, for example, Bert Eutemey was part of the nearly 69,000 "Negroes" who resided in Brooklyn, as opposed to the 1,400 Chinese who lived in the borough. How many of these individuals could also claim mixed ancestry is unclear. Bert and Louise had to figure out a different kind of strategy for creating community for themselves and their children.

Louise Holmes Eutemey maintained unequivocal ties with the African American working-class community in Brooklyn. The eldest daughter of Harry and Bertha Holmes, Louise was born around 1900, the product of a small but well-established black community in Brooklyn.[47] As was typical in a gendered and racially segmented paid labor force, Louise's parents and grandparents were employed in service jobs. Her father found work first as a chauffeur for a private family and then as a factory clerk. Her maternal grandfather, Henry T. Savage, was a cook, and her grandmother, Emily Savage, was a laundress.[48] When Louise was a baby, her family was one of a handful of black families living in Brooklyn. By 1910, with the birth of a second daughter, Beatrice, the family moved from Broadway to Atlantic Avenue, a busy thoroughfare between what would become the predominantly black neighborhoods of Bedford-Stuyvesant and Crown Heights. The move symbolized both the increased racial segregation of Brooklyn as greater numbers of blacks moved to the borough and the creation of a semblance of community, which may well have included Bert Eutemey's family. Enos had also married a black woman, Leila, and lived north of Atlantic Avenue on Halsey Street. Although they changed residences several times, Bert and Louise never moved more than a few blocks away from her parents.[49]

The Eutemeys experienced Jim Crow segregation on different levels. Living openly as a black–Chinese couple in Manhattan's Chinese community risked social and economic marginalization for themselves and their children. In his work life, Bert encountered another obstacle. He was interested in providing undertaking and funeral services to the Chinese population in Manhattan, but state law restricted certain occupations, including undertaking and funeral directing, to U.S. citizens and those who were eligible for citizenship. The exclusion laws, which remained in effect until 1943, forbade Chinese immigrants from applying for U.S. citizenship. As a result, Bert circumvented federal immigration and citizenship laws by using a British passport to obtain an undertaking license; ironically, he became known as the first undertaker of Chinese ancestry in New York.

Although it is impossible to know with any certainty that Bert adopted an exclusive Chinese identity or whether Chinese Manhattanites knew he was married to a black woman, it is clear that he chose to keep his home and his work separate. He became an active member of lower Manhattan's Chinese community. In addition to operating his funeral parlor on Mulberry Street, he organized the second Chinese Boy Scout troop in New York City. His facility in Chinese and English also enabled him to serve as an interpreter for the Chinese Consolidated Benevolent Association, the most powerful clan-based Chinese organization in the city.

Bert was able to literally move back and forth between the Chinese and the black communities in Manhattan and Brooklyn relatively easily. Bridges that linked the two boroughs helped him keep his feet in two worlds. With the opening of three bridges between the 1880s and 1920s—the Brooklyn Bridge (East River Bridge) in 1883 and, later, the Manhattan and Williamsburg bridges—and the subway system, commuters and tourists did not have to rely solely on the ferry to cross the East River.[50] The entrance to the Brooklyn Bridge on the Manhattan side was close to the Lower East Side via Park Row and Centre Street, while the Williamsburg Bridge, pejoratively called "Jews Bridge," connected Delancey Street, the heart of the predominantly European Jewish neighborhood in Manhattan, to the Williamsburg neighborhood in Brooklyn.[51] For business owners, the bridges provided a more efficient way to ship agricultural and manufactured goods from Brooklyn to other parts of the city.

But the bridges did more than serve as physical thoroughfares. They held symbolic meaning, as well, in terms of how New Yorkers identified themselves—by their boroughs and by the specific neighborhoods in which they lived. The Brooklyn Bridge in particular, as the first structure to link the two boroughs, has been hailed as both a technological and a cultural achievement. In addition to its physical features, complete with a promenade for walking and a thoroughfare below for vehicles, the bridge symbolized the link between two worlds that Brooklynites saw as distinct: the densely populated and bustling life of recent immigrants and finance versus the rural, bucolic setting that Brooklyn had represented since the eighteenth century. For Jews, Brooklyn served as an extension of the Lower East Side for first- and second-generation immigrants. By the 1920s, blacks, European immigrants, and a small community of Chinese people had enhanced Brooklyn's diverse ethnic character.[52]

Bert Eutemey's migration experience exemplifies the fluidity of ethnic identity and community formation. The decision to ensconce the family in Brooklyn while he worked and socialized in Manhattan illustrates the fractures that existed between blacks and Chinese by the 1920s. Thus, at the same time that the Brooklyn Bridge functioned as a symbolic and literal link between co-ethic groups, it also served as a way to facilitate the separation of people living and working in the two boroughs.

The bridge served the latter function for Margaret Hart. Although she and Jung Que were able to combine work and family on the Lower East Side, Margaret's marriage to a Chinese man apparently alienated her from her father and stepmother.[53]

By the time Margaret and Jung Que married, Margaret's family had relocated to Brooklyn. The Wongs resided on Doyers Street, among several other interracial households in the "Chinatown" neighborhood. Their son, James, born in 1923, grew up in the neighborhood, one of the few mixed-race children in Chinatown. In addition to her role as mother and housewife, Margaret, like many other wives of small-business owners, ran the cash register at her husband's restaurant. The possibility of out-marriages among Chinese men and women of Irish ancestry persisted into the twentieth century. But unlike Ah Fung and his wife, whose very existence as an interracial couple had drawn commentary from the local newspaper more than a generation before, Wong Jung Que and Margaret Hart lived a relatively uneventful existence in a neighborhood that continued to gain popularity as a tourist destination. Like many other working-class families, then as now, daily life meant scratching out a living in low-wage jobs or small businesses that sustained family and friendship networks, as well as the budding tourist industry.

The fine line between "white" and what Karen Brodkin refers to as "not quite white" shaped the migration experiences of Ethel Gross. Yet despite the debates over the gradations of whiteness as a racial category, under the law both Gross and Hopkins were "white" regardless of cultural differences and the persistence of anti-Semitism in the United States. Gross was a Hungarian Jew who had immigrated to the United States with her widowed mother, Celia, and several siblings in the 1890s, the height of the new immigration from Southern and Eastern Europe. Like many new immigrants, Gross's family settled among a diverse population of working-class European Jews on the Lower East Side. Unlike many immigrants, however, the Gross family experienced downward mobility when they immigrated to the United States. Both of Ethel's parents were educated and, despite the intense anti-Semitism in Hungary, had enjoyed a middle-class life. Ethel's mother, Celia Rich Gross, was a widow when she brought her children to the United States. Celia struggled to adjust to her new life and the responsibility of supporting her family in an era when few choices were open to women; Celia committed suicide when Ethel was twenty-one. Presumably, Ethel and her siblings contributed to the family economy the best they could. Ethel attended school until the eighth grade; then she found clerical work and, later, a job with an electrical company.[54] As a child, Gross had participated in the activities offered at Christodora House, located in the northeastern sector of the Lower East Side. As a young woman, she worked at Christodora in the hope of pursuing a career as a settlement house worker.

Harry Hopkins had come from a very different background. Even though he and Ethel may have been classified in the census as "white," one could argue that Harry was "whiter" than Ethel. Born in Sioux City, Iowa, in 1890, Harry Lloyd Hopkins was the fourth of five children born to David A. Hopkins and Anna Pickett Hopkins. The elder Hopkins began work as a harnessmaker but lost his business in the Panic of 1893. In an effort to secure steady employment, the elder Hopkins moved his family several times, first to Grinnell, Iowa, then to Nebraska and to Chicago. Religious devotion maintained the emotional and spiritual stability of the Hopkins family as they migrated from place to place within the Midwest. Harry grew up in a world of strong Protestant social activism. His mother was a former schoolteacher from Ontario, Canada, and an active member of the Methodist church. She once served as president of the Methodist Home Missionary Society in Iowa. Methodism boasted a long history of activism among the Protestant denominations, from the Second Great Awakening earlier in the nineteenth century to the Social Gospel movement after the Civil War in both Canada and the United States.[55] Thus, it was no surprise that Harry Hopkins chose to attend Grinnell College, an academic center of Social Gospel reform.[56]

Inspired by ideas of Progressive-era urban reform and the Social Gospel, Hopkins moved to New York City after graduating from college in 1912 to supervise the Northover Boys Camp in Bound Brook, New Jersey, which was sponsored by Christodora House.[57] Hopkins was one of many young, college-educated white men and women from small towns and villages who were eager to apply the ideas emerging in the new field of social work to improve the conditions of the poor through the social settlement house movement in cities throughout the United States. Embedded in the social settlement house movement were theories of assimilation and acculturation to white, middle-class ideas about education, hygiene, and motherhood. After his stint at Northover, Hopkins continued on to Christodora House, where he met Gross. Following a brief and furtive courtship, Harry and Ethel married in October 1913 at the Ethical Culture Society, a reform organization established by Felix Adler and other activists as part of the Ethical Culture movement.[58] Although the couple shared a strong commitment to urban social reform, gender politics, Harry's roving eye, and cultural differences proved to be an unending source of friction in their marriage.

Marriages between Jews and non-Jews were less common than marriages between other ethnic groups.[59] Despite the comparative numerical realities, the numbers of such marriages that did exist were too high in the eyes of some Jewish writers. In his memoirs, the Jewish social reformer David Blaustein recalled that the number of out-marriages among Jews was not only "quite large" but a problem. Blaustein blamed the factory workplace as the prime venue for young Jewish men and women to meet non-Jews, which he considered a "social problem—a racial problem—a religious problem." The purpose of settlement houses that catered to Jews, such as the Educational Alliance, where Blaustein served as superintendent in the 1890s, was to provide a social and religious venue for Jews to meet and marry. The ultimate goal was "the preservation of the Jew."[60]

Interest in and concerns about Jewish–non-Jewish romances and marriages gained increasing popularity in literature and the theater. Relations between the Irish and the Jews were particularly popular. Perhaps the best-known stage representation of such marriages was *Abie's Irish Rose*. Although Anne Nichols's play received lukewarm reviews from critics when it opened on Broadway in 1922, it was wildly popular among audiences and enjoyed a run of more than 2,000 performances. In 1928, the film version of the story premiered.[61]

The significance of their interfaith relationship was not lost on either Gross or Hopkins. In one letter, he jokingly requested that she not fall in love with his friend, who was an Irish Catholic, because "you know you can't play every instrument in the band!"[62]

To Gross's family, the romance was no laughing matter. Ethel's siblings expressed apprehension about their sister's growing romantic interest in a non-Jew. Their letters suggest the tension as well as the passion that surrounded their courtship. For Ethel's sister, the problem was not so much about breaking faith or that Ethel was four years younger than Harry but about anti-Semitism, which she believed always potentially lurked below the surface of non-Jews. In a long letter to Harry, Ethel recounted her sister's misgivings: "She said she would always welcome and like anybody that I chose for a friend—but she 'does not believe in inter marriages because that born prejudice against the jew [*sic*] might be slumbering sometimes but it is never dead no matter how broad-minded they are.'"[63]

In some ways Ethel's sister was correct: Anti-Semitism could emerge

from anyone at anytime. Ethel, however, newly in love and more ideal-
istic that her sister, was adamant that such relationships could succeed
if the couple were "in perfect harmony and absolutely suited to each
other—in spite of the fact that they were born to different faiths."[64] The
next month, Harry responded optimistically: "Ethel dear—I love you
so that I don't see how they can object. Every interest I have is centered
on you—everything I do is done for you dear and we will be happy no
matter if the whole world objects."[65]

Gross's impending engagement to Hopkins apparently caused Christina MacColl, the founder and supervisor at the settlement, to worry
about how *his* family would react to an upcoming marriage to a Jew.[66]
Having worked closely with both Gross and Hopkins, MacColl apparently had been a strong supporter of the couple's engagement. Hopkins
especially had sought MacColl's approval. In one letter to Gross in early
March, he joked, "Poor dear—how she [MacColl] will regret wrecking
your life for a Methodist settlement worker—and a poor Methodist at
that. Ten years from now we'll show her it wasn't so bad—won't we
Ethel?" Throughout the month, he still seemed afraid to be forthright
with MacColl about his new love. Hopkins wrote to Gross that he had
finally told MacColl he was going to be married but that he had not yet
told her to whom. A few days later, he wrote excitedly that he was "crazy
for her to know." He finally told MacColl about their engagement but
requested that she keep the news a secret.[67]

As working-class interracial couples settled into married life, they
negotiated specific forms of race, gender, and class politics at the local level—within their families, among one another, and in the workplace. The degree to which they could combine work and family varied.
Ethel Gross's circumstances brought her a degree of public recognition
through her participation in the Settlement House Movement and a
rocky marriage to Harry Hopkins, who later rose up in the ranks of
national public policy in Franklin Delano Roosevelt's administration
during the Great Depression.

One might see Ethel Gross's marriage to Harry Hopkins as a continuation of her desire to assimilate into middle-class American society. Ironically, once married, she found herself marginalized from both
her husband and the work in which she had actively participated before
her marriage. Ethnic differences apparently had been a source of attrac-

tion at the beginning of their courtship and marriage. According to a friend and fellow social worker, John Kingsbury, Hopkins claimed he had courted Gross out of pity for a "poor Jewish girl" but that her "Jewish relatives and customs" contributed to the breakup, not the presence of another woman. According to June Hopkins, the idea that Hopkins pitied Gross is unlikely, given her active participation in a number of political causes, including suffrage and the labor movement. His claim that another woman was not involved in the breakup of his marriage was also untrue. By the time Hopkins and Gross separated, he had been seeing Barbara Duncan for two years. They married in 1931.[68]

For Harry and Ethel Hopkins, ethnic and class differences, as well as gender conventions, shaped both their marriage and their eventual divorce. Like many women of her generation, Ethel, despite her professional aspirations and their different backgrounds, married the man she loved. But marriage and children, while fulfilling family and, perhaps, her own expectations of adult womanhood, ultimately limited the degree to which she could continue her work as a reformer. In many ways, she remained in the shadow of her husband, who was quickly expanding his personal and political circles.

Marriages and household configurations provide a glimpse into the development of interracial and cross-cultural relations in the private lives of working-class people who lived and worked in southern Manhattan. In this densely populated, ethnically and racially diverse part of the city, it is hardly surprising that such relationships existed, despite the hostility that interracial and cross-cultural families may have endured from the larger society and from their own ethnic communities and extended families. Prevailing racial ideologies, which provided the structure within which systems of inclusion and exclusion functioned in the daily lives of mixed couples, help us understand the forces that shaped people's choices of whom to marry and where to live in the city.

Living in the city was a double-edged sword. On the one hand, it provided an opportunity for many to create new lives and identities and to seek a degree of anonymity. With its mix of immigrant and native-born people of diverse ethnicities and races, the city could provide a haven for some couples to create niches for themselves and other mixed couples in the face of structural inequality and societal disapproval. Yet this same urban space could be alienating for those who found that national racist narratives seeped into daily life at the local level. Those who may have wanted to bring their spouses into their families and ethnic communities risked compromising their full identities, family ties, or economic opportunities by out-marrying.

The intersections of race, gender, ethnicity, class, and nation had specific effects on mixed couples during the early twentieth century. As individuals and as a couple, husbands and wives negotiated national ideologies of race, gender, and class within multiple social configurations—with each other; with their immediate and extended families, friends, and co-workers; and with the state.

Unfortunately, sources do not reveal the daily tensions and dynamics that most couples, regardless of race and class, faced as individuals and as part of a couple. What is clear is that mixed-race couples negotiated a racial system based on a black–white binary and in which the terms of race were still unresolved. Associations with whiteness through kinship ties or marriage could potentially broker racist practices and policies and in some cases provide a wider set of opportunities. Conversely, the taint of "color" could impede any privileges whiteness could bring. How did urban working-class families survive?

The next two chapters explore the ways in which the urban workplace facilitated or limited the formation of social and economic relations across cultural boundaries. As these chapters demonstrate, families and households were integral components of the urban workplace as workers and consumers.

2

Building Commercial Relations

On 10 February 1921, James M. Miller and William Chambers each sat before the Chinese immigration inspector's office in New York City to testify on behalf of Lee Chong Ho to confirm that Lee was a "merchant" and not a "laborer." A week earlier, Lee had arrived in Seattle, Washington, from China, claiming that he was a partner in the Chip Kee Company. Located at 11 Mott Street, Chip Kee was one of many Chinese-run businesses that sold a variety of imported and local foodstuffs, clothing, and sundries.[1] Each witness maintained a particular relationship to Lee Chong Ho and the Chip Kee Company. Miller ran a pharmacy on Greenwich Street, a long thoroughfare in what is now the Tribeca neighborhood of New York City, about a mile away from Mott Street. He traveled each month from his shop to take and deliver orders. Chambers worked as a truck driver for Chip Kee, delivering goods to and from the store. While Miller depended on Chip Kee to sustain his pharmacy business, Chambers depended on the company for his wages. Both men proved their worth as witnesses by successfully confirming Lee's role as a partner in the firm.[2]

Lee Chong Ho's case was not unusual. As the previous chapter indicates, non-Chinese as well as Chinese witnesses routinely testified on behalf of Chinese people who sought to re-enter the United States under the exclusion laws. Even though Chinese applicants or the Chinese Consolidated Benevolent Association typically paid people to testify as "stock witnesses," all of whom were expected to be upstanding citizens and not involved in illicit activities, witnesses were not strangers to Chinese applicants. Male witnesses included clergymen, businessmen, tradesmen, or employees. Women were usually friends, neighbors, missionaries, or teachers. Although testimonials by white witnesses did not guarantee a good outcome for the applicant, they benefited many Chinese people seeking re-entry into the country. The interviews provide a glimpse into interactions between Chinese "merchants" and non-Chinese male workers, retailers, and other businessmen and the world of interracial/ interethnic networks that operated alongside and, in fact, helped sustain co-ethnic businesses. Retail establishments, hand laundries, restaurants, and saloons functioned simultaneously as work sites and as places within which a mostly male workforce created social, economic, and political networks with co-workers, bosses, and consumers across racial/ethnic lines.

Exclusionary policies and practices that regulated citizenship and occupations tell a larger story about how gendered and racialized immigration laws affected individuals and urban ethnic businesses during the late nineteenth century and early twentieth century. National debates over the Fourteenth Amendment after the Civil War, over whether to extend citizenship to blacks and all those born in the United States, signaled the coming of further discussions over whether to exclude certain immigrant groups from eligibility for naturalization. The growing anti-Chinese movement fueled the passage of Chinese exclusion laws designed to limit both Chinese immigration to the United States and claims for citizenship. The Page Act of 1875 had targeted Chinese women, and the Chinese Exclusion Act of 1882 reflected concerns by white working-class men about the migration of Chinese male labor. Hence, the laws restricting immigration, not surprisingly, were tied to gendered definitions of paid labor. The labels "laborer" and "merchant" typically referred to male workers, even though throughout history women also have earned wages in low-paying occupations and operated their own businesses. In the daily practice of administering the exclusion laws, the distinction between the two types of occupations also seemed arbitrary. For example, a restaurant worker could qualify as a "merchant" if he did not mop floors or wipe down tables but owned or managed the business, kept the accounts, or acted as a cashier.

Although existing records do not reveal the depth of relations between Chinese and non-Chinese, they do provide an opportunity to examine the workplace as a locus for examining the breadth of interactions within the context of exclusion. How did groups marginalized by race, ethnicity, class, and gender manage to survive in a local urban economy? How did structures of inequality operate in daily life? William Chambers, for example, was an American-born white man who worked as a truck driver for a company owned and operated by Chinese immigrant men who by law were non-citizens and channeled into a racist occupational system that limited Chinese to a handful of livelihoods. How did his status as a white male citizen matter in a work environment in which he was a subordinate to non-citizens? How did federal and state laws shape the degree to which urban working-class men and women exercised power over and within the workplace? All of these questions underscore the nuances of power relations at the local level.

Retail and leisure commercial enterprises provide one set of spaces to examine various webs of social and economic relations. Such establishments in New York City catered to an ethnically diverse clientele within and across class lines, often resulting in social mixing among people of different ethnic backgrounds, despite efforts to reify racial boundaries during the era of Jim Crow segregation.[3] Interracial/interethnic interactions occurred routinely in small businesses in lower Manhattan—shops, restaurants, laundries, and drinking establishments—that served and employed immigrant and working-class people, as well as middle-class tourists. The degree to which interracial/interethnic relations occurred in these establishments depended in large part on their physical location within particular neighborhoods and the kind of fare they offered consumers. Chinese laundries, shops, and restaurants, for example, catered to, employed, and did business with Chinese and non-Chinese. White-run saloons varied according to neighborhood location: Those located near the "Chinatown" neighborhood catered to a more diverse working-class clientele, while others served a mostly white, working-class set of male customers.[4]

Ethnic enterprises have been critical components of co-ethnic community development. Founders of these businesses and those who labored within them carved out a special niche in a local economy in which racism severely limited economic opportunities.[5] But instead of being acknowledged as a vital part of a larger commercial economy, small retail and service industries fueled the popular perception of immigrant communities during the post–Civil War period as backward and isolated from the modern city and from U.S. society in general. Small ethnic enterprises functioned in different types of spaces, including tiny "hole in the wall" nooks, basements, ground-floor units in apartments and tenements, where businesses displayed meats hanging in the windows, with racks of produce and non-perishable items placed on the narrow sidewalks outside the stores, and more spacious quarters that accommodated large groups of customers.

The exclusion of Chinese and Japanese people from most trades resulted in a system of mutual dependence between Asian and white businesses. White merchants in California relied extensively on Chinese and Japanese consumers for household merchandise. The reverse, however, was also true. Chinese small businesses supported non-Chinese retailers and tradesmen. By the 1950s, in large cities that had developed a large and diverse industrial base such as San Francisco, Chicago, New York, and Boston, Chinese ethnic enterprises stood a better chance of survival by catering to both Chinese and non-Chinese clienteles.[6] As others have written, non-Chinese patronage facilitated the growth of a thriving tourist industry in the nation's "Chinatowns."At the same time, immigrant business owners relied on social, political and economic ties in their co-ethnic communities at the local, national, and international levels. Transnational relationships, for example, were critical to the survival of Chinese immigrants by facilitating the flow of goods necessary to sustain Chinese foodways and other familiar cultural practices in addition to maintaining contact with friends and family in China.[7] Local connections were also important for Chinese restaurants, which required the assistance of local Chinese and non-Chinese people in the immediate area for perishable items such as meat, fish, and produce. Local business relations between Chinese and non-Chinese people often extended beyond transactions between retailers and other businesses. As the case of Lee Chong Ho illustrates, employer–employee relations constituted another kind of configuration, illustrating the limits of chain migration processes in hiring within trades and businesses. Daily operations also required interactions with men associated with occupations such as law, insurance, and brokerage that kept businesses in line with tax laws and the like.

Interracial/interethnic economic interactions were gendered as much as racialized in the structure and daily operations of small businesses. The ethnic and gender configuration of workplace interactions varied according to the type of establishment as well as according to job segmentation within and between businesses. In most cases, the husband was recognized as head of both the family and the business. The work performed by wives and younger children was often invisible and went unrecognized in official documents such as the census, which typically listed these individuals as having no occupation. Gendered migration patterns shaped the extent to which women could participate in family businesses. Unlike European immigrants, Chinese men significantly outnumbered Chinese women. As a result, Chinese women appeared less frequently in Chinese-run enterprises. In family-run enterprises where both men and women participated, members of immediate and extended family contributed their labor as part of an unsalaried workforce in exchange for room, board, and the benefits that came with the economic success of the family's business. With the death of a husband, widows or elder sons typically took over businesses.

That the Chinese, more than European immigrants, depended on non-Chinese people for economic survival is not surprising, given the gendered and racialized structure of New York City's paid labor force by the late nineteenth century. The composition of occupations by ethnicity and gender can be attributed to several factors, such as the timing of migration, federal immigration laws, state laws that imposed citizenship requirements on certain occupations, the recruitment of cheap immigrant labor into industry, and the anti-Chinese stance of craft-based unions. The results were predictable. According to the federal census, among males age ten and older, whites dominated the major occupational categories in Manhattan during the period under consideration. In 1900, for example, of the 666,308 males age ten and older, whites constituted 99 percent of those employed in agriculture, 98 percent of those in professional service, 91 percent of those in domestic and personal service, 98 percent of those in trade and transportation work, and 99.5 percent of those employed in manufacturing and mechanical work. The combination of four factors accounts for this situation. The most obvious is the population ratio. The total white population in New York far outnumbered those classified as "colored." In 1900, for example, whites, who included those born in the United States and elsewhere, constituted 98 percent of the total population of Manhattan borough (N = 1,808,968), while those classified as "colored" made up 2 percent of the total population (N = 41,125 "colored," which included 36,246 "Negroes").[8] The timing of migration between the seventeenth century and the late nineteenth century and the institution of the Chinese exclusion laws, beginning with the Page Act of 1875, contributed to the even smaller numbers of Chinese in the non-Negro "colored" category. As a result, men of European ancestry dominated many occupations by the time the Chinese arrived in New York City, relegating a predominantly Chinese male population to home manufacturing and peddling cigars and candy, restaurant and laundry work, and shopkeeping.[9]

Second, the formation of informal networks among working-class European immigrant men since the early nineteenth century resulted in the concentration of European ethnic groups in certain lines of work. For example, men from the British Isles dominated the building trades, with English men concentrating in carpentry and cabinetmaking and Irish men in bricklaying. Third, urban, white, working-class identity formation in the United States during the nineteenth century facilitated the continuation of this process and its systemic exclusionary practices. Entering white-dominated jobs often brought disastrous results, as the upsurge of the lynching of blacks after the Civil War attests. The Chinese found themselves in a similar situation. As Peter Kwong has written, the Chinese in the United States were virtually locked into their "chosen" occupations and did not often bother to look for employment other than in restaurants, grocery stores and curio shops, and laundries.[10] In 1930, 3,582 Chinese men (nearly 47 percent of all employed Chinese men in New York State) were engaged in some aspect of the restaurant business, which included proprietors, cooks, waiters, and dishwashers.[11]

Finally, state policies supported federal citizenship restrictions in the occupational realm. Many states, including New York, had adopted laws that restricted entrance into certain trades and professions to citizens or those eligible for citizenship, a practice that explicitly excluded the Chinese and, eventually, all Asian immigrants until the 1940s and early

1950s. Such laws augmented Jim Crow practices that were already in place to exclude blacks from skilled trades and high-paying occupations. The intended and actual consequence of state-sanctioned restrictions in employment was the further concentration of people of European ancestry in most trades and occupations. The configuration of citizen–noncitizen contributed to the racialization of the paid labor force. But as the history of women and African Americans so clearly demonstrates, gaining citizenship does not eliminate systemic inequality.[12] The particular types of relationships in the workplace, whether between businessmen or between employers and employees, highlight the complex role of intersectionality in urban community formation.

In response to exclusionary practices at the local, state, and federal levels, well-established Chinese kinship networks, which functioned similarly to those of European immigrants, helped Chinese men find work that did not compete with that of white men. For example, in contrast to the new immigrants from Southern and Eastern Europe who dominated New York's garment industry and needle trades, Chinese men did not usually find employment in factory work except for cigar and candy making, instead concentrating in restaurant and laundry work and small shops. In 1900, for example, most Chinese men were merchants, cooks, or laundrymen. A few were barbers and, in a rare instance, one Chinese man who lived on Pell Street listed his occupation as "carpenter." In many rural areas, Chinese men operated small truck farms, which supplied restaurants with Chinese produce.[13]

The Chinese Consolidated Benevolent Association (CCBA) assisted Chinese men who wanted to open small businesses on their own or join in partnerships with other Chinese men. The CCBA, also known as the Six Companies, was a clan-based organization begun in California in the 1850s that functioned similarly to other ethnic mutual aid societies. Designed to help newly arrived immigrants, the CCBA provided loans, sick and death benefits, and money to pay white witnesses to testify on the behalf of those who had applied for return certificates. Through its rotating credit system, many Chinese men started businesses as part of partnerships with other Chinese men who pooled their money, out of which came the funds to begin their enterprises.[14]

The proprietor–customer relationship was one of several configurations of economic relationships that emerged within the walls of Chinese-run enterprises. Each set of interactions represented different social and economic stakes. Restaurants, laundries, and shops took on competing images that illustrated the simultaneous fears of and fascination with the foreign and exotic.

Eating establishments had been an integral part of New York City's landscape since the colonial period. "Restaurant" typically referred to upscale places to dine; their working-class counterparts were known simply as "oyster houses," "eating establishments," or "refectories." Many of the latter were located near the wharves, catering to sailors, artisans, and laborers. By the mid-nineteenth century, most were operated by white men and women, although at least two notable eating houses in lower Manhattan were run by African American men: Benjamin Bradley on Dover Street, near the South Street Seaport, and Thomas Downing, who ran a popular oyster house at Broad and Wall streets. When Downing first arrived from his home state of Virginia in 1819, he sold oysters at his home at 33 Pell Street, which later became part of the "Chinatown" neighborhood.[15] By the late nineteenth century, much of the black population in the city had moved out of lower Manhattan northward to Harlem or across the East River to Brooklyn.

Despite the proliferation of eating establishments over the course of the nineteenth century, the Chinese restaurant has occupied a special place in the American popular imagination. As the historian Donna Gabaccia writes, "No enclave businessmen enjoyed greater success attracting culinary tourists in search of inexpensive exoticism than Chinese restaurateurs in the Chinatowns of New York and San Francisco."[16] Chinese restaurants regularly served a mixed clientele, and many establishments offered both Chinese and "American" food in "two-cent" all-night establishments located in darkly lit basements in places like the famous "Mulberry Bend," a term the reformer Jacob Riis made famous to describe the impoverished area in the Five Points district of southern Manhattan.[17] More spacious, ornate, and brightly lit establishments catering to a wealthier clientele included the Chinese Delmonico on Pell Street, the Chinese Tuxedo restaurant on Doyers Street, and the famous Port Arthur restaurant on Mott Street. With its expansive rooms and long tables, Port Arthur was a perfect place to host business meetings and other large gatherings among Chinese and non-Chinese alike.

Christian missionaries and clergymen often met at the restaurant to discuss the problems brought on by the Tong wars.[18]

The Chinese premier, Viceroy Li Hung-chang, first popularized Chinese food among non-Chinese Americans when he visited the United States in 1898.[19] Negative stereotypes about Chinese food, however, persisted. One writer, in an effort to capture the "truth" about the Chinese in New York in a survey of "Chinatown" in 1893, challenged the popular stereotype of Chinese as eaters of domesticated animals and vermin: "There is a popular notion, so false that it is surprising that it should obtain among people with any pretensions to culture or education, that in matters of cooking the Chinese are unclean, and, more absurd, that rats, cats, and mice enter into their ordinary bill of fare." The writer goes on to describe the actual staples offered in Chinese restaurants, which included pork, rice, and noodles.[20] Despite pervasive stereotypes, Chinese restaurants remained popular among non-Chinese if only for the experience of entering an exotic and forbidden cultural domain.[21]

Fictional works, guidebooks, and newspaper and magazine essays emphasized the restaurants as interracial/interethnic spaces, gathering places for blacks, whites, and immigrant groups who were out "on the town." New York newspapers kept readers up to date about the latest eating establishments in the city. By the 1920s, the number of Chinese restaurants had increased throughout New York City.[22] Although the Great Depression resulted in the demise of many Chinese eating establishments, some managed to survive the economic crisis. Of the 447 Chinese restaurants established across the five New York boroughs between 1928 and 1935, only 140 survived the first year.[23]

Descriptions of the food and the ambience at Chinese eating establishments abound in guidebooks, magazines, and fiction about New York City. Nicholas Brooks, a New York City policeman, combined his role as a keeper of order and as an "expert" on the comings and goings of visitors to Chinatown establishments: "Slummers drop in occasionally to see the natives eating their food with their chop sticks, and generally order a native dish so as to be able to say they ate in a Chinese restaurant."[24] By the 1930s, such descriptions had become standard in popular histories of New York City. Charles Towne's *This New York of Mine* summarized what by then had become a habit among so-called slummers: "People of wealth and fashion used to go 'slumming' in the old days, and it was considered quite smart to have a supper party in some mean little saloon down on the Bowery, and watch the strange goings-on of the underworld, see Chinatown and dens of iniquity, and sit, in dinner coats and ermine and evening gowns, on the benches of the night courts."[25]

Earlier in the century, writers had expressed an awareness of the increase in the number of Chinese restaurants in the city, but a few maintained their loyalty to the downtown establishments. An article published in the *New York Tribune* in 1901 noted the increase in the number of Chinese restaurants in northern Manhattan but argued that the ones downtown were still the best places to obtain Chinese food and served more reputable customers:

> These new uptown places are not so good, either in a moral or culinary way, as those down in Chinatown. It is usual to speak as if Mott and Pell [streets] were the city's sink of iniquity, and so they are in some respects; but there are no Chinese restaurants in the neighborhood as disreputable as one or two uptown. The clientele of the downtown places is above suspicion. . . . Uptown the bills of fare are more limited.[26]

Margherita Arlina Hamm, a well-known suffragist and journalist who wrote extensively about her travels around the world, reported on her forays into New York City's local neighborhoods. In 1900, she informed readers of the *New York Evening Post* that a Chinese baker and confectioner on Doyers Street was famous for his many sweet creations that were "appetizing to an American."[27]

Chinese restaurants as interracial spaces also found their way into fictional writings about race, identity, and New York. In his novel *Auto-biography of an Ex-Coloured Man*, James Weldon Johnson's reference to a Chinese restaurant on Sixth Avenue, adjacent to a speakeasy, accentuates the mysterious and secretive world of illicit alcohol and interracial socializing during Prohibition: "We stopped in front of a house with three stories and a basement. In the basement was a Chinese chop-suey restaurant. There was a red lantern at the iron gate to the area way inside of which the Chinaman's name was printed. We went up the steps of the stoop, rang the bell, and were admitted without delay."[28]

While the "culinary tourists" to whom Gabaccia refers were non-Chinese, mostly white, middle-class patrons, Chinese restaurants were also popular among working-class people who enjoyed the inexpensive fare. Many Jews and Italians found Chinese restaurants appealing, even though many opened delis, grocery stores, and restaurants that catered to other Jews and Italians. Chinese restaurants were particularly popular among many Jews in New York City throughout the twentieth century, partly because they remained open on Christian holidays and offered a night out for Jewish families.[29] Even among observant Jews, Chinese food, unlike other non-Kosher cuisines, was considered "safe treyf." Some Chinese restaurants even began offering kosher items on their menus, which suggests that, although Jewish delicatessens, butchers, and grocers provided kosher meats and groceries to a predominantly Jewish clientele on the Lower East Side, they also supplied Chinese restaurants.[30] For Elliot Willensky, who grew up in the Jewish community in Brooklyn during the 1930s, visiting Chinese restaurants was a memorable treat, a diversion from the Eastern European Jewish cuisine to which he was accustomed: "What promptly came from the kitchen was always accompanied by a pair of tiny dishes of dark, thick duck sauce and hot mustard guaranteed to clear your nostrils better than Vick's VapoRub."[31]

In an era of Jim Crow segregation, the Chinese restaurant was of particular significance to blacks, who were often excluded from white-owned eating establishments. In a survey of Chinese restaurants in 1901, the *New York Tribune* reported that black workers were regular customers in "disproportionately large numbers" at Chinese restaurants. The writer concluded that the black patrons "seem to like the Chinese," that the restaurants were somehow familiar spaces for blacks, and that "the noise of the kitchens remind[s] one of the similar condition of Southern kitchens under negro management."[32] Serving a black clientele was a common occurrence at Chinese eating establishments throughout the country. In the Mississippi Delta, poor blacks and whites patronized Chinese lunchrooms, often located in Chinese-owned grocery stores. Black sharecroppers, who faced exclusion from white establishments, made up much of the clientele at Chinese grocery stores, which provided supplies, lunches, drinks, and snacks at affordable prices.[33] By the 1930s, however, some Chinese restaurants in

New York City refused to serve black patrons in an effort to maintain their white clientele.[34]

Patrons of Chinese restaurants and downtown saloons, whether white middle-class and wealthy "slummers" or local working-class people, had a different relationship to these establishments from those whose livelihoods depended on them. To feed customers, Chinese restaurants relied on men from other trades and occupations for essential items. The grocery trade was critical to Chinese restaurant owners. Chinese grocers, who imported many of the ingredients they sold in their shops, provided necessary staples for Chinese cooking for individuals and for proprietors of the restaurant trade. Chinese vegetables—bok choy, bitter melons, and special types of cabbage—came from Chinese truck farmers who hauled these perishable goods in from farms on Long Island, in Queens, and in New Jersey.[35] Chinese and non-Chinese wholesale businesses provided non-perishable food, mostly dried herbs and condiments, from China.

The economic relationship between Chinese and non-Chinese businesses illustrates both a system of mutual dependence built on structures of inequality and the particular historical legacy that Chinese and European ethnic groups brought to urban commercial life. In lower Manhattan between the 1880s and 1920, Irish and Italian retailers were regular suppliers of Chinese eating establishments. The Randles family, for example, had been in the wholesale grocery business between at least 1880 and the 1920s.[36] Born in 1844, John Randles arrived in the United States sometime in the late 1870s, the tail end of the Great Migration from Ireland. He obtained citizenship in 1878.[37]

The location of Randles's business may have helped him maintain a regular and ethnically diverse clientele. He first opened his store on Cherry Street. A large concentration of Irish immigrants lived on the western end of Cherry Street; Eastern European immigrants gradually filled out the rest of the street. By 1900, Randles had moved the business to Water Street, located closer to the wharf and a variety of eating establishments, including Chinese restaurants, that catered to sailors and ship galleys.[38]

Unlike many immigrant business owners, Randles and his wife, Anne, did not live in or near the store. Rather, they had set up residence in an apartment at 89 Madison Street, where they raised their son and four daughters. Most of their working-class neighbors were also of Irish ancestry, but a small number of new immigrants from Russia and Poland also settled there. Within the next twenty years, Eastern European Jewish immigrants and their families would come to dominate Madison Street, as they had Cherry Street. By 1910, as the poor and immigrant population increased in that area, the Randles family moved northward to a home John Randles had purchased on East 60th Street.

John Randles was fortunate to find work as a merchant when most Irish immigrant men who settled in U.S. cities still mainly found employment as manual laborers.[39] Men far outnumbered women as "traders and dealers," but men of Irish ancestry did not outnumber all groups of European men in this line of work. German merchants living in Manhattan and the Bronx numbered nearly 9,000 in 1880 and 13,000 twenty years later, compared with the number of men of Irish immigrant parentage in this line of work, which dropped from about 5,500 to 4,124 in the same period. By 1900, men from Russia/Poland working as merchants also surpassed the Irish by more than 2,000.[40]

After his death, several of his children took over the firm of John Randles Inc. By 1920, George F. Randles and his sisters, Adelaide and Julia, were running the firm. George by then was one of 9,000 U.S.-born white men in the retail trade in Manhattan. Adelaide and Julia were among a smaller number of women in the trade—only about 600 in that same census year. The concentration of Chinese restaurants a few blocks away helped the Randles family enterprise continue to flourish. By the 1920s, customers included the Wing Yee Yuen Wah Kee Company on Mott Street and the Imperial Restaurant on Third Avenue. The Randles company also eventually expanded to include Chinese customers in other parts of the city and in New Jersey.[41]

Louis Coppola, Frank Buonocore, and Joseph Molinelli were second-generation Italian immigrant retailers whose regular customers also included proprietors of Chinese restaurants.[42] Coppola and Buonocore delivered supplies to Leong Gar's restaurant on Sixth Avenue, which was located close to their businesses. By the early 1920s, Buonocore and his son, Frank Jr., regularly delivered groceries to Leong Gar from their store on Eighth Avenue.[43] Coppola, who was seventeen years old when he testified on behalf of Leong Gar, worked at his father's fish market on Seventh Avenue. Dominick Coppola had established the business in the early 1900s, after he had emigrated from Italy in March 1896 at the age of twenty-five. Like many immigrants, Coppola had taken advantage of the chain migration process by securing employment from a fellow Italian immigrant, where he likely got his start in the food retail business. When he arrived, Coppola worked as a driver for Anthony Spaduzzi's grocery business in Brooklyn.[44]

The Molinellis resided near the Chinese restaurant they had supplied since at least 1910. They were longtime residents of the section of Mott Street where Chinese as well as Russian Jewish and Italian immigrants had settled. Joseph Molinelli lived at 50 Mott Street and ran a grocery store with his father, John, who started the business at the turn of the century at nearby 43 Mott Street. The Molinellis delivered items regularly to Sun Kwong On and Company, located down the street at number 28.[45]

Trade in items besides food between "Orientals" (Chinese and Japanese, in particular) and "non-Orientals" in U.S. towns and cities was also a typical part of urban commercial life in lower Manhattan.[46] Interactions with non-Chinese dealers who came into the shops to buy and sell wares date back to the early nineteenth century, when U.S. involvement in the China trade intensified.[47] To many outsiders, ethnic working-class communities may have seemed isolated from the "modern" city, dwarfed by large-scale industries and retail businesses that had blossomed during the late nineteenth century's so called Gilded Age. Certainly, by the 1920s small enterprises contrasted sharply with the growth of opulent and elaborate large-scale department stores that catered to the middle and upper classes and the bargain stores aimed at "the masses." Department stores such as Gimbels, Saks, R. H. Macy and Company, and A. A. Vantine's, which specialized in "Oriental" wares, experienced a decline during World War I but then burgeoned during the postwar period.[48] Smaller enterprises, however, still served local, working-class people as well as middle-class tourists and "slummers" who visited immigrant neighborhoods to purchase "exotic" objects and to partake of food and entertainment.

Although few accumulated the kind of wealth gained by prominent businessmen such as John Jacob Astor, smalltime dealers earned a decent living by trading in "Oriental" goods. Grocery stores provided food staples, and Chinese curio shops, often operated by non-Chinese salesmen, sold "Oriental" clothing, jewelry, and other commodities. Harry Meyer and Solomon Satosky were two of several Jewish purveyors who sold jewelry, clothing, and shoes throughout lower Manhattan and included among their clientele Chinese shop owners. The son of German immigrants, Meyer had been selling jewelry since 1880 and was a frequent visitor to Moy Toy's jewelry shop on Mott Street in the early 1920s, selling precious stones and, in exchange, purchasing jade to add to his collection of wares. Meyer was one of thousands of traders who combined street peddling with the emerging occupation of "traveling salesman." Like many urban sellers, Meyer limited his travels to shops within walking distance from his home and shop and in the process established regular economic relations with a diverse population of people living in the area.[49] Solomon Satosky and his sons ran a wholesale ginseng import-export business on Third Avenue. Their enterprise, the International Ginseng Company, was a large establishment that sold supplies of ginseng to Chinese herb shops and grocery stores, including the Wing Fat Company on Catherine Street.[50]

Just how much cordial social relations and friendship may have motivated white witnesses to testify on behalf of Chinese merchants and employees is impossible to determine from the case files. That a mutually dependent economic relationship factored into the decision to testify was a probable factor, for just as the Chinese relied on trade with non-Chinese business owners, the reverse was also true. As was typical of small-business owners, retaining customers was critical to their survival. Non-Chinese butchers, grocery suppliers, and liquor dealers benefited from the success of Chinese businesses, which since the end of the nineteenth century had grown in popularity. Italian, Irish, and Jewish retailers contributed to their own survival and success, as well as to the ability of Chinese restaurants, laundries, and shops to flourish. At the same time, Chinese proprietors relied on the cooperation of white businessmen to testify as witnesses, a reminder that even if Chinese and whites depended on each other for the success of their respective businesses, white assistance was often a key to transnational travel, for Chinese merchants also relied on contacts in China to sustain business and family relations.

That non-Chinese retailers were of European ancestry was not unusual. Although most men fell into the broad classification "laborer," there were a fair number in a host of other occupations, including retail and various skilled trades. As Thomas Kessner points out in his study of Italian and Jewish mobility rates, the urban paid labor force was not a static entity but a dynamic one among people of European ancestry. By the late nineteenth century, new European immigrant groups began to displace German and Irish male workers in certain unskilled and semi-skilled occupations, such as construction and transportation.[51] The Italian population had grown significantly between 1880 and 1900. In 1880, 12,000 Italian immigrants resided in New York City. By 1900, the number of first- and second-generation Italians who were employed in an occupation numbered 319,665 in the United States. Of that number, 52,159 males and 9,342 females over age ten resided in Manhattan and the Bronx combined.

According to the 1900 census, most first- and second-generation Italian men found employment in the rather vague category "laborer," which usually referred to unskilled and day labor. In that year, the census counted 15,486 Italian male laborers, second to immigrant and second-generation Irish men, who numbered 24,738 in this category. Non-wholesale "merchants and dealers," such as the Buonocores and Molinellis, ranked third among first- and second-generation Italian men in Manhattan.[52] In 1900, out of 42,507 men living in Manhattan and the Bronx, 41,606 were classified as "white" in the category "merchants and dealers." Of this number, European immigrant men predominated, totaling 27,804. In that year, 3,885 Italian men were classified as merchants and dealers, behind 3,935 in the tailoring trade.[53] Although most Irish men were laborers, men of Irish ancestry, who as a group had resided in the United States for a longer time, found a broader range of employment opportunities than either Italian or Chinese men. By the late nineteenth century, the increased concentration of the Irish in New York City politics led to greater economic opportunities for many Irish men, who could be found in skilled trades, as well as in hauling and carting, livery, law enforcement, and the saloon business, to name a few.

In addition to crossing ethnic and cultural borders to do business, some of the more prosperous Chinese men had set up businesses in several cities in the United States. In a study of thirteen Chinese merchants in New York City's Chinatown conducted in 1909, John Stewart Burgess found several men whose business interests extended well beyond

New York City. One respondent was the keeper of "the largest retail and wholesale store of Japanese and Chinese goods on Mott Street." According to Burgess, "He makes frequent trips to China. Two years ago he returned to the United States after a four years' visit. He has traveled extensively for business purposes, and has branch stores in Changhai, Yokohama, Hong Kong, and Vancouver. His New York store, having 32 employees, is large and well fitted, neat and of American style. His clerks are well dressed and speak English fluently."[54]

To sustain their businesses by ensuring the continuing importation of goods, immigrant businessmen interacted regularly with customs brokerage houses and insurance companies. Shop owners in particular depended on customs brokers to facilitate the importation of goods. Customs and insurance brokerage were also dominated by white men, as illustrated in the 1920 federal census for the State of New York. In that year, out of a total of 16,510 men engaged in the insurance business, 11,815 were native-born white; 4,652 were foreign-born white; 43 were "Negro"; and none were "Indian, Chinese, Japanese." In the commercial brokerage trade, out of a state total of 4,564 men in the business, 3,311 were native-born white; 1,245 were foreign-born white; 2 were "Negro"; and 6 were "Indian, Chinese, Japanese."[55] William D. Gilbert sold insurance to Chinese shop owners. James V. Storey and William Luders, themselves sons of English and German immigrants, respectively, represented the brokerage firm of W. A. Brown on Pearl Street, which dealt with several Chinese clients. All three men testified on behalf of numerous Chinese clients who had applied for return certificates.

By the 1920s, Storey had established his own company on State Street in Manhattan and retained his connection to the Chinese community. In a letter to Chin You Jung of Pell Street, Storey responded to Chin's request for help in bringing his wife, Wong Shee, and his daughter, Chin Ping Jean, to the United States. From his letter, it is clear that Storey empathized with Chin's frustration that his family was being detained in Seattle, their port of entry. It is also evident that Storey had long been familiar with such cases: "There used to be a time when Chinese women and children were given preference. I appreciate your anxiety in connection with this matter, and I assure you that I am doing everything possible to facilitate the final disposition."[56]

In addition to trading with fellow merchants locally and transnationally, Chinese business owners hired Chinese and non-Chinese workers and did business with deliverymen as part of the daily workings of the business. It is in this configuration that the incongruity between enfranchised citizenship as a racialized status and class hierarchies within the workplace become more apparent.

It was not unusual for Chinese immigrant business owners and managers to supervise non-Chinese workers. It also was not uncommon for European immigrants who were not yet U.S. citizens to hire U.S.-born or naturalized citizens. By the late nineteenth century, the male citizenry included black men such as Clarence G. Rollans, who worked for the Canton Company at 49 Mott Street. Among non-white businessmen, however, hiring working-class male citizens was less common. One of the best examples was James Forten Sr., a black businessman and abolitionist in Philadelphia who supervised dozens of white journeymen in his successful sailmaking enterprise decades before the Civil War. While most of the white men in his employ could vote, Forten witnessed his own disenfranchisement when Pennsylvania rescinded the right of black men to vote in 1837. Still, as one of the wealthiest blacks in the North, he wielded considerable power over his employees, who were dependent on him for their regular wages. It was common knowledge, for example, that Forten pressured his workers to vote in certain ways.[57]

Again, the Chinese Exclusion Act case files provide a glimpse into the conditions under which non-Chinese people came into contact with Chinese merchants and workers. In the 1920s, working-class men such as the truck drivers Charles F. Bartels Jr. and Clarence G. Rollans regularly wove in and out of Chinese neighborhoods. Bartels, who lived with his parents and siblings in a predominantly German block of Rivington Street, delivered ice to the Chip Kee Company at 11 Mott Street as part of his father's wholesale ice company. Rollans may have been one of the few African Americans to testify on behalf of Chinese merchants who had applied for return certificates.[58] In some cases, non-Chinese workers were married to the business owners. Chinese-run businesses were no different from most family enterprises, as in the case of Margaret Hart Wong, who often assisted her husband, Wong Jung Que, as the cashier in the Mea Gen Restaurant on Pell Street during the 1920s and 1930s.

Chinese men who operated hand laundries typically also served a

Chinese and non-Chinese clientele.[59] Laundrymen typically set up their shops in residential areas inhabited by "white-collar" workers, although one-man laundries existed in the poor neighborhoods, such as Chicago's "Black Belt."[60] Although the number of urban occupations had increased significantly during the period under consideration, as had degrees of specialization within existing occupational categories, men of color did not gain access to them to the same degree as did white men, whether U.S.-born or immigrant.

Chinese hand laundries were so numerous in New York City by the 1880s that the *New York Times* reported an "army" of 610 Chinese laundry men working in the city. One business directory established a separate subcategory, "Laundries, Chinese," in 1888. Out of the hundreds listed, only two were designated by name: Lee Sing on West 37th Street, and Wah Hop nearby, on West 38th Street. The rest were known only by address. As in Chicago, the Chinese in New York set up hand laundries in white neighborhoods as well as in predominantly Chinese neighborhoods. In 1888, more than 600 establishments could be found throughout Manhattan, most of which were located on the Lower East Side. Clusters of hand laundries were listed on Allen, Attorney, Baxter, Bayard, Catherine, Cherry, Chrystie, Clinton, Division, Canal, Eldridge, Elizabeth, Henry, Ludlow, Mott, Mulberry, Norfolk, and Orchard streets.[61] Only about twenty were located in the "Chinatown" neighborhood.

Local newspapers were quick to emphasize the mixed clientele who frequented Chinese hand laundries. The unsolved murder of one Chinese laundryman, Hop Lee (also known as Lee Ling and Sam Sing), on Clinton Street generated the usual deployment of popular gender, ethnic, and class stereotypes in the local papers. The *New York Times* reported that several days after the death of Hop Lee, two Polish Jews had visited his laundry demanding their shirts, apparently impervious to the news that their laundryman had been murdered. Using ethnic vernacular popular among many urban journalists, the *Times* quoted the elderly customer as saying, "But my zwei shirts, he exclaimed piteously, you vill keep zem for me. I must haf them. It ees not right to hold them back."[62]

Despite being scattered throughout the city, Chinese hand-laundry operators were able to organize with relative ease, undoubtedly because their very entrance into the industry had resulted from the extensive kinship and friendship networks that had facilitated their immigration into the country and their finding employment in Chinese-dominated areas. They were the first Chinese service workers to unionize, forming the Chinese Hand Laundry Alliance in 1933, independent of the CCBA.[63]

Unlike in restaurants and retail establishments, cross-cultural relations at Chinese hand laundries were limited to customer–proprietor and employer–employee relations within a tiny workplace, where there was just enough room for the laundryman and, perhaps, an assistant and washtubs. At most, six laundrymen would work together in areas where boardinghouses rented to working-class men who needed clean shirts every day. In many cases, the proprietor lived in a small room in the back of the laundry. In some cases, Chinese laundrymen hired non-Chinese female assistants. Perhaps because of the solitude of the hand laundry business, the popular press viewed Chinese laundrymen with more suspicion than those who ran bustling shops and restaurants. Representations of the laundrymen in popular theater and film drew on negative stereotypes of Chinese men as a danger to innocent white women and children in the neighborhood.[64]

Conflicts sometimes erupted between Chinese laundrymen and non-Chinese people within a range of social contexts. Until the Chinese Hand Laundry Alliance was organized in the 1930s, laundrymen could do little to prevent harassment from locals, including children who came around to taunt them and customers who refused to pay. Although Chinese laundrymen and non-Chinese employees, customers, prostitutes, neighbors, wives, and girlfriends formed a varied set of economic and social networks out of both necessity and desire, these relationships were often fraught with tension.[65] By the 1920s, the racial and ethnic composition of southern Manhattan had changed as a result of a steady pattern of black migration northward to Harlem. The social and physical distance between blacks and Chinese, for example, had grown to such a degree that by the 1940s, when members of the Chinese Hand Laundry Alliance attempted to rally Jews and blacks to the cause of "oppressed nations," many blacks hesitated to ally with the Chinese, whom, they argued, had discriminated against them.[66]

Just as Chinese hand laundries functioned as sites of potential friction between Chinese and non-Chinese people, so did local watering holes, run mostly by men of European ancestry. The presence of alcoholic beverages as the main staple of saloons often intensified both co-ethnic bonding and interethnic and interracial tensions. Since the early days of the republic, taverns symbolized emerging class distinctions among male patrons. The classic image of polished mahogany bars, decorative inlaid tile floors, and beveled mirrors mostly characterized taverns that catered to middle-class businessmen and politicians. In southern Manhattan, the Bowery, the "half-humorous, half dreaded portion of the city," was well known for its numerous saloons catering to "Bowery bums."[67] Photographs from the early twentieth century depict a more charming setting of local workingmen's bars as simpler, small spaces with well-worn wooden plank floors. Group photos underscore the masculine culture of saloons; saloonkeepers, their patrons, and bartenders posed together proudly with drinks and cigars in hand, often with the owner's dog sitting prominently in the foreground on the floor or on top of the bar. Rarely were women included in these photographs, even though women as well as children were present in the daily operation of saloons.[68]

Saloon operators in New York City were of European ancestry, mostly first- or second-generation German and Irish men. In 1890, of the 4,859 "restaurant and saloon keepers" in the city, 3,744 were immigrants, 2,292 were from Germany, and 621 were from Ireland. Ten years later, German and Irish men still outnumbered all other ethnic groups in this occupation in Brooklyn, Manhattan, and the Bronx.[69]

Unlike restaurants and shops, where families could visit and partake of the wares, saloons catered to a predominantly adult male clientele looking for alcohol, a place to gamble, female prostitutes, and sexual encounters with other men. European immigration throughout the nineteenth century resulted in the increase of taverns in the nation's cities. Many taverns, eating houses, and "stale-beer dives" were located in poor, working-class, and immigrant neighborhoods and attracted both local clienteles and urban middle-class men and women who were curious about how the "other half" lived. Popular spots included Steve Brodie's saloon and P. J. Kennedy's eating and drinking house, where patrons ate cheap ten-cent meals and imbibed alcoholic beverages.[70]

In the eyes of reformers, saloons presented a bigger social problem than did other forms of commercial enterprises. They provided not only venues where mostly white working-class men gathered to drink but also social and political spaces for labor organizing, gambling, prostitution, and brawls between customers, male and female. Since the early nineteenth century, temperance advocates had argued that saloons perpetuated overindulgence and social depravity. According to a report issued by the Committee of Fifty in 1901, based on an extensive investigation of the "Liquor Problem" in New York City, "The craving for liquors is what makes the saloon." Such establishments attracted the "lowest forms of social life . . . ex-convicts or embryonic criminals."[71] One such place was Callahan's Saloon at 12 Chatham Square, a popular place for drinking, gambling, and prostitution. Callahan's operated out of one of several buildings in the Bowery that housed hundreds of single working men. The Committee of Fifteen, another privately funded and operated anti-vice organization, conducted frequent raids on the bar.[72]

Drinking establishments were unique commercial enterprises in which co-ethnic and interracial/interethnic relations took particular forms. In New York City, taverns served sailors and resident poor and working-class populations in ethnically mixed streets near the wharves. In these establishments, the sex trade flourished, as did gambling and a subculture of criminality across lines of race and ethnicity.[73] In Manhattan's Sixth Ward, Irish and black working-class people frequented the same taverns, where they built friendships and fought with each other.[74] Young children fetched "growlers" of beer to take home or served as lookouts when illegal gambling took place. Women were also present as servers and sometimes as owners of saloons, and wives and girlfriends of male clients often gathered in the back rooms. As Madelon Powers has shown, most of the male clientele in saloons created a homogenous culture, where men bonded along lines of ethnicity, occupation, and class. Since the 1850s, German immigrants had operated biergartens in the "Kleindeutschland" neighborhood in lower Manhattan. As male-dominated spaces, saloons served as places for forging and maintaining ethnic solidarity among white working-class men and often served as venues for political and labor organizing. In the saloons, relations between ethnic groups were often fragile; in a place where strong drink flowed freely, it took little to spark an argument or brawls among patrons. Cross-cultural interactions were limited to illicit activities that often took place in the back rooms, such as the sex trade and gambling. In many saloons, a line existed between ethnic solidarity and cross-cultural interactions.[75]

Social dynamics that emerged in a range of small businesses illustrate how the racialized, gendered, and ethnic segmentation of the urban paid labor force resulted in the concentration of ethnic groups in certain enterprises and shaped interactions across lines of gender, race, and ethnicity. The next chapter brings into sharper relief the tradesmen who helped maintain urban communities by sustaining the physical infrastructures and providing necessary social services. In many cases, the need for such services brought people of different cultural backgrounds into contact with one another daily.

3

Sustaining Life and Caring
for the Dead

When William H. Kennedy expanded his livery and stable business into the undertaking trade in the 1860s, the Irish-born undertaker, who later boasted of his longtime association with the Chinese in lower Manhattan, was not alone. Kennedy was part of a larger community of Irish men who had entered the funeral business in the mid-nineteenth century. That men from the British Isles dominated this occupation was no accident; it resulted from a combination of structural and cultural factors that led to a system of exclusion and dependence.

As the previous chapter illustrates, economic networks forged among co-ethnics and between ethnic groups facilitated urban commercial relations by supporting local businesses and serving both the people in the surrounding neighborhoods and the growing tourist trade in southern Manhattan. Other services, however, such as birthing babies, caring for the sick, burying the dead, and maintaining a healthy environment, required different sets of skills. In cities like New York, Boston, and Chicago, microcosms of the public health and settlement house movements, a predominantly white cadre of physicians, midwives, nurses, and various tradesmen, served an ethnically diverse working-class urban population.

This chapter argues that chain migration patterns, the administration of state occupational laws, and Jim Crow segregationist practices adopted in institutions of higher education and professional schools together shaped co-ethnic and interracial/interethnic relations. What resulted were varying relations of dependence between those who dominated certain trades and professions and those who were in need of basic services. As with the commercial trade, interracial/interethnic interactions often occurred out of necessity as much as personal desire, as national, state, and local policies and practices often placed people of European ancestry in positions of power over the lives of poor and working-class women, men, and children. But as much as structural inequality denied them access to many trades and professions, women, the poor, immigrants, and non-whites made the most of the limited choices available to them. Neighborhood residents were not completely at the mercy of licensed health practitioners who worked in their midst; many people carved out their own ways to care for themselves. At the same time, the exclusion of non-whites from many "skilled" trades resulted in a reliance on white tradesmen to maintain and improve their living environments.

I begin this discussion with those who tended to the most intimate aspects of the lifecycle. Providing health care to the urban poor and to working-class people was a daunting project and fell to licensed and unlicensed physicians, herbalists and apothecaries, nurses, and midwives. For centuries, the responsibility for caring for the sick, assisting birthing mothers, and preparing the dead for display and burial often fell on the shoulders of women, particularly midwives. Even with the systematic exclusion of women and non-whites from university education and professional schools by the late eighteenth century, women remained central players in the daily work of dispensing health care to their families and communities in both rural and urban areas of the United States. Even in the censuses of the early twentieth century, enumerators recognized midwifery as a women's occupation. At the same time, the professionalization of nursing was on the rise and, not surprisingly, was dominated by women of European ancestry. Nursing schools followed the lead of the country's medical schools in their admissions policies and practices. Although they did not exclude on the basis of gender, they maintained the color line and established quotas for the admission of blacks, Jews, and Catholics.

In 1900, nurses and midwives facilitated half of urban childbirths. Most of these women were European immigrants. In New York City, the number of foreign-born white women who identified their occupations as midwives and nurses outnumbered U.S.-born white nurses and midwives by 3,640 to 2,751 in the boroughs of Manhattan and the Bronx. Among the immigrant female population in 1900, Irish and German midwives/nurses significantly outnumbered midwives/nurses from all other immigrant groups.[1] It is unclear from the census whether these women had received any formal education. Many likely did not, for as the profession of nursing evolved as a women's occupation, formal training was reserved mostly for U.S.-born white Protestant women.

The public health movement, advancements in the education of white native-born women, and the professionalization of nursing increased the presence of educated white women in nursing by the early twentieth century. The work of public health nursing is well known in the historical literature on Progressive-era reform. Inspired by images of the new woman—college-educated, independent, and civic-minded—professionally trained public health nurses were an integral part of urban reform aimed literally at cleaning up the streets.

The institution of ethnic/racial quota systems were common practices in New York's nursing schools, based on long-held assumptions about qualities that supposedly constituted a "proper" and "genteel" woman. Many of the early nursing students came from farming communities. The New York Hospital Training School, established in 1882, gained the reputation for admitting only "mature" (age twenty-two to thirty-three) unmarried women from middle-class backgrounds. In its list of regulations in 1887, the Committee of the Training School for Nurses stipulated that the "preferred" applicant was a woman who possessed "superior education and cultivation." A letter from her clergyman would attest to her "good moral character," and one from her physician would affirm her "sound health."[2] Long-standing stereotypes of black women as hypersexual and intellectually inferior to whites, as well as Jim Crow segregation, virtually barred black women from access to nursing education. In the State of New York, only two nurse- training programs were available to blacks during the era of segregation, both in Manhattan: the Lincoln Hospital for Nurses, established in 1898, and Harlem Hospital, which opened its nursing program in 1923.[3]

Public health nurses cared for a diverse population and assisted midwives in birthing children. Lillian D. Wald (1867–1940) and her nursing-school classmate Mary Brewster (1865–1901) founded the Visiting Nurse Service at the Nurses' Settlement at 261 Henry Street on the Lower East Side in 1893.[4] Both Wald and Brewster had come from middle-class families. Born in Cincinnati, Wald was the daughter of Polish and German immigrant parents. When she was a child, her parents, Minnie and Max D. Wald, moved to Rochester, New York, where they became part of a growing middle-class German Jewish community and where Max ran a successful optical business. Lillian Wald was one of a small number of Jewish women admitted to New York Hospital's School of Nursing (now part of New York–Presbyterian Hospital). After graduation in 1891, the two women worked at the College Settlement on Rivington Street, not far from the future site of the Nurses' Settlement. Once they established the Henry Street settlement, Wald, Brewster, and several other well-known nurses—including Lavinia Dock of Pennsylvania, the Canadian-born nursing educator M. Adelaide Nutting, and Annie Goodrich, who later established the first nursing school at Yale University—joined the Visiting Nurse Service. The nurses made daily rounds among the Italian, European Jewish, and Chinese residents throughout lower Manhattan.[5] Wald stayed on for several more decades, serving as the primary spokeswoman for the settlement until her death. The foci of the settlement's activities ranged from public campaigns to eradicate political corruption to eliminating contagious diseases among the poor through the application of new scientific ideas about sanitation, hygiene, nutrition, and childbirth practices.[6]

Interracial/interethnic relations took several forms at the Henry Street settlement. The first and most obvious was the nurse–patient dynamic between the all-white visiting nurse corps and the immigrant patients, whose willingness to interact with outsiders varied. Some were loath to admit strangers with "modern" views of helping and healing into their homes.[7]

Male physicians, who often supervised nurses in the hospitals and in the streets, also worked among the urban immigrant population, sometimes offering part-time services at settlement houses. When in need of a doctor, impoverished immigrants did not always have one from their own ethnic group to call on. White, native-born men dominated the occupational category "physician and surgeon" by 1900.[8] The numbers of physicians among the new immigrants were small—81 Italians, 244 Russians, and 28 Poles. In the years before immigrant Jews could go to their own physicians, those who lived on the Lower East Side often went to non-Jewish practitioners such as Harry James, an obstetrician who was born in New York. James resided on Broome Street, not far from the clusters of immigrant Jews he served. Over the course of his career, James learned Yiddish, a skill that undoubtedly facilitated relationships with his patients.[9]

Other physicians were not so accommodating. Prevailing race and class stereotypes shaped Cyrus Edson's view of the immigrant poor. The son of a former mayor of New York City, Edson operated a clinic at 301 Mott Street and served as the city's public health inspector under the Tammany regime. He gained local fame for averting a typhus epidemic in 1892, which he blamed entirely on the immigrant Eastern European Jewish population. In an interview later that year, he expressed simultaneous disdain for and sympathy with the mainly Jewish and Italian people who sought free medical care from his office. He described Russian Jews as "phlegmatic, dull and stupid" and noted, with marked impatience, the difficulties he faced in attempting to gather information from Italians, whom he viewed as "sullen and suspicious."[10]

By 1920, the number of physicians and surgeons who were first- or second-generation European immigrants had grown significantly.[11] The number of Jewish physicians increased from 450 to about 1,000 between 1897 and 1907, despite quotas that had long kept many Jewish men from seeking careers in medicine. Hungarian, German, Russian, Polish, and Austrian Jews were now able to locate physicians from their own ethnic groups, who often spoke their language and were familiar with Jewish religious and health-care practices.[12] Abraham Jacobi, for example, was a leader in pediatric medicine. Born in Germany, Jacobi immigrated to the United States in the 1860s. After settling in New York, he established a thriving practice and held regular salons for young physicians in his home. He married Mary Putnam, one of the few female physicians during the late nineteenth century. Both concentrated their medical practices among the immigrant poor.

Although Jews tended to seek out Jewish physicians, some of these physicians saw non-Jewish patients, as well. Such was the case of Harry

Philip Schlansky, a second-generation Russian Jew who had moved to New York from Germantown, Pennsylvania. Like most doctors, he made home visits to an ethnically diverse set of patients, including the Chinese in lower Manhattan. In 1917, for example, he assisted in delivering Lung Som Moy, whose story appeared in the Introduction to this study. In the early years of his practice, Harry and his wife, Blanche Lissner Schlansky, opened an office in their home on Madison Street, near his patients and the immigrant Jewish community. By World War I, he and his family had moved to the Bronx.[13] It is unclear whether he continued to see patients from his former neighborhood.

That Schlansky and other white physicians cared for Chinese patients is not surprising, given the dearth of licensed Chinese physicians in New York. State law excluded non-citizens and those ineligible for citizenship from practicing medicine and other professions, such as law. Although the New York State legislature had passed a law that enabled non-citizens to bypass the original requirement through "waived alienage," only a handful of Chinese physicians could practice medicine in the state, and those who could were allowed to treat only Chinese patients. Jin Fuey Moy and Joseph Chak Thoms practiced medicine at the Chinese Hospital in Brooklyn, established by the Chinese Hospital Association in 1890, until it closed in 1892.[14] Both men had been born in China in the early 1860s and graduated from American medical schools in 1890, Thoms from the Brooklyn College Hospital and Jin Fuey Moy from Jefferson Medical College in Philadelphia. Moy eventually returned to New York City to work with Thoms.

When the Chinese Hospital closed, Thoms continued his private practice in Brooklyn. In 1929, he was murdered by one of his patients.[15] In addition to seeing Chinese patients in Manhattan's "Chinatown," Moy worked as the first superintendent of St. Bartholomew's Chinese Guild on Mott Street and as an interpreter for the Office of the District Attorney.[16] In 1914, after relocating to Pittsburgh, Moy was arrested and indicted for violating the Harrison Anti-Narcotic Act of 1914, which intended to exert federal control over the sale of narcotics—especially opium, which served as the chemical basis of morphine. Moy was charged with writing prescriptions for morphine for people who were not his patients and supplying opiates to drug addicts. He was eventually acquitted and continued to practice in Pittsburgh until his death in 1924.[17]

Although many non-Chinese were arrested under the Harrison Act as part of the resurgence of temperance and anti-drug movements during the Progressive era,[18] as a Chinese physician accused of indirectly "selling" opiates by writing false prescriptions, Moy practiced medicine under the shadow of Chinese stereotypes. Popular associations between the Chinese and opium persisted into the early twentieth century, even though the bulk of the opium trade did not come from China, and the British, not the Chinese, introduced the drug to the United States.[19] Sensationalist literature of the period, such as Norr's *Stories of Chinatown*, abounded with references to opium dens operating in Chinese neighborhoods and the danger they posed to the health of the nation and, specifically, to innocent white women, who supposedly were easily lured by Chinese men into the illicit drug and sex trade. The white pharmacist who testified in Moy's case underscored the link between the Chinese and opium by consistently referring to Moy as the "Chinaman."[20]

Within the climate of increased federal drug regulation during the 1910s, people continued to consult pharmacists and apothecaries, who sold medicine to a diverse clientele.[21] For these tradesmen, retail was an integral part of health care and often required the development of business relationships between suppliers and dispensers of medicine. Solomon Satosky's ginseng import business, for example, was a regular supplier of herbal medicine to Chinese groceries and herb shops in lower Manhattan. Some observers found the Chinese herb shops alienating, at best. The journalist Louis J. Beck, who wrote extensively about New York City's Chinese community, expressed doubt about the effectiveness of Chinese medicines, arguing that the wide variety of herbs available "possess no particle of virtue." The physical surroundings of the shops fared no better in Beck's mind: he described them as similar to a "witch's cave."[22] He also expressed doubt about the reliability of Chinese doctors who had received no formal medical training. Regardless of such attitudes, Chinese herbalists and doctors were an integral part of the cultural and economic networks between Chinese and non-Chinese clients, shopkeepers, and retailers.[23]

Chinese people sometimes sought help from settlement house workers in childbirth cases. The small number of Chinese women in the city— fewer than 150 in 1900—likely resulted in the request for non-Chinese assistance during labor.[24] A Nurses' Settlement report noted that most of the cases among the Chinese involved child birthing as opposed to other health needs, which the writer attributed to the self-sufficiency of the Chinese, who "rarely summon aid in ordinary illnesses." The report, however, added that when Chinese people agreed to see white nurses, the patients were "cooperative" and "endeavor[ed] to get well [as] quickly as possible."[25]

Co-ethnic hospitals and dispensaries provided the ill with "modern" medicines, as well as familiar curatives and healing practices. In 1896, for example, the Baptist Home Mission Society opened a dispensary on Doyers Street. The establishment was headed by Fung Mow, an evangelical Christian from the mission. A non-Chinese physician, however, Dr. C. F. Mills, provided actual medical services to the local Chinese.[26] The Chinese population in Brooklyn could go to the Chinese Hospital, if only for the year or so that the facility existed. Chinese people who lived in southern Manhattan probably preferred to go to the new Chinese hospital in "Chinatown." The Chinese Six Companies founded the Chung Wah Kong Sor E Sang Fong in 1906, a hospital that catered exclusively to the Chinese. Located at 105 Park Street, across from the rear of the Church of the Transfiguration, the hospital was housed in an unassuming two-story brick building. While patients occupied the first two floors, the basement served as the pharmacy, where one could find the Chinese medicines that Beck had decried in his description of Chinese herb shops. At the hospital, shelves held "the mysteries of the powdered toad and cockroach, of snake skins and frog skins, oil of snails, and herbs."[27] According to one journalist, the relatively small institution was "off the beaten path" of tourists, who tended to participate in "Chinatown" tours on the more popular streets—Mott, Pell, and Doyers. Apparently, only one man, Joseph Chung Hoe, served as the proprietor and chief "nurse" at the hospital.[28]

Jewish immigrants also founded their own hospitals. Mount Sinai Hospital in Manhattan was one of six Jewish hospitals in the United States by the early 1880s. Unfortunately, it was located in the northern area of Manhattan on West 71st Street, far from the Lower East Side. Closer to the immigrant poor was Beth Israel Hospital, where physicians dispensed free health care to the predominantly European Jewish population. Located at 206 Broadway when it was founded in 1890, the hospital moved to a larger building at Jefferson and Cherry five years later. By 1919, the facility accommodated 150 beds for lying-in patients.[29] The founding of Har Moriah Hospital on 2nd Street on the Lower East Side in 1908 illustrated the growing attention to ethnic diversity among European Jews. The new facility's founders praised the collective efforts of workers and merchants in the Galician Jewish community as much as the support of German Jewish leaders for gathering the necessary funds to build the hospital.[30]

Hospital facilities for Italian immigrants came under the auspices of the Catholic church. Catholic women in particular were active in dispensing health care to other Italian Catholics. One of the best known was Mother Francis Xavier Cabrini, who immigrated to the United States in 1889. Born in Italy, Cabrini and six other nuns had established the Institute of the Missionary Sisters of the Sacred Heart of Jesus several years before they arrived in New York. Included in the institute's mission was the provision of health care to the poor. In New York, Cabrini helped establish Columbus Hospital in 1892, to which a children's pharmacy was added two years later. The hospital, located at 41st and East 12th streets, served mainly the poor Italian population in southern Manhattan. Italian Hospital, founded in 1905, provided similar services on the West Side at 165–167 West Houston Street.[31]

Racial, ethnic, and gender segmentation in the medical profession rendered Italian hospital patients dependent on non-Italian male physicians. In 1900, the federal census recorded only 150 physicians of Italian ancestry in the entire United States; 82 of this number worked in Manhattan, only one of whom was a woman. Not surprisingly, in many cases doctors required the help of translators, an important service provided by Italian Catholic nuns who worked in the Catholic-run hospitals.[32]

While physicians, pharmacists, midwives, and nurses tended to the bodily needs of the living, undertakers assisted families with the proper care of the dead. Female family members and friends saw to immediate tasks, such as bathing and dressing the deceased. By the early twentieth century undertakers, most of whom were male, transported bodies from the home to the funeral parlor and arranged funeral rites.

The business of death among the urban working classes illustrates the impact of ethnic migration and occupational patterns between the mid-nineteenth century and the 1930s. Conducting a proper funeral was important to working-class people. Relatives of the deceased relied on mutual and immigrant-aid associations, insurance companies, contributions from friends, and labor organizations to help pay for funeral expenses.[33] According to a study conducted under the auspices of the Greenwich House Committee on Social Investigations in 1907, it was not uncommon for families to use up all of their investment in insurance or mutual aid society accounts and go into additional debt to pay for a funeral. To make matters worse, the lack of regulation or standards during this period resulted in the emergence of unscrupulous undertakers who overcharged their customers for myriad services. Part of the reason for the lack of regulation was that the business of undertaking had emerged out of a number of other types of trades rather than as a singular occupation on its own. Nevertheless, families were willing to pay what they could to provide a funeral complete with pallbearers, food, and flowers.[34]

On the surface, undertaking resembled other small business enterprises. They were usually run by male heads of households or widows and used the labor and partnerships of family members and friends of the same ethnicity. The physical location of these businesses in part determined the composition of the clientele. As the story of Ah Fung illustrates, the undertaking business in lower Manhattan provides insight into the social and economic consequences of a racialized and gendered occupational structure that rendered marginalized groups dependent on dominant groups for necessary services.

The racial and ethnic stratification of undertaking as a local and a national phenomenon already existed by the time the Chinese immigrated to New York City in the nineteenth century with the gradual exclusion of African Americans from the business. Although black migration patterns had shifted to Harlem and Brooklyn by the early twentieth century, African Americans constituted an "absent presence" in lower Manhattan. The discovery in 1991 of the African Burial Ground in southern Manhattan serves as a reminder of the presence of slaves and free blacks in this area of New York City dating back to the colonial period.[35]

The footprints of black coffin makers and the role of the black church in burying the dead serves as a reminder of slavery, segregation, and the physical mobility of populations in the history of New York City.

Free blacks who worked in trades related to undertaking advertised their skills in southern Manhattan in the early nineteenth century. One such tradesman was Adam Suder, who advertised the opening of his cabinet business, which included the construction of custom-made coffins, on Duane Street in 1828.[36] By the mid-nineteenth century, Irish undertakers greatly outnumbered blacks in the business. In 1855, for example, there was one black undertaker in New York City, compared to twenty-two Irish undertakers.[37] When blacks began to enter the undertaking and funeral home industry in large numbers in the 1920s, they struggled financially, especially in areas where the white population outnumbered blacks. Except in emergencies, well into the present day, whites typically patronize only white-run funeral homes, leaving the relatively few black families in the area to support black undertakers.[38] In other areas, black undertakers were valuable and trusted resources for the black community; they knew the families, attended the same churches, and belonged to the same social organizations.[39]

In 1900, out of a total of 858 undertakers in Manhattan, 5 were "colored" or African American.[40] The small number of African American undertakers in the borough signaled a system of racial exclusion that had already been mapped out by the time Chinese people settled in New York City. Although African Americans in New York were not excluded from undertaking and funeral work as a result of state citizenship laws governing occupations, they, like Asians, sought work in which they did not compete with whites. When they did try to enter white-dominated trades, they often faced violence and intimidation, as Karla Holloway demonstrates in her study of blacks and the "death care" industry in the United States. Consequently, to bury their dead, black families frequently had to rely on white-owned funeral establishments that discriminated against them in various ways. Under Jim Crow segregation practices, blacks were often required to enter white-run funeral establishments through the basement, and they paid the same prices as white customers for inferior and limited services.[41]

Black undertakers had a different historical relationship to the development of the trade than did other groups—one that was rooted in slavery. Under slavery, blacks often had to bury their own dead as well as the deceased in the white families they served. In the North, the black churches, mutual aid organizations, and insurance companies enabled blacks to serve their own community, providing funds to help bury the poor and to supply hearses, horses, and coffins. In one significant case, free blacks assisted both the black and white populations during the yellow fever epidemic that swept Philadelphia in 1793.[42]

Within the slave and free black community, people took great pains to ensure respectful care for deceased loved ones both in the preparation and in the burial of the bodies. Excluded from church burial grounds within the city limits, black New Yorkers had a separate burial ground that dated back to the colonial period, located at what is now 290 Broadway and in the Five Points district at Pearl Street. Excavators discovered the cemetery, known as the Negroes Burial Ground, in 1991 as they dug the foundation for a new bank building. The artifacts from the cemetery, which was renamed the African Burial Ground in 1993, and hundreds of skeletal remains suggest a devotion to African burial rites.

William Kennedy's funeral parlor on Pearl Street was located a few blocks south of the so-called Chinese Quarter. Since the early nineteenth century, Pearl Street had housed an ethnically diverse working-class population who worked as seamen and longshoremen and in other skilled occupations. The area around the street had also been a starting point for wholesale dry goods dealers, hatters, and cotton and fur merchants. By 1850, there were three undertaking establishments on Pearl Street, a necessity given that the death rate during the decade just among the city's Irish population was 21 percent.[43] Businesses continued to thrive, despite a huge fire that destroyed many residences and businesses in 1854.[44] The ethnic demographics had changed by the 1870s, although the population remained predominantly working class. Businesses had also come and gone. By the time of Ah Fung's murder, Kennedy was the only undertaker on Pearl Street.

In an interview with the *World*, Kennedy described his interactions with Chinese clients, portraying himself as somewhat of an authority on Chinese funerary customs. "'Chinamen,' said Mr. Kennedy, as he complacently seated himself at the foot of one coffin and lifted his feet to a comfortable position on the head of another, 'don't go in for very ostentatious funerals, but they generally have a cheap, respectable affair. . . . His funeral won't cost more than $60 or $70—a hearse and four or five carriages—and I'm blessed!'" Kennedy added that he trusted his Chinese customers, who helped his business succeed, noting that only twice did they ever try to cheat him.[45] Over time, Kennedy's reputation as a businessman grew. Known as the "liveliest man in the sixth ward," he was elected coroner under the Tammany administration in the 1880s.[46]

White journalists across the country found Chinese funeral practices in the city a fascinating topic. Similar writings on Chinese funeral practices in California appeared in popular magazines such as the *Overland Monthly*. The Reverend A. W. Loomis, one of many missionaries in the San Francisco area, not surprisingly focused on the spiritual aspects of the Chinese funerals he observed while working among Chinese immigrants in that city, noting that many aspects of the practices were "pleasing in the care bestowed by the Chinese on the burial-places of their dead, and in the various devices for preserving the fragrance of their memory." Like other writers, Loomis described in great detail the adornments that were placed at the burial sites, including varieties of food and "mourning women," who were hired to follow the carriage to the grave, wailing loudly along the way.[47]

These writings tend to address the most visible part of funeral rites; they do not address the deeper, more complex cultural meanings attached to such rituals, from the preparation of the body to the use of incense, paper money, and food at the services. For the Chinese, turning dead friends and relatives over to people outside the ethnic community was yet another concession to Chinese exclusion in the workplace. As in many cultures, the task of preparing the deceased for a proper burial had been the responsibility of family members, particularly the women.[48] In the United States, where care of the dead was shifting from the home to the funeral parlor, putting a loved one in the hands of those who did not have an intimate understanding of Chinese culture must have been difficult.

One writer known only as "An Old Californian" or "A. T." included his observations of Chinese ways to handle illness and death in New York City in 1882 in *The "Heathen Chinee,"* his book on the Chinese in the United States. He wrote that, immediately after a Chinese man's death, friends of the deceased took "a series of semi-holidays, governed exclusively by the amount of money taken during life by the dead man which did not go up in opium fumes or into the gamblers' coffers."[49]

The format and content of the book was similar to that of other books and articles on the Chinese written by journalists who had staked out southern Manhattan as part of their "beat" during this period. Given the propensity to include "fact or fancy" in such stories, it is impossible to determine the accuracy of the authors' descriptions. Adding local color was a standard part of the new urban journalism. For example, A. T.'s deployment of popular stereotypes of Chinese men as inveterate gamblers and opium smokers was common to popular descriptions of the "Chinese Quarter."

Frank Moss noted that, for many Chinese in New York, funerals often combined Chinese and American practices, suggesting a willingness to adapt. Beck observed that "there is an exceedingly curious mixture of Chinese customs and American methods. . . . There is no crape [*sic*] on the door and no appearance of overpowering grief." At the same time, he added, hearse drivers participated in Chinese rituals by allowing a man to sit next to them at the graveyard and "[throw] red papers stamped with prayers that confuse and mislead the devils and give them plenty of diversion in chasing them as they are whirled about by the breezes."[50]

Wong Chin Foo, a journalist who was born in China and came to the United States in 1868 as a student, provided the only published Chinese voice in the United States on Chinese funerary customs. Wong, who had written a corrective to popular stereotypes of Chinese people and customs in 1888, provided a detail that Kennedy had overlooked: that the Chinese usually wore white clothing for mourning.[51]

Kennedy provided a number of services, including gravesite rites and burial:

> At the cemetery, we put the corpse in the grave and then all the Chinamen and their wives get in line and marching past the grave each throws in a handful of dirt. In the summer time they put in a sprig of evergreen. When the grave is filled up they put bunches of incense on it and set the incense afire, and sometimes they put in a row of joss-sticks the whole length of the grave, and setting them afire leave them burning.[52]

Although the CCBA provided financial help to families to bury the dead, care for tombs, and send the bones back to China,[53] this powerful network of Chinese merchants could do little to change the structure of the labor force by helping other Chinese enter the undertaking business.

When Kennedy first advertised his services with his business partner, a man named Malone, in 1861, he followed a long line of Irish male undertakers in New York City.[54] Irish men in the funeral trade could be found in lower Manhattan as early as the 1820s. Several others were located on Pearl Street, where Kennedy would later open his funeral parlor. Henry McCadden and John L. Dillon, for example, offered "ready-made" coffin service during the early nineteenth century. By the 1840s, Dillon dominated much of the funeral business in the area. The trade expanded among the Irish in the next two decades. By 1900, of the 441 undertakers in Manhattan and the Bronx who had at least one foreign-born parent, 285 had Irish surnames.[55]

By the 1880s, the Naughton funeral home on Mott Street had begun to compete with Kennedy's establishment, particularly as the Chinese community began to concentrate in the area around Mott, Doyers, and Pell streets. Although there were other funeral homes in the immediate area, including Whelan and Riordan, run by William J. Riordan, at 51 Mott Street; Francis Quigley, at 252 Elizabeth Street; and Charles and Patrick McCollum's establishments on Mulberry Street, Naughton's was the best known for serving the Chinese community by the end of the nineteenth century.

The Naughtons were familiar faces in the "Chinese Quarters" in lower Manhattan. James Naughton was an Irish immigrant who, like other undertakers, had begun his career as a stable keeper and then expanded his business to include funeral goods and services. He established his funeral home and livery business at 33 Mott Street, next door to the historic Church of the Transfiguration. Later, the business expanded into contiguous spaces at 31 and 35 Mott Street.[56] Surrounding Naughton's building were several Chinese businesses and apartments that housed both Chinese and non-Chinese.

Naughton provided funerals for both the ordinary and prominent people who lived in the neighborhood. For example, in 1888 the establishment provided the funeral services General Lee Yu Doo, a prominent Chinese soldier who had died in his home at 28 Mott Street, just a block away from the funeral parlor. The general's funeral was an elaborate and expensive service, which apparently had been rare when Kennedy was serving the Chinese community.[57]

That Kennedy, Naughton, Riordan, and Whelan had first worked as proprietors of livery stables was not unusual for male undertakers.[58] The expansion of livery work, in particular, to include care of the dead was directly related to the change in funeral practices in the United States. Between the eighteenth century and the late nineteenth century, many livery and carriage proprietors, sextons, and carpenters had expanded the scope of their tasks to include funeral and undertaking services.[59]

Operators of livery and carriage houses, whose business was hauling goods, could also use their equipment to transport bodies from the homes of the deceased to funeral parlors, as well as rent their horses and carriages for funeral processions. The livery business was attractive to working-class men who had little capital to spare, because stables were not difficult or expensive to set up. Irish immigrant men who had come from farms in Ireland also brought with them some experience with handling horses and operating stables. In the United States, however, these men struggled to enter the hauling business, which in the early nineteenth century was categorized as "unskilled" labor. Eighty-seven percent of Irish men in New York City had found employment in low-paying and sometimes dangerous and irregular unskilled jobs. Many of those in the livery business had begun as unlicensed cart men, who, according to a city ordinance in 1818, could haul only "dirt and nothing else" so as not to compete with licensed cart men. By the mid-nineteenth century, men of Irish and English heritage dominated carting and livery work.[60]

In addition to carrying the dead from homes to the funeral parlor, undertakers prepared bodies for embalming and display, secured caskets from local furniture or cabinet makers, provided public spaces for viewing and services, and, finally, transported the deceased and family to the cemetery. By the mid-nineteenth century, many municipalities required cemeteries to be located outside the city limits as a way to eliminate overcrowding in city, family, and church cemeteries. In the process, they hoped to curb epidemics like yellow fever, which they associated with the odors from city cemeteries and private family crypts. Most used the two public burial grounds in Brooklyn: the Cemetery of the Evergreens, referred to by whites as "Celestial Hill," or the Chinese section of Cypress Hills Cemetery.[61] Many Chinese did not want to be buried in New York; they preferred final interment in California, thus rendering the mortuary business transnational and transcontinental. The Naughtons, for example, were regular customers of the Canadian Pacific Railway Company, which transported Chinese bodies back to California.[62]

The Naughton family business adapted to the changes in American funerary practices and eventually prospered enough from its "Chinatown" business to move the family out of lower Manhattan to a larger home in a less racially and ethnically diverse neighborhood on Lexington Avenue, although the family retained the business on Mott Street. The Naughtons' prosperity can be attributed to several factors. First, because undertaking had involved other types of trades, such as livery, horse dealing, and carpentry, families in the undertaking business could augment their income by providing services other than caring for the dead, such as renting out their livery equipment and horses. Second, James and Ann Naughton had a relatively large family that included several sons, which facilitated the expansion of the businesses at least to the next generation. In this sense, undertaking was similar to other small businesses that used children and other relatives as cheap or unpaid labor and encouraged male descendants to take on the family business.[63] By 1900, the Naughtons' business would include several other Naughton men, including James's four adult sons, Laurence (also sometimes spelled Lawrence), James Jr., John, and Joseph, and a cousin, Francis.

Most important, as the only undertaking business in the center of "Chinatown," the Naughtons virtually held a monopoly on the increasingly lucrative and specialized undertaking and funeral home business.[64] The Naughton men, therefore, were not unusual in that they were a part of the population who dominated most of the urban men's trades. White men dominated all of the major categories of men's occupations in Manhattan during the period under consideration. Two factors account for this trend. The most obvious is that the total white population outnumbered those classified as "colored."

In addition to the uneven population ratio, state occupational laws and local Jim Crow practices resulted in the concentration of "colored" men, including Chinese, Indian, Japanese, and African Americans, in the category of domestic and personal service, while the majority of white men found employment in "skilled" trades and transportation.

Within the "unskilled" category, most African American men, who made up 77 percent of the "colored" male population in Manhattan, were servants, waiters, and laborers.[65] By 1920, the picture had not changed significantly. Out of the total population of 2,284,103 in Manhattan, those classified as "white" numbered 2,168,906, or 95 percent of the borough's population.[66]

Few non-white men took up the undertaking trade for some of the same reasons that women were excluded. Unlike white men, few men of color found steady work in the related trades of livery, carpentry, and furniture making. Many of those trades maintained exclusionary apprenticeship practices. For example, in 1900, out of a total of 2,115 cabinetmakers in Manhattan and the Bronx, only four were "colored"; all of them were "Negroes." There were also only four black men in the livery stable business out of a total of 594 in the two boroughs. The same held true for furniture manufacturing: two black men, who again made up the total number of "colored" men in this work, were employed in furniture manufacturing out of a total of 346. No Chinese men were in any of these occupations.

Exclusion on the basis of non-eligibility constituted another layer of discriminatory practices in the occupational structure and created a system of dependence for essential services and maintenance of the infrastructure of the urban built community. Chinese men had been officially locked out of many occupations and professions, including undertaking and the funeral home business, by state laws that required citizenship status. The only Chinese man listed in the undertaking businesses in 1870 resided in San Francisco. By 1900, there were only nine in the country. Twenty years later, a national total of 23,342 men and 1,127 women had taken up the trade, but in New York State, the number of Chinese in the undertaking business remained at zero, compared with 55 African Americans, 1,114 U.S.-born whites, and 1,274 European immigrants in the trade.[67]

Until the 1930s, when the first person of Chinese ancestry received an undertaker's license, the Chinese community depended on non-Chinese undertakers to care for their dead and they usually went to the Naughtons.[68]

The Naughtons' business weathered and likely even profited from street violence that often erupted in the neighborhood. When the laundryman Hop Lee was murdered in January 1884, the funeral parlor served as the site for his autopsy and subsequent burial. The funeral parlor then became a scene of what ended up as a minor contestation between a representative from the Chinese consul and the New York City coroner. Both men inspected the body but arrived at very different conclusions about a possible culprit. Although three Chinese men were questioned, the Chinese consul denied that the crime could have been committed by a Chinese man, deploying popular stereotypes of both Chinese and white working-class men. According to the consul, no Chinese man was physically capable of inflicting such an extensive knife wound, and "an American loafer" was undoubtedly the murderer.[69]

In October 1912, the funeral home and livery stables were one of several businesses and apartment buildings riddled by gunfire between members of rival Chinese gangs, the Hip Sings and the On Leongs.[70] In a hail of bullets, a man in Naughton's office was wounded, and one of the horses was killed. Although the Naughtons' funeral home sustained damage during this incident, the business survived.

The fighting continued intermittently throughout the first two decades of the twentieth century. Conflict between the two gangs had gotten so bad that in 1924, when two Hip Sing members, Eng Hing and Lee Duck, were executed for the murder of an eighteen-year-old member of On Leong, the police demanded that the funeral be held outside "Chinatown." As a result, in this rare instance, Naughton lost out to C. Baciagalupo, which ran one of its funeral parlors on Spring Street.[71]

Although the Kennedys and the Naughtons gained local notoriety for their connection to instances of street violence, they were not unusual in the history of undertaking in the United States. They were both insiders and outsiders to the Chinese community they served. The services and items they offered revealed an accumulation of knowledge over the years about Chinese funereal practices. At the Naughtons' funeral home, for example, in addition to obtaining funeral services, Chinese customers could purchase items that were an important part of those services, such as incense, flowers, candles, and artificial paper money at the adjoining shop.[72] The Naughtons' undertaking business organized long funeral processions favored by the Chinese.

The maintenance of funeral and burial practices among Chinese immigrants was a crucial part of everyday life. Adam McKeown's analysis of the Chinese diaspora and migration patterns during the early twentieth century is useful here. McKeown's focus on the Chinese in Peru, Chicago, and Hawaii illuminates the extensiveness of transnational economic and social networks between Chinese people. An important part of Chinese migration was the maintenance of a religious cosmology that rooted "overseas Chinese" squarely back in China, regardless of where in the world they lived and worked. The transplantation of cultural practices included preparing and disposing of the dead. The maintenance of proper funeral and burial practices was a critical dimension of this belief system, and the Chinese took great pains to ensure that the community followed certain customs. One important custom was to dig up the bones of the deceased after one year and send them back to China for permanent burial. Although the distance the bones had to travel underscored the diasporic experience of the Chinese and the perception that to die in a foreign country was considered a tragedy, the practice itself was in keeping with Chinese funerary practices during the late imperial era. The final burial of the bones in China, however, varied by region.[73]

Naughton and other undertakers of Irish ancestry undoubtedly noticed both the similarities and the differences between their own Irish cultural practices surrounding death and funeral rites and those of the Chinese to whom they catered. Although the placement of items and the sequence of events may have differed, both groups, for example, as did many other cultures, provided food and expressed concerns about protecting both the living and the dead from ghosts and demons. For the Chinese, food was placed at the gravesite or in front of the casket at the funeral parlor, and coins and paper money were placed with the body so that the deceased would not go hungry in the afterlife. For the Irish, food and drink were staple components of wakes. In the words of the historian Jay P. Dolan, "To bury an Irishman was as much a social event as a religious one."[74]

Over the years, members of the Naughton family had developed further connections with many Chinese in the area as they expanded their real-estate holdings in the neighborhood. The Chinese relied on the Naughtons not only to bury their dead and provide housing for Chinese tenants but also to support their applications for return certificates under the Chinese exclusion laws. In January 1908, for example, Laurence Naughton testified on behalf of Lau Din, a Chinese merchant who worked across the street at Sam Kee and Company, which sold groceries and clothing. Lau Din had applied to bring his wife, Pang Ah Gum, into the country the following October. Naughton not only worked as an undertaker and livery but was also a landlord. He owned the building where Sam Kee and Company was located and had come to know Lau Din over the fourteen or fifteen years that Lau worked at the company.[75]

The Naughtons' establishment thrived until its buildings were purchased and then demolished to expand the facilities of the Church of the Transfiguration in the 1920s. Sometime during the 1920s or 1930s, the Baciagalupo family established the Chas. Baciagalupo Resting Parlor at 36 Mulberry Street, which serviced the needs of parishioners at Transfiguration.[76] John and Joseph Naughton later adapted their father's livery business to the new automobile culture by renting limousines to local funeral homes from a large parking garage they owned on Lexington Avenue.[77] Thus, the Naughtons had done well financially after decades of running a successful business that depended to a great extent on a Chinese clientele.

The history of the undertaking business in southern Manhattan exemplifies the ways in which racial categorization shaped the composition of certain occupations and in the process created relations of dependence within an urban setting. That the Kennedys, Naughtons, and Baciagalupos could enter the undertaking and funeral home business attests to the workings of whiteness at the federal and state levels. The immigration restriction laws determined who would or would not be eligible for U.S. citizenship based on race. States such as New York followed the lead of the federal government by enacting laws of inclusion and exclusion in certain occupations.

While racial segregation in the trades resulted in Chinese and black dependence on white undertakers, many European immigrant groups could, to a greater extent, serve the funerary needs of their own ethnic groups. By the 1920s, other European ethnic groups were also establishing undertaking businesses on the Lower East Side, although it is unclear whether they also served the Chinese community. In most cases, these groups could serve the funerary needs of members of their own ethnic group, although they may have identified with certain regions of the country of origin. The funeral business grew, albeit slowly, among the Italian population in Manhattan. Italians and Sicilians clustered on several streets contiguous to "Chinatown" on Mulberry and Elizabeth streets.[78] Although most Italian men and women earned wages in trades, factories, and piecework, many, men, in particular, also ran small businesses, including undertaking. In 1890, for example, Hunt's business directory listed three undertaking businesses designated by Italian surnames. By 1926, Phillips's business directory listed forty-seven such businesses. Several were located on Mulberry Street, long considered the center of "Little Italy."[79]

In 1890, Charles Baciagalupo ran two funeral homes: one at 95 Park Street, and one at 26 Roosevelt. He had immigrated to the United States from Italy with his family when he was a boy and was a parish leader at Our Lady of Pompeii Roman Catholic church on Bleecker Street. His sons and his brother-in-law, Giovanni Battista Perazzo, took over and expanded the business to include the branch on Spring Street. The undertaker who served the Chinese community during the Tong wars in the 1920s was probably Eugene Baciagalupo, who lived nearby on Mulberry Street.[80]

A few Jewish funeral homes dotted the eastern section of the Lower East Side by the early twentieth century. Unlike the Chinese, Jews and other European immigrant groups could obtain undertaking licenses and thus serve the needs of their own communities. In addition, as had occurred with the Irish and Italians on the Lower East Side, the training of family members in Jewish household in the trade facilitated the continued growth of undertaking and of the number of undertakers in these ethnic groups. For orthodox Jews, the presence of a Jewish undertaker and funeral home in the neighborhood ensured that certain cultural practices were followed. Observing traditional burial practices was an important dimension of daily life among Jewish immigrants, as it was among the Chinese.[81] The noted writer Abraham Cahan told the story of a Jewish man found dead on a sidewalk. No one knew the cause of death, but friends and neighbors feared that the man might have committed suicide, which meant that he could not be buried in a

Jewish cemetery. After a local and trusted physician confirmed that the death was not a suicide but an accident, friends and family breathed a collective sigh of relief that the man, Harris Friedman, could be buried as a Jew.

Jewish funeral establishments also followed the pattern of most family businesses in which sons assisted their fathers and other family members contributed their time and energy to some aspect of the business. For example, Abraham Fielman ran an undertaking business near his home on Montgomery Street during the early twentieth century. His youngest son, Isaac, worked as the manager of the funeral home, and the eldest son, Jack, later left his job as a bank teller to take over the family business. Jacob Finkelstone, who resided on East 57th Street, operated a funeral home on St. Mark's Place. His son Isaac worked as a bookkeeper for a cemetery.[82]

Jewish mutual aid societies were critical to tending the burial needs of impoverished Jews. The first was the Hebrew Free Burial Association, formed in 1888 by Barnett Friedman, a tailor who resided with his family at the southern edge of the predominantly Sicilian neighborhood on Elizabeth Street.[83] By 1917, the association had several branches, each of which was responsible for arranging burials at specific cemeteries. Friedman went on to serve as president of the Agudath Achim Chesed Shel Emeth, Gustave Hartman was president of the Hebrew Free Burial Society and Israel Orphan Asylum, and Fannie Krakow served as president of the Harlem branch of the society. Jewish undertakers were highly visible in the New York Jewish community and created networks between their businesses and the community they served. The Fielmans and the Finkelstones were active in the mutual aid societies. Abraham Fielman served as president of the Brisker Ladies Burial Association in 1917–1918, and Libby Finkelstone, one of Jacob's daughters, was a social worker who also served as secretary for the United Hebrew Charities.[84]

Funeral homes, mutual aid and burial organizations, and burial sites among Jews served as important places for social interaction. Between 1888 and 1909, many Jewish mutual aid and burial organizations were organized along ethnic lines. For example, the Austro-Hungarian Hebrew Free Burial Society, organized in 1889, served Austro-Hungarian Jews, and B'nai B'rith provided for the needs of secular German Jews. These societies remained active during the early twentieth century, even as Jewish funerals, following the trend of most funerals in U.S. cities, moved from the private home or synagogue to commercial funeral homes like those run by Fielman and Finkelstone.[85] What remained was the ability of Jewish residents to rely on other European Jews to see to the proper burial of loved ones.

By 1918, New York Jews could arrange for burial in a number of Jewish cemeteries in Brooklyn, Queens, Long Island, and New Jersey. Customers could make the arrangements in cemetery offices that were conveniently located in Lower East Side neighborhoods on Grand Street, Norfolk Street, and Second Avenue. By 1920, there were approximately fifteen Jewish cemeteries in New York City, many of which were subdivided and decorated according to regional affiliation, such as Galicia and Austria-Hungary.[86]

Thus, European immigrants could establish funeral homes that catered to diverse ethnic populations. The funeral homes owned by Irish and Italians served the Chinese and white populations until the Chinese could create their own institutions. For the Jamaican-born undertaker Bert V. Eutemey to do so during the period of exclusion, however, meant that he had to use his official identity as a non-Chinese British citizen. Once in the United States, Eutemey could reclaim his Chinese identity and participate in New York's Chinese community.[87] His bilingual skills and close connection with the most powerful organization in the Chinese community undoubtedly smoothed the path to establishing himself at 22 Mulberry Street as the first Chinese undertaker in the city. As both a non-Chinese citizen and a successful member of the Chinese community, he could open an important line of work previously closed to the Chinese and serve the local Chinese population.

World War II was an important turning point for both women and ethnic minorities in the United States. During the postwar period, the color bar against the entrance of Chinese men in a variety of trades and professions slowly lifted, resulting in the increase, especially of second-generation Chinese men, in professions such as chemistry and various areas of engineering. Changes in legislation—most significantly, the repeal of the Chinese Exclusion Act in 1943—allowed Chinese immigrants to become U.S. citizens and enabled them to gain access to professions in states that retained citizenship restrictions in certain occupations. Since the late 1970s, three Chinese-run funeral homes have operated on the same block of Mulberry Street, although ownership has changed hands among Chinese families in recent years. Eutemey's Cheung Sang Funeral Corporation at number 22 is now the Wah Lai Family Funeral Corporation; next door, at number 26, is the Wah Wing Sang Funeral Home; and at number 36 is N. G. Fook Funerals Incorporated, established in 1976 when the Chen family replaced the Baciagalupo funeral parlor.[88] The "ethnic succession" of the inhabitants of 26 Mulberry Street is evident in the façade of the building, which is decorated with carvings of Christian imagery immediately above the Wah Wing Sang awning.

Sustaining the physical urban infrastructure was just as necessary as providing health and death care, although it required less intimate interactions across lines of ethnicity, race, and culture. As with other occupations, the building trades exemplify how a racially and sexually stratified occupational structure shaped the degree to which such interactions occurred. For example, the exclusion of the Chinese and other non-whites from most trades until the 1930s resulted not only from overt threats or intimidation (as in the case of railroad work or mining in the western states) but also, especially in urban areas, from the transplantation of experiences and skills that white men already possessed (such as carpentry and stable work) and from the evolution of trades over time, which white men already dominated.

By the late nineteenth century and early twentieth century, well-established chain migration processes that led mostly Northern European men into the majority of trades and professions merged with new social reform movements aimed at improving the health and well-being of the working class and poor in the nation's cities. Plumbers, carpenters, and electricians were critical to the maintenance of residences and businesses.[89] Although electricity and advancements in indoor plumbing had begun as novelties for the rich, housing advocates quickly saw their value to the improvement of living spaces among the urban poor. As electricity replaced gas lighting in businesses and factories, the need for electricians increased. Most of these tradesmen were white. In 1900, 7,639 electricians in Brooklyn, Manhattan, and the Bronx were "white"; the remaining 18 were listed as "coloured." By 1920, the total number of electricians in New York City had increased to 18,987, only 130 of whom were Negroes and seven of whom were "Indian, Chinese, Japanese, and all other."[90] As a result, Chinese business owners relied on white electricians such as George W. Davis, who resided at 42 Mott Street. Some trusted Davis enough to ask him to testify on their behalf when they applied for return certificates or for the admission of family members into the country. In 1920, for example, Davis testified on behalf of Chon Cum Sim, a poultry dealer for the Chinese firm of the Kwon Sang Company on Pell Street, when Chon applied for the admission of his wife, Chin See.[91]

Louis Scheinmann provided plumbing services to Chinese clients and, like Davis, was often called on to assist Chinese merchants when they requested necessary documents under the exclusion laws. Perhaps even more than electricity, improved plumbing was critical to the health of the population. In the cities, public health reformers targeted contaminated water, cesspools, and poorly maintained outhouses as a main cause of disease, which resulted in tenement reform, city garbage collection, and revisions in municipal health codes. That urban immigrants were associated with disease and filth only exacerbated the perception that Old World burial practices threatened a healthy, modern society, a view that coincided with the public health reform movement during the Progressive era.[92] The longtime housing and tenement reform activist Lawrence Veiller proclaimed in the early 1920s that even though no one could yet prove that a causal relationship existed between bad plumbing and the spread of disease, it was "unquestionably true that modern sanitary plumbing makes greatly for better living conditions."[93] Changes in the city health codes directly affected the trades of plumbing and care of the dead. Municipal and individual efforts to provide services to residents and businesses were part of a larger Progressive-era reform agenda to maintain both the physical and the moral health of the city's urban population.

As much as they were able, immigrant and working-class people found ways to provide health care and burial services through co-ethnic organizations and institutions. The degree to which they sought outsiders depended to a large extent on structural factors. Exclusion from certain trades and professions sometimes resulted in the reliance on interethnic/interracial relations to care for both the living and the dead, as well as to maintain a decent living environment. Relations across class, race, ethnicity, and gender were not always antagonistic; rather, they reflected a more complex set of social dynamics that operated within larger systems of inequality.

The next two chapters explore the ways in which interracial/interethnic relations emerged as a result of efforts by social reformers to create a more healthful social and moral environment through the elimination of vice and the establishment of settlement houses. In the process, male anti-vice agents and settlement house reformers came into daily contact with the immigrant poor and working classes, creating different kinds of social relations and different modes of interaction.

4

Mixing with the Sinners

The Anti-vice Movement

Late on a July evening in 1901, William C. Steele Jr., Arthur E. Wilson, and Isaac Silverman scoured the Lower East Side looking for prostitutes. They were no ordinary men looking for a good time; they had recently signed up with the city's newly formed private moral reform organization, the Committee of Fifteen. Their job was to locate known houses of prostitution and report the addresses and exact locations of the prostitutes' flats and to describe the physical features of the buildings and of the women and girls who solicited them. Two of the men had been active in the city's anti-vice campaign. Wilson had been an investigator for the Anti-Saloon League. Silverman, a New York County detective, participated in gambling raids and later served on the staff of the new reform-minded and controversial District Attorney William Travers Jerome.[1] Steele was likely the son of a prominent Methodist minister in the city who was a strong temperance advocate.

Investigators like Steele, Wilson, and Silverman traversed the streets after most businesses had closed for the night. But the streets were not empty; saloons and Chinese restaurants remained open until the early-morning hours, catering to workers coming from their night shifts, local residents, theatergoers, and late-night "slummers." As was typical during the summer months, residents chatted, argued, and played on the sidewalks and front stoops late into the night. With temperatures rising into the high eighties and nineties by the late afternoons that month, poor families brought their mattresses out of their stifling flats and camped in the streets at night to escape the "heat holocaust."[2] Despite the heat, reform agents were ardent in their quest to end—or, at least, curb—the sex trade.

This chapter and the next examine the ways in which urban reformers and local immigrant and working-class residents together shaped race and ethnic relations during the Progressive era. This chapter focuses on neighborhoods in lower Manhattan—that were frequent targets of anti-vice raids and investigations. In their quest to eliminate prostitution, illegal gambling, and "white slavery," reformers made themselves an intentionally disruptive presence in the daily lives of working-class and poor urbanites.[3]

Most studies of private anti-vice organizations have explored their impact on city politics, particularly police corruption and the struggles between Tammany and anti-Tammany forces. Scholarship on settlement house workers, which includes those involved in anti-prostitution, has expanded our view by illustrating the role of female reformers in literally carving out "redemptive spaces" in the city. But urban reform was not a completely one-sided phenomenon. Many people who lived and worked in the neighborhoods under surveillance at times intentionally interacted with reformers by mail or in person; some sent notes expressing support for the anti-vice crusade or seeking employment with reform organizations, while others visited anti-vice offices, missions, rescue homes, and settlement houses to help locate missing daughters. Thus, while prostitutes kept an eye out for anti-vice agents, some of their neighbors participated in the movement by working as agents. In so doing, they not only blurred the line between reformer and targets of reform but also complicated the classic characterization of moral reformers as uniformly native-born, educated, white middle-class men and women.

Many reform *leaders* were, in fact, from the privileged classes of urban society: the clergy, settlement workers, missionaries, scientists, and social scientists. Among these educated professionals swirled new ideas about the source of criminal behavior. While a new strain of thought proposed that one's physical environment was at the root of bad behavior, older ideas that blamed inherent characteristics of individuals and certain ethnic groups persisted. A number of prominent scientists and social scientists argued that the new immigrants from Southern and

Eastern Europe had an inherited propensity for criminality. Charles B. Davenport, an instructor at Harvard University and the founder of the Eugenics Record Office at Cold Spring Harbor, New York, argued that the influx of Southern and Eastern Europeans would result in an increase in criminal behavior because they were "more given to crimes of larceny, kidnapping, assault, murder, rape and sex-immorality" than the "old" immigrants from the British Isles. Although Davenport's credibility would fade by the 1940s, he and other eugenics leaders were instrumental in the passage of the immigration restriction acts of 1921 and 1924.[4] But even those who may have opposed the passage of an immigration restriction bill did not necessarily reject basic eugenicist arguments that certain ethnic/racial groups were inclined toward specific types of behaviors.

An explicitly gendered component of anti-prostitution rhetoric was its association with immigrant women, a line of argumentation that extended from more general views of heredity that reinforced existing assumptions about women's inherent weakness made worse by genetic flaws.[5] As Benjamin O. Flower, a clergyman and editor of the social reform journal *Arena*, argued, young women, through "pre-natal influences" and having fathers as "moral lepers," were destined for sexual immorality.[6]

In the minds of many reformers, moral debasement, combined with poverty, led poor immigrant women into prostitution. In a lengthy report, the tenement house activist Lawrence Veiller wrote that the "most terrible" feature of tenement life was the "indiscriminate herding of all kinds of people in close contact . . . with the drunken, the dissolute, the improvident and the diseased." He worried that the spread of prostitution and gambling beyond the boundaries of "red-light districts" into residential areas posed a danger to "respectable" working-class families and posed a particularly corrupting influence to children.[7] Veiller's solution was to improve the physical infrastructure of buildings and at the same time discourage "immoral" acts within dwellings.

In addition to finding a range of solutions for deterring criminality among the poor and immigrant population, a growing number of activists targeted corruption in the municipal government and the police for supporting and profiting from houses of vice through bribes, intimidation, and kickbacks. The organization of private anti-vice committees like the Committee of Fifteen and Committee of Fourteen, headed by influential men in the city, sought both to solve the problem of the sex trade and to end police corruption through street-by-street investigations and reportage.

Prostitution was not a new social phenomenon when Progressive reformers came onto the urban scene in the late nineteenth century. It had flourished in New York City since the earliest settlement by Europeans. The sex trade had long provided tantalizing fodder for fictional stories, tourist guides, and the press. Nathaniel Hawthorne's short story "My Kinsman, Major Molineaux," published in 1832, was one of the earliest works to connect New York City with prostitution. During his journey through the streets of lower Manhattan, Robin Molineaux, a youth "of barely eighteen, evidently country bred," narrowly escapes a number of unsavory characters, including a woman dressed in scarlet who tries to lure him into her rooms.[8] Although prostitutes were part of the neighborhoods in which they plied their trade, they lived a precarious existence. The murder of the New York prostitute Helen Jewett in April 1836, which was covered extensively by the local press, highlighted the vulnerability of prostitutes to violence. By midcentury, popular guidebooks such as George G. Foster's *New York by Gas-Light* cited prostitution as part of the city's corruptive influence.[9]

Efforts to combat vice in American cities began as early as the eighteenth century. Clergy and reformers viewed prostitution as a symbol of urban moral decadence. Anti-vice organizations emerged periodically until the early twentieth century and focused mainly on prostitution but also included gambling and alcohol.[10] These groups emerged within the context of larger social reform movements, such as the Second Great Awakening, which "awakened" the Protestant clergy and their congregations during the early decades of the nineteenth century to an "immediatist" agenda of eliminating sin in the wake of the second coming of Christ. Reformers targeted prostitution, excessive drinking, and, for the first time, slavery. By the 1830s, clerical and lay activists had organized against vice through the establishment of rescue homes, proselytizing, and the publication of reform journals that addressed a range of issues, including temperance, domestic violence, and illicit sex.[11] After the Civil War, moral reform resurged in U.S. cities, shaped by new ideas concerning public health and the notion that municipal government had a responsibility to regulate or eliminate the sex trade.

Historians tend to characterize reform activities as primarily a middle-class endeavor; however, a diverse population of women and men in rural and urban areas participated in reform. Gender conventions prevailed in most cases. Many women worked under the visible leadership of their clergymen. Others worked on their own by establishing houses of refuge for women who had left the sex trade. For example, Hetty Reckless, a black working-class abolitionist in Philadelphia, transformed her boardinghouse into such a refuge, calling it the Moral Reform Retreat. Catholic nuns also organized to persuade immigrant Irish girls to eschew prostitution in favor of more respectable, albeit lower-paying, employment as live-in domestic servants.[12] Protestant missionaries, toting Bibles, "visited" prostitutes in the hope of rescuing them through "moral persuasion." Late-nineteenth-century reformers continued the practice of "visiting" but also launched investigations into police and government collusion that many believed sustained the sex trade and other forms of urban vice.

The Progressive-era reform movement represented a dramatic step away from viewing prostitution as a "necessary evil" to a "social evil," even though its association with sin remained. The concept of "social evil" combined the earlier emphasis on morality with new scientific and medical concerns about the spread of venereal disease. While many reformers in the United States followed European models, regulating prostitution through strategies such as requiring prostitutes to submit to medical testing for the presence of venereal disease, others sought to end the sex trade and the municipal corruption that supported it by passing legislation at the state level and hoped that the reports issued as a result of investigators' visits to prostitutes would buttress the affidavits and oral testimony at committee hearings.

The first step toward the passage of such legislation was to gather evidence through the surveillance of local female residents, most of whom were working-class and poor immigrants. The effort to collect data on prostitution was not new when the Committee of Fifteen organized in 1900. In 1858, William W. Sanger, a New York physician, interviewed thousands of prostitutes who were incarcerated on Blackwell's Island to determine why women entered the sex trade.[13] Sanger published his findings in *The History of Prostitution* the following year. That the Eugenics Publishing Company reissued the book in the 1930s illustrates the popularity of the belief in a link between heredity and sexual behavior.

Others took more drastic and sensational measures. While anti-vice agents such as Steele, Wilson, and Silverman simply posed as "johns," others took the performative even further, donning elaborate disguises and venturing into bars and dance halls. Sara J. Bird, founder of the Gospel Settlement, for example, often went to the local dance halls and music halls masquerading as a prostitute to mingle and talk with the women in an attempt to convince them to leave the trade.[14] The Reverend Charles H. Parkhurst, pastor of the Madison Square Presbyterian Church in Manhattan, also donned elaborate costumes to document various illicit activities in saloons, brothels, gambling houses, and dance halls.[15] On at least one occasion, Parkhurst left his house on East 23rd Street in what is today Manhattan's Chelsea neighborhood to investigate vice activities for himself. Charles W. Gardner, a private detective and the superintendent of the Society for the Prevention of Crime (SPC), sometimes accompanied Parkhurst. Gardner recounted their adventures in *The Doctor and the Devil*. His work can be read in at least two ways: as an example of sensationalist urban narratives of the times and as a set of informal strategies for anti-vice investigations. Popular writing such as Gardner's book highlighted the so-called lights and shadows of life in the Great Metropolis and helped shaped tourist images of "forbidden" quarters throughout the city, typically working-class and poor neighborhoods. Like many of these "true to life" fictional works of the period, Gardner's book took readers along into the nightly adventures of "respectable" middle-class men. At the same time, the book introduced readers to the use of "slumming" as a legitimate form of gathering information for the sake of a moral cause.[16]

Parkhurst had laid much of the groundwork for collecting information on prostitution, especially in southern Manhattan. Born and educated in Massachusetts, Parkhurst took over the pastorate in 1880. Soon after his arrival, he expressed concerned about the proliferation of the commercialized sex trade. After discovering that the police were actually profiting from the "social evil" through payoffs from brothel operators, he initiated his own organization to investigate prostitution. In 1890, he organized the City Vigilance League (CVL), which rivaled the SPC. Parkhurst had been frustrated with the SPC, formed in 1878, for its inability to stamp out immoral activities. The SPC had collaborated with the city police in rooting out relatively minor cases of morals charges against individuals or citing saloonkeepers who refrained from paying excise taxes on alcohol.[17] From his pulpit, Parkhurst railed against police and government officials who lined their pockets from kickbacks that protected brothels from raids.

In early March 1892, shortly after Parkhurst delivered his famous sermon in which he once again publicly condemned municipal and police corruption, he donned shabby clothes and, along with Gardner and twenty-six-year-old John Langdon "Sunbeam" Erving, headed for brothels, dilapidated lodging houses, gambling establishments, saloons, and opium parlors.[18] The trio traveled as far south as Water Street, northward to the Bowery and to Mott, Catherine, and Pell streets. After dinner at a Chinese restaurant on Mott Street, the men were guided by a Chinese interpreter named Lee Bing to the popular haunts that had begun to give the neighborhood its reputation as a tourist attraction. Later that evening, they ventured southward to Cherry Street. As described previously, Cherry Street was home to working-class, poor, and immigrant populations; boardinghouses provided lodging to unmarried seamen, and laborers who co-existed with families residing in apartments along the thoroughfare. Finding a saloon that provided a range of leisure activities to the local people was not difficult. Gardner and Parkhurst entered a racially mixed saloon and dance hall, where they were immediately solicited by a young female prostitute. In their depositions to the city, Gardner and Parkhurst reported that men and women at these places were "engaged in drinking, dancing, carousing, using vile, indecent and lascivious language and otherwise disturbing the peace."[19]

The "adventures" of Parkhurst and his compatriots resulted in two well-publicized trials of women accused of operating "disorderly houses." White working-class women were central to these cases both as prostitutes and as operators of brothels. Hattie Adams and Maria Andrea had claimed that their establishments were legitimate boardinghouses in the Tenderloin district, even though the local police testified otherwise. Adams admitted that she ran a "free and easy" boardinghouse for actors but vigorously denied that it was a "disorderly house," which was a misdemeanor. Both women were found guilty within a week of their trials and sentenced to jail.[20] What is significant about these cases is that the sensationalism surrounding it rested partly on whether Parkhurst, Gardner, and Erving had crossed the line in their efforts to identify vice. Erving testified that during their visit to the Adams place, Gardner had raised his hat in the air, and the women in the house kicked at it. Afterward, the private detective played a game of leapfrog with the women as they drank beer and Erving danced with one of the women. According to "Sunbeam," he danced with the woman only because he believed he had to do it as part of the investigation. In the end, the trials proved to be too much for Erving; shortly after his testimony, he withdrew from participation in the trial and remained ensconced in his family's country house in Rye, New York, suffering from "brain fever."[21] On the day of her sentencing, Adams continued to proclaim her innocence in a public statement she submitted to the judge, citing the intrusion into her home and the subsequent accusation and conviction as "unfair."

Investigators sometimes overstepped their boundaries in ways that were more insidious. Gardner's shady interactions with the locals ultimately ended his association with Parkhurst and other moral reform leaders in the city. In 1892, Gardner was charged with, and initially convicted of, blackmailing Lily Clifton, alias Catherine Amos, for keeping a disorderly house on West 53rd Street. Although he was originally convicted and jailed in the Tombs, legal technicalities resulted in his release. Parkhurst's committee did not solicit Gardner's assistance again, especially given that the former detective was subjected to another indictment for an unrelated crime. The notoriety of the case undoubtedly also rendered him ineffective as an undercover agent.[22]

The Lexow Committee and the Mazet Committee, formed in 1894 and 1897, respectively, brought the issue of police collusion with the sex trade to the state level. The New York State Senate held numerous hearings on the issue of police corruption, interviewing prostitutes, non-prostitutes, informants, and owners of tenement buildings. In some cases, people who were often targets of reformers tried to use the committee to further their own interests. In one case, several Chinese Tong men testified before the Lexow Committee as a way to attack rival gangs by handing over the names and addresses of opponents.[23] Although these committee hearings publicly exposed the corruptive power of Tammany Hall and the persistence of the "social evil," reformers saw few concrete results.

Frustrated with the lack of permanent reform measures, a group of prominent New York businessmen took it upon themselves to collect information on prostitution by sending agents posing as customers to the tenements and apartment buildings where prostitution was known to flourish.[24] Formed in December 1900, the Committee of Fifteen operated out of an office on Park Row, conveniently located near the major New York newspapers, where it could gain access to the numerous reporters who worked the streets and knew where illegal activities were located. William H. Baldwin Jr., president of the Long Island Railroad, chaired the committee. George Wilson Morgan, a young attorney, served as secretary. Morgan had worked closely as a legal adviser with social reformers since graduating from Cornell University Law School in 1897. He participated in the East Side Committee on Public Morality, headed by Professor Felix Adler of Cornell University, and served as an assistant to District Attorney William Travers Jerome, whose public antics included storming saloons with an ax.[25]

The collusion between the police and owners of brothels, commonly referred to as "disorderly houses," was a major focus of the committee's work, as noted by the publisher William Abbott, who nominated Frank Moss to join the organization: "The Committee will be practically fighting the [Police] Department (or its leaders) and needs such a man as him."[26] In many ways, Moss was a perfect candidate to serve on the committee. Born in 1860 and having grown up in lower Manhattan, he knew the area well. He also had extensive experience in anti-vice activities, including joining Jerome on an ax-wielding rampage against local saloons. Moss also served as an associate counsel for the Lexow Committee and maintained a long association with Parkhurst. Later in his career, he served as police commissioner of New York.[27]

Although the new committee would enjoy support from many quarters, it also drew criticism from the beginning, much of it focusing on the elite composition of the organization and its focus on the poorest sections of the city. Moreover, although its members claimed not to operate as a political group, the committee clearly targeted the existing Tammany regime, arguing that city corruption contributed to illicit activities. Anonymous criticism of the committee may have been as much politically motivated as a defense of working-class neighborhoods. In one letter, "A Citizen" proclaimed that the committee had little basis for perceiving tenements as dens of vice and that its efforts eventually would backfire by ensuring a Tammany victory in the next election. The writer, who claimed to be an evangelist among the poor, also chastised Baldwin for his elitism, claiming that "the occupants of the tenement houses are no more immoral than those of Fifth Avenue."[28]

The composition of the committee did not escape notice among labor leaders, either. Although some doubted the effectiveness of anti-vice crusades in general, others supported the idea. A number of labor spokesmen criticized the upper-class composition of the Committee of Fifteen, not because they opposed targeting poor and working-class neighborhoods, but because they wanted to play a formal role on the committee. At a meeting of the Central Federated Union (CFU), one speaker argued for increasing the breadth of representation on the committee and for the organization to investigate not only the residents of tenements but also the owners of buildings in which vice activities took place. At the same meeting, the chairman of the CFU warned that Parkhurst's earlier crusades had done nothing but move vice activities to other locations: "Brooklyn was a moral city . . . but the Parkhurst raids drove many vicious people across the river and multiplied disorderly houses in the City of Churches [Brooklyn]."[29]

As historians have pointed out, anti-vice organizations imposed middle-class values on poor and immigrant people. But to a certain degree, a social and economic exchange also took place between the Committee of Fifteen and local residents. People who lived in the neighborhoods under surveillance sometimes called on the organization for employment or for help in searching for missing daughters.

The Committee of Fifteen served as a site for coalition building among various social reformers, some of whom simply wanted to destroy Tammany Hall and others who were interested in better law enforcement; the elimination or, at least, control of the sex trade; and saving "fallen" women from lives of disease and immorality.[30] Unlike the settlement houses, discussed in the next chapter, the Committee of Fifteen was a mobile force that sent male agents into certain neighborhoods to "visit" alleged prostitutes, interview them, and submit detailed reports to the committee. The committee did little if anything to provide guidelines for investigators to follow or to supervise their activities; it was assumed that they would not engage in sex with the alleged prostitutes, although no evidence suggests whether or not they did. In the relatively short time between the dissolution of the committee in 1901 and the formation of its successor, the Committee of Fourteen, four years later, the composition of the organization changed, as did its methods of collecting evidence.

The Committee of Fifteen enjoyed the support of a diverse group of men and women who worked or volunteered in the organization's investigations. Buoyed by the financial backing of influential men on the committee, who were bankers, industrialists, and financiers, as well as donors from throughout the city, the committee was able to hire several agents to conduct investigations. In addition to conducting investigations, working-class and middle-class men and women from diverse ethnic backgrounds performed many of the daily tasks of the committee, including office work, donating small sums of money, or providing information on the location of prostitutes, gambling, and opium parlors.

Men from all walks of life regularly wrote to the committee in search of employment or to volunteer their time. Most emphasized their high moral standards. One man who lived several blocks north of the Lower East Side inquired after a position with the committee "because I don't or never did I drink a drop of liquor in my life . . . also I don't smoke or chew." C. Botkin, a physician at the New York Magnetic Sanitarium and School of Psychology, volunteered to help the committee, even though he was a newcomer to New York. According to Botkin, his devotion to law and order, his Christianity, his anonymity, and his investigative experience made him uniquely qualified to assist the committee in its investigations. "While I am a stranger to this City, having lived here less than one year," he wrote, "now this is my home and as a citizen, loving law and order, and from a Christian position, I am willing to do my part, in enforcing the laws of good government. Having spent some little experience in detective work, and a stranger in the city, if I can help your noble work, command me."[31] Ecumenical ties were also evident in the composition and work of the Committee of Fifteen. In one letter to Morgan, Reverend Robert Paddock introduced the Reverend H. P. Faust, a former rabbi and now an attorney who had visited poor families in the tenements. According to Paddock, Faust had prosecuted "some nice cases" in his career and thus was a valuable ally and informant.[32]

The committee's alliances extended to several other citywide organizations dedicated to the elimination of prostitution and the municipal corruption that maintained the "social evil." One such ally was the American Purity Alliance (APA). In January 1901, O. Edward Janney, president of the APA, wrote to Baldwin from Baltimore to express his hearty support for the committee's work, decrying those who had supported regulation rather than the outright elimination of the sex trade. Janney also hoped the committee would come out in support of the APA: "We feel strong assurance in the character of those who constitute your Committee, that we have your sympathy in the object of this letter, and may count on its serious and conscientious consideration." Janney then got to the heart of the matter: "In the effort to suppress social vice there is constant danger of the advocacy of methods which aim at the regulation of vice, in the hope of bettering civic conditions. Against such methods the American Purity Alliance has firmly maintained an opposition for twenty-five years."[33]

The Salvation Army also supported the committee's work. The evangelical character of the organization, with its goal of redemption and reform, comes through clearly, as does the notion that women and girls were seduced into "dens of infamy": "We are watching this movement with great interest and are ready to do all on our part to receive, as far as our capacity will permit, the unfortunate victims that are desirous of escaping from the condition that they are in, and to lead lives of reformation . . . and forsaking the life of shame."[34]

A number of organizations led by women offered their help. In January 1901, the Quaker suffragist Anna W. Jackson, representing the Society for Political Study composed of New York Quakers, requested "any reliable information" on the work of the committee "to purify our city" and extended any help her club could offer. Jackson resided with her husband, William, at the Penington Friends House on East 15th Street.[35] In some cases, reformers helped create networks between the committee and other groups who were interested in reform.

There were limits, however, to cooperative relations. Although the committee welcomed tips on potential locations for investigation, its members were hesitant to share the information with activists outside the organization. When Josephine Shaw Lowell, a prominent philanthropist and reformer, requested information on prostitution from the committee, Morgan responded cordially that he thought it was "inadvisable" to release information that had not already been made public.[36]

Not all local residents were happy about the presence of investigators in their neighborhoods. Those who operated poolrooms and saloons, especially those who regularly paid off the police to run their businesses, not surprisingly were wary of the presence of reformers. Agents often ran the risk of sustaining bodily harm from proprietors, as was the case when one poolroom owner beat up an agent who had entered his establishment to collect evidence.[37]

Despite the risks, neighborhood residents did much of the committee's work by conducting regular surveillance of their neighbors. Some informants were business owners themselves and saw the sex trade as a danger both to their families and to "legitimate" businesses in the area. Such relations reveal the economic need of committee agents and informers, who received payment for their work, and the support among local residents for certain aspects of moral reform. The Committee of Fifteen received numerous letters, signed and unsigned, from people in the neighborhood requesting assistance in eliminating the sex trade from their buildings and streets. Just one month after the committee officially organized, it had received twenty-one written and verbal complaints about prostitution and complaints about forty-seven different gambling establishments and poolrooms.[38] One group of property owners that called itself the "Citizens of Mott Street" looked to the committee, not the police, to help quell the "nuisance" on their block. In a letter to the committee, the group stated that it consisted of "fathers of children from ten to twenty years of age all living in the street," whose daughters and wives were continually insulted day and night by visitors of the house [at] 116 Mott St. conducted by J. Fegelle, a saloon keeper who allegedly operated a brothel in the rooms above the bar.[39]

One unnamed resident of Mott Street sent a letter of endorsement based on his own status as a U.S. citizen and as a father of four daughters. The man supported the "purification and destruction of all Houses of shameful business" in the city. In particular, he wanted the sex trade eradicated from his neighborhood and accused "an Italian woman," Teresa Gitare, as the keeper of three girls "of very bad reputation" at 133 Mott Street, an apartment building situated in a predominantly Italian immigrant neighborhood near Hester Street. According to the unnamed writer, Gitare hid the girls in the basement whenever she knew that detectives were going to visit the house.[40] The writer also pointed the committee to apartments at 116 and 118 Mott Street. It is not clear whether the committee followed up on the first address or whether Gitare really was involved in the sex trade, but agents had reported the latter two addresses as houses of prostitution. Number 116 was a regular site of complaint and investigation.

Seemingly innocent venues also came to the committee's attention. On at least one occasion, the committee was called on to investigate candy shops as places where schoolchildren gambled. A few weeks after the committee was formed, it received a letter from Carlotta Russell Lowell of the Public Education Association regarding the problem of gambling among children at candy shops near the schools and the lack of intervention by the police to attend to the issue. At its meeting in December, the association resolved that "the attention of the Committee of Fifteen be called to this instance of police neglect & that the Committee be requested to include these shops in the scope of its investigations."[41]

Committee members also passed on information they had gathered on their own. Particularly valuable was a list that Moss had provided on gambling parlors and poolrooms from a previous investigation. In a memo in which he notified William Baldwin of Moss's contribution, Morgan included his own observations of vice around the city: "I might add that from my own investigation, gathered accidentally from the fact that my home is now in Capt. Diamond's precinct, I might say that soliciting has rather increased than diminished in this precinct. It would be a comparatively easy matter to locate the house occupied by those women." Morgan added that Officer Herlihy's twelfth precinct was "infested" by prostitutes.[42]

Under the auspices of the committee, investigators produced dozens of lists of addresses and detailed descriptions of their ventures into known sites of prostitution. Steele's report typified the emphasis on class and ethnicity. According to Steele, the group entered the building at 100 Mott Street at 10:50 P.M. and left at 11:15 the same night. There they met "Rosa," an Italian woman, and two young boys whom she claimed were her sons:

We were solicited on Mott Street near the house by two women who took us up to said house in the rear side of the said house, up one flight of stairs to a room in the rear of the north side of the house. In this room, in the presence of A. E. Wilson and I,

Silverman paid one of these women, calling herself Rosa, fifty cents and went with her to a bed room in front of the rear room. In the bed was a young boy about eight years old and in the room in front was another boy sleeping on a sofa, about eleven years of age. This woman, Rosa, informed me that they were her children and that her husband was away in the country and did not support her.

The investigators described Rosa's physical features in detail: "She was about 38 years of age, five feet six inches high and weighs about 140 pounds: dark complexion: Italian." Steele went on to report that Rosa then "threw herself on the bed beside the young boy and exposed her person to me for the purpose of prostitution." Horatio S. Conklin, Jake Kreiswirth, and Max Moskowitz apparently visited the same address shortly after Steele, Wilson, and Silverman had left. Conklin reported that the prostitute was "an Italian woman in a family way." After the woman "offered herself" to Conklin, he paid her seventy-five cents and left the apartment fifteen minutes later.[43]

All of the men who posed as potential customers for the committee were of European ancestry, immigrant and non-immigrant, who came from diverse class and ethnic backgrounds. In addition to the agents mentioned above, others included Sylvester Carfolite, twenty-one, an Italian immigrant; Henry Masterson Leverich, a forty-seven-year-old attorney from Brooklyn; and Max Moskowitz, a thirty-three-year-old hotelkeeper from Ludlow Street, where he lived with his wife and children.[44] Carfolite's world revolved around the very establishments that were coming under increased scrutiny by the Committee of Fifteen and, later, the Committee of Fourteen: restaurants, liquor, and gambling. His father, Genero, was a liquor dealer when Carfolite began working for the committee. Carfolite himself was no stranger to trouble. In 1901, he was arrested for operating a dishonest roulette wheel for children. Later in his life, he seemed to "go straight." Between 1910 and 1930, he managed a restaurant and worked for the city's Department of Licensing.[45] Leverich came from at least two generations of New Yorkers and therefore was familiar with the local neighborhoods.

Like other investigators, these men walked a fine line between morality and temptation. Isaac Silverman was aware of this when he sent his report to the committee in July 1901, noting that he did not engage in sex when he investigated the flats at 100 Mott Street: "I noticed on the first floor front left hand side that women were in the rooms; one of the women asked me to have sexual intercourse, which I refused." In a similar report, Moskowitz noted that after he had interviewed the prostitute, he told "my girl" that she could keep the 50 cents for luck, "as I wanted to get out as quickly as I could."[46]

In its fight against prostitution and other vices in public sites of leisure within the Chinatown and Bowery neighborhoods, the Committee of Fifteen frequently hired Chinese men as informants whose assistance facilitated outsiders' ability to enter "forbidden" and unfamiliar urban spaces. Wong Aloy, for example, was a regular informant for the police and the committee. In a lengthy report, Arthur Wilson described in detail how Wong had led him through Callahan's Saloon at 12 Chatham Square, where prostitution and illegal gambling flourished. According to Wilson, "Everything in Chinatown is wide open." Wong Aloy allegedly promised to secure additional evidence about gambling and prostitution for the committee and would even bring "5 or 8 of the best entrusted large and able bodied Chinamen" to assist in a raid. The police, however, were apparently also part of the vice problem. Annie Gilroy, who solicited male customers at the bar, told the investigators that the police received regular payoffs of twelve to twenty dollars from each prostitute to avoid arrest. She also informed Wilson that if he and his friends wanted sex, they could call on her to arrange meetings with both Chinese and non-Chinese women at her building at 11 Mott Street.[47]

Wong communicated regularly with the committee and seemed to enjoy a cordial social relationship with committee agents. He once invited Wilson and Morgan to the Chinese Theater at 23 Chatham Square, ostensibly to "return some your gentlemen's kindness to me while I am in New York." Although it is not clear how exactly the committee men helped Wong, their meeting provided an opportunity to both partake of an evening's entertainment and share information on vice activities in the area.[48] Since the late nineteenth century, the Chinese Theater had served as a venue for theatrical performances before a predominantly Chinese male audience. The police frequently raided the theater for infractions that ranged from illegal gambling to allowing performances on Sunday.[49]

Quan Yick Nam was also a regular informant to the committee, as well as an employee of the New York City police. Quan provided long, detailed lists of opium dens hidden in Chinese shops throughout the city, including nearly all of the addresses between 7 and 32 Mott Street and between 12 and 34 Pell Street, where various types of gambling took place. Most of these buildings were boardinghouses that housed Chinese men and thus were very visible to both informants and investigators. Number 20 Pell Street was the supposed headquarters of the Chinese lottery. At some of these addresses, one could also solicit prostitutes.[50] In addition to assistance from men like Quan Yick Nam and Wong Aloy, whose motive, according to Wilson, was to "destroy the gambling houses and stop [their] countrymen from being robbed by Chinese expert gamblers," the committee received tips from other organizations. Although it is unclear whether either Wong or Quan was motivated by Tong affiliations, their sustained work with the anti-vice organizations and with the municipal police illustrates the networks these organizations had built within ethnic communities for the sake of urban reform. The Young Men's Chinese Christian Association (YMCCA) sent a list of illegal gambling venues in Chinatown and the names of their proprietors, as well as the size of the operations. One letter identified Tom Lee, the "ex-Mayor of Chinatown," as one of the more important figures in the neighborhood to receive ten dollars a week from each table. Chinese benevolent societies were also recipients of payments, such as the Chinese Yue Mason Society, which received an extra dollar per table at the Pell Street location. The members of the YMCCA noted that the association would "cheerfully" provide further information to the committee on gambling among the Chinese.[51]

Lillian Wald, head of the Nurses' Settlement on Henry Street, notified Morgan about a group of men who could help root out vice activities in local poolrooms and saloons. According to Wald, a number of these men had been "victims" of these establishments but were unsavory characters themselves. The kind of victimization the men suffered, besides being swindled at pool games, is unclear from Wald's note. She recommended that the committee use a go-between to gather information:

Some of the men belonging to the club in connection with the church could undoubtedly give information regarding pool rooms and saloons that might be valuable to the Committee. The general membership is that of the victims of these places and therefore it would appear safer to have the "co-operation" through Mr. Jeliffe presumably who could "solicit" the individuals whose testimony could be relied upon and whose co-operation would not reflect upon the serious character of the work. Summed up—some of the men could be made probably valuable reporters of conditions. The Club as a whole I would consider unsafe—Mr. Jeliffe has discretion.[52]

As part of its work, the Committee of Fifteen often assisted families whose children had run away or had been abducted into the sex trade and, hence, allied itself to the broader movement to end "white slavery." The anxiety over the fate of young daughters was part of a larger concern about what many saw as the negative result of the new woman phenomenon as it was enacted by young, unmarried women and girls. Such concern did not rest on the shoulders of parents alone. In addition to church-sponsored rescue missions, the state enacted measures to regulate the physical mobility of female youth. "Delinquent" daughters could find themselves in the new juvenile court system, designed to deal with wayward urban children and teenagers.[53]

Since the early nineteenth century, the term "white slavery" had been used in several different social and political contexts at particular moments in history, from consumerism and working-class labor to prostitution during the post–Civil War period. The use of the term "white" was never coincidental or accidental. In all of these contexts, whiteness took on a clear racial and class dimension. After the end of slavery, the term was used to distinguish between the legal enslavement of blacks in the United States and the involuntary entrance of young women into prostitution during the late nineteenth century and the early twentieth century, regardless of race. In addition to the historical juxtaposition to black slavery, the white slave narratives revealed complicated racial dynamics by the early twentieth century, which increased the vigilance of the police and moral reformers to shore up the boundaries around the geographic and cultural zones that separated the races.[54]

Writers and political cartoonists expressed the fear that young women would find themselves in the hands of non-white men. The non-white men in question were usually Chinese. Images of young white women being seduced or kidnapped by Chinese men appeared frequently in popular magazines. In the Chinatown narratives, white slavery was a common theme, prompting writers such as William Norr to wonder why "comely" white women would cast their lot with the "repulsive Chinese." Regardless of whether they came from middle, working-class, or poor families, and regardless of the fact that they had been forced into prostitution, the social respectability of these young women plummeted once they entered the sex trade. Their social standing was further tainted if they also had entered into sexual relationships with non-white men. Thus, their moral downfall resulted as much from crossing the color line as from their entrance into the world of prostitution, drugs, and violence. Following the lead of racy printed material such as the *Police Gazette*, white slavery as a genre made its way to the stage and screen. In addition to a number of Broadway performances, the emerging film industry began capitalizing on the fear that young, innocent white women would be kidnapped or lured into the sex trade. This resulted in such popular movies as *Traffic in Souls* (1913) and *Little Lost Sister* (1917).[55] The theater and the movie houses provided vicarious interzones for audiences, for these performances contributed to the popular consumption of negative narratives of the city and its snares, which had existed since the early nineteenth century.

In southern Manhattan, incidents of "white slavery" typically involved young women from European immigrant families. In one case, a woman visited the committee's office requesting assistance in her search for her daughter, who had run away from their Lower East Side tenement apartment on Hester Street. Committee agents located her in a boardinghouse. When she was interrogated in Morgan's office, with her mother present, the girl (whose name was never identified) denied being a prostitute and claimed she had run away from home because she could not stand the filth of their tenement any longer. The committee agreed with the girl's account after conducting an investigation of her former home. Morgan concluded that the source of the conflict between the young woman and her family was both generational and an issue of acculturation:

> It is the old story over and over again, of the foreign parents who do not at all appreciate the average American standards of living,

Wah Wing Sang Funeral Corporation, Mulberry Street, New York.
(Courtesy of A. Church.)

Margaret Hart Wong, New York, 1921.
(From the Chinese Exclusion Act Case Files. Courtesy of the National Archives and Records Center, Library of Congress.)

Wong Jung Que, New York, 1921.
(From the Chinese Exclusion Act Case Files. Courtesy of the National Archives and Records Center, Library of Congress.)

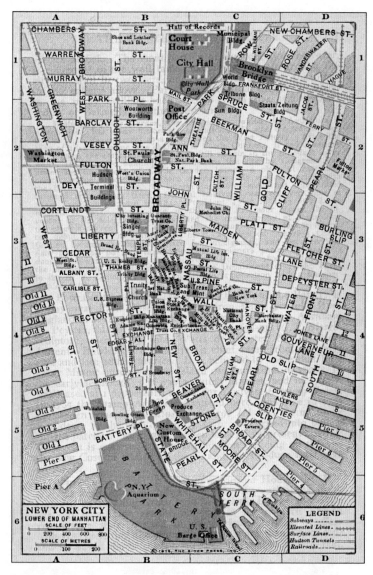

"New York City, Lower End of Manhattan," 1916. *(From Rider's New York City. Courtesy of Henry Holt and Company.)*

Christodora House. *(Courtesy of Roberta Gold.)*

Christodora House, front entrance. *(Courtesy of Roberta Gold.)*

Marriage of James Wong to childhood Chinatown neighbor
Barbara K. Moy, 1955. *(From the author's private collection.)*

but whose children have become thoroughly Americanized and are thus out of touch with their home surroundings. I do not blame the girl for not desiring to return to those conditions, especially in view of the fact that she is an expert demonstrator and can command a salary of about fifteen dollars per week.[56]

Morgan's recommendation was to remand the young woman to the Clara de Hirsch Home for Working Girls, a settlement house established in 1897 by prominent German Jewish women in New York City. Both Morgan and Edwin R. A. Seligman pleaded the woman's case to Rose Sommerfeld, the head worker at Clara de Hirsch. Seligman described the case as "peculiarly interesting" and echoed Morgan's assessment of the young woman as unusually bright: "The girl is represented to me as an exceedingly able, even brilliant, young woman with a seeming desire to lead a decent life in the future."[57]

Unfortunately, prevailing gender expectations led Sommerfeld to reject the young girl. According to Sommerfeld, her story had been leaked by a detective who had been looking for her to other female workers at Erlich's department store, where she had applied for work. The narrative that the detective passed on was that she had left home and taken up with a man, posing as his wife. It did not matter whether the story was accurate. It was the woman's reputation, now publicly sullied, and that of the Clara de Hirsch Home that was at stake. This indiscretion, wrote Summerfeld, would undoubtedly prevent the young woman from finding legitimate employment in the city and "has made it impossible for me to keep her here. . . . You can imagine the effect it would have on this Home if it were once noised around that we had that girl in the house. We would never again be able to get a respectable girl to come either as boarder or trainee." As an alternative, Sommerfeld reported, Lillian Wald had agreed to take the young woman to "The Rest" in South Nyack, New York, "where she will be well taken care of."[58]

In this case, the young woman had two counts against her. In Morgan's view, although he described her as a "bright girl," her poverty and immigrant parentage served as the primary explanation for her wayward actions. As a second-generation, "Americanized" young woman who strove for a clean life, she ended up an "unclean" woman by running away from home allegedly to live with a man. To Morgan, the young woman was simply trying to escape filth and poverty but had found few healthy alternatives. Such conclusions were not unusual among middle-class reformers, who often viewed housing conditions as the fault of ignorant immigrant parents as much as they also blamed unscrupulous landlords. At the same time, as Sommerfeld suggested, the young woman now had a tainted reputation, brought on by an indiscreet detective who had made her story public. Otherwise, as the head worker noted, "perhaps in this instance we might have made an effort and kept her."

Although in this instance Sommerfeld rejected the committee's recommendation, the Clara de Hirsch Home maintained regular contact with the committee and often did accept the "East Side girls" whom it sought to rescue from the sex trade. A month after the unsuccessful placement of the young girl, the home accepted one of these young women.

The Committee of Fifteen essentially ended its work with the untimely death of Baldwin and the publication of *The Social Evil* in 1902. Within a few years, the Committee of Fourteen, another citywide anti-vice organization, was established. Several members of the earlier committee worked with the newly organized committee when it formed in 1905, lending their experience, political and business connections, and data to the new organization. Historians have done much to underscore the new committee's importance as part of the social purity movement and the effort to bring about housing and tenement reform and addressing more broadly the application of criminal laws. They have devoted less attention, however, to how changes in academic research—in particular, the rise of the social sciences—shaped the way it gathered its data. The research process highlights another important dimension of cross-cultural interaction that was more systematic and "scientific" and "objective" than the Committee of Fifteen's approach to the anti-prostitution campaign and literally covered a lot more ground in its attempt to root out the sources of prostitution. In this process, new women—college-educated female social reformers—applied their training in the new social sciences to the urban "field."

While the Committee of Fifteen's agents hired reform-minded activists and men from the neighborhoods to "visit" prostitutes, saloons, and gambling houses and provide detailed reports, the Committee of Fourteen sought more sophisticated and systematic methods of gathering information. The new organization expanded its cadre of investigators by hiring college graduates who were trained in the new social-science methods of data gathering. They also cast their net wider to include hotels and restaurants that were in violation of the Raines hotel law. At the same time, however, the committee retained the undercover practices adopted by earlier reformers, blurring the lines between investigator and subject. Clothed in the garb of their subjects, they practiced a kind of "passing" and "slumming" through performance and imitation of the people from whom they gathered information.[59] One writer saw little difference between the new social-science approach and the older practices of anti-vice surveillance: "They used to call themselves 'slummers,' but now they're all sociologists and carry notebooks, and are more of a nuisance than ever. There'd be Yale sociologists on Mondays and Vassar sociologists on Tuesdays, Columbia sociologists on Wednesdays and Princeton sociologists on Thursdays."[60]

The Committee of Fourteen was the longest-running anti-vice organization in the city. During its twenty-seven-year lifespan, it helped usher in significant federal and state legislation, such as section 79 of the Page Act, which was designed to eliminate "diseased" prostitutes by requiring them to undergo medical examinations. Its members were also instrumental in pushing for enforcing and expanding the scope of state and municipal policies, such as the Raines hotel law, and the elimination of the red-light districts in New York City.[61] Although they fell short of passing an amendment to the state vagrancy laws, also known as the "customer" law, the leaders of the city-based society gained national and local attention in their attempt to regulate the sexual behavior of both men and women. In so doing, they developed an unlikely alliance with feminists in the National Women's Party.

In its initial gathering of documentation on the sex trade, the Committee of Fourteen, not surprisingly, used the Committee of Fifteen's report as a starting point. However, the new committee quickly deviated from its predecessor in a number of important respects. First, the new committee shifted its focus away from the semi-private spaces of the tenements and apartments as the root of prostitution and "white slavery." Instead, it turned to the public establishments, primarily the Raines Law hotels, as well as saloons, poolrooms, and dance halls. Second, its composition was more diverse, especially in terms of religion and professional experience, although it remained all white. George Haven Putnam was the only member who had served on the Committee of Fifteen. The board of the Committee of Fourteen included two women—William Baldwin's widow, Ruth Baldwin, and Mary Simkhovitch, director of the Greenwich Settlement House—a Catholic priest, a rabbi, and a Presbyterian minister.[62] The founding members of the committee also included college-educated men and women with experience in social work and social-science methods, such as Simkhovitch and Lawrence Veiller, whose main focus was tenement reform. In 1911, he would serve as the director of the National Housing Commission.[63]

When the committee was formally incorporated in 1907, it added several more prominent men, including Police Commissioner William McAdoo, as well as those well versed in business and industry, such as Isaac Seligman, a banker whose older brother Edwin had been a member of the Committee of Fifteen; William Jay Schieffelin, heir to the Schieffelin wholesale drug company;[64] and Francis Louis Slade, a lumber merchant and a major financier of the Christodora settlement house. Most of the committee members were not strangers to one another. They traveled in the same social, intellectual, and business circles. Some members had worked on philanthropic and social reform projects together. For example, Schieffelin and William Baldwin had been longtime supporters of Booker T. Washington and served as trustees of the Tuskegee Institute. Simkhovitch and Veiller were active participants in housing reform and knew the Seligman brothers from their participation in discussions in the Simkhovitches' home.[65]

In contrast to the earlier committee, the Committee of Fourteen was shaped by the expertise of professionals—social workers and scholars who would gather evidence in the most systematic way possible, using the new social-science methods of data gathering. The committee immediately established a research subcommittee composed of Baldwin, Simkhovitch, and Francis M. Burdick, a law professor. Frances Kellor, well known for her studies on incarcerated women and unemployment, was recruited as secretary. The women who participated on the subcommittee offered a range of expertise and experiences working across lines of class and race.

Ruth Baldwin was not simply a widow who carried on the work of her late husband. She was an activist in her own right; she had been one of a handful of white reformers who had devoted much of their work to improving the social and economic conditions of blacks, particularly black women workers. Ruth Standish Bowles Baldwin had grown up in a family that was deeply involved in national politics. Her father, Samuel Bowles, was a newspaper editor and the proprietor of the *Springfield Republican*.[66] Ruth enjoyed a comfortable middle-class lifestyle. She graduated from Smith College in 1887 and later served on its Board of Trustees. Undoubtedly, her years as a student at Smith introduced her to the opportunities available to the new women of the middle classes, many of whom entered various women's professions, such as social work, nursing, and teaching. Like many of the elite women's colleges, Smith nurtured and encouraged its students who were beginning to develop a passion for social reform. According to its founder, Sophia Smith, the "Christian education of women" would result in their increased status in society, and "their weight of influence in reforming the evils of society would be greatly increased as teachers, as writers, as mothers, as members of society, their power for good will be incalculably enlarged."[67]

Mary Simkhovich and Frances Kellor emerged from the ranks of college graduates who had received training in the new social sciences. Sinkhovich, who was born Mary Melinda Kingsbury in 1867 into a middle-class Congregationalist family in New England, was introduced to sociology and settlement house work during her student years at Boston University, when she visited Denison House. On the visit, she and her classmates met Emily Greene Balch, well-known peace advocate and sociology professor at Wellesley College.[68] She pursued graduate studies at Radcliffe and in 1898 won a scholarship to study in Berlin. In 1902, with the support of her husband, Vladimir, and other settlement colleagues, she founded Greenwich House on Barrow Street on the Lower West Side of Manhattan (known now as Greenwich Village).[69] Simkhovitch served as director of Greenwich House until her retirement in 1946.

Frances Alice Kellor had a decidedly different background from that of Simkhovitch and Baldwin. She was born in 1873, and her father abandoned the family when she was an infant. Her mother and elder sister moved from their home in Columbus, Ohio, to a small town in Michigan, where her mother worked as a laundress. At an early age, Kellor displayed a penchant for defying prescribed gender roles; she participated actively in sports and could best any boy in her class. Living on the edge of poverty, she was unlikely to obtain an education beyond the primary grades, even though she had developed a passion for books. A chance meeting with the wealthy Eddy sisters, however, changed the course of her life: They nurtured her love of books and eventually sponsored her enrollment at Cornell University's women's coordinate, Sage College, in 1895.[70] Kellor's initial interest was to assist Southern black women who had migrated North in search of employment but who were often met by unscrupulous employment agents and procurers of prostitution.

While prominent white social scientists and reformers constituted the Committee of Fourteen, African American reformers established an auxiliary organization, illustrating the segregationist practices of urban social reform during this period. Black activist women throughout the country, many of whom were active in the black women's club movement, focused on education, the protection of black workers, and racial discrimination in housing, schools, and settlement organizations such as the Young Women's Christian Association (YWCA). A number of black female activists also would have brought expertise to the committee had they been included in the founding of the Committee of Fourteen. For example, Victoria Earle Matthews was a former slave who became a journalist. She was an active participant in the National Association of Colored Women. In 1897, she opened a settlement house for black women, the White Rose Home, on East 97th Street in Manhattan.[71] Some white and black activist women attempted to collaborate on common social problems. While many white women dealt more extensively with immigrant populations, others, such as Kellor and Baldwin, considered themselves allies to black women's causes.

This new generation of activist reformers were politically minded and mobilized for changes in public policy. Although both sexes participated in Progressive-era reform, the movement held a special significance for young college-educated women, who represented the coming of age of the new woman. As part of the cohort of the first female college graduates, they differed from those who had participated in moral reform earlier in the century. Armed with the theory and methods of the new social sciences, they combined advancements in the education of women with older images of white, Protestant, middle-class women as inherently more moral than men or working-class and poor women. Through the concept of "enlarged housekeeping," female reformers argued, they could clean up the cities, literally and figuratively.

Within the movement, male and female reformers carved out distinct types of roles. Female reformers, many of whom were now educated professional women, worked in missions and settlement houses and visited prostitutes and the poor. Under the auspices of the more social-science-oriented Committee of Fourteen, college-educated female researchers found entry into the saloons, pool halls, and hotels that offered prostitution and gambling. While many reform-minded men found a niche in the movement by posing as "slummers" and "johns," female investigators by the 1910s regularly posed as prostitutes to gather data on the numbers of men who solicited them.

In 1910, the Research Committee of the Committee of Fourteen published its findings in *The Social Evil in New York City: A Study of Law Enforcement*. Although bearing the same root title as its predecessor's report in 1902, the new report exemplified the application of the new social-science methods that had been taught at the University of Chicago and Columbia University. Its data-gathering methods were far more sophisticated, although not necessarily unbiased, than those employed by the Committee of Fifteen. Trained in the relatively new methodology, which championed objectivity and systematic forms of gathering data, the subcommittee members—Kellor, Simkhovitch, and Burdick—had interviewed hundreds of prostitutes and saloonkeepers. In contrast to the Committee of Fifteen's report, Kellor's committee was much broader and included lengthy discussions of industrial conditions, the rape and abduction of impoverished children, and the state of poor immigrant families in an effort to demonstrate the links among poverty, violence, low industrial wages, and deplorable housing conditions that, they argued, led many women and girls into the sex trade. Throughout the document, the moral judgments of the research committee were clear, frequently referring to prostitutes and dance-hall "spielers" (dancers) as "immoral."

The nature of the research project obviously required cross-cultural interactions, as subcommittee members approached and talked to poor immigrant women and their families. The researchers were not the first educated female social scientists to interview this population. For example, during the late 1890s, the historian Lucy Maynard Salmon's national survey of female domestic servants became a standard work on the experiences of domestic servants in the United States.[72]

Kellor knew firsthand how difficult this kind of social-science work could be and that informants were sometimes suspicious and hostile toward the privileged white women who knocked on their doors seeking information. Several years earlier, Kellor had interviewed female prisoners as part of her study of criminality in eight different prisons in the South. She also administered physical and psychological tests to a predominantly black female prison population. Kellor based her recommendations for developing preventative crime measures on a critique of institutional racism that meted out longer sentences for black offenders and on emerging environmental arguments for improving the social and economic conditions of the poor in general and of poor blacks in particular. Like other Progressive reformers of her generation, however, Kellor also embraced assumptions about the inferiority of blacks, which, she argued, was not inherent but could be remedied through middle-class standards of education, parenting, and moral behavior.[73] Not surprisingly, Kellor brought to the Committee of Fourteen her expertise in sociological methods of data gathering, support for social reform, and dominant cultural conceptions of morality.

Initially, Kellor and her fellow researchers followed earlier reform practices. Like the male agents of the previous committee, the subcommittee women took to the streets to gather their data. Unlike the Committee of Fifteen, the subcommittee did not confine its investigation to obvious sites of vice—tenements, gambling joints, and saloons, but fanned out to include places where the "immoral women" might be less visible to the public, such as massage parlors, cafes and lunchrooms, cigar and candy stores, and ice cream parlors.[74] In the course of their investigation, they interviewed neighborhood residents, families, and shopkeepers. In its investigation of hotels, the research committee established a standard by which it would judge a hotel worth further study, based on the operation of the registration desk and on the behavior of its patrons:

> The Committee of Fourteen has a secretary and assistants constantly in the field investigating and reporting on prevailing con-

ditions. The following standard is observed as a basis for making complaints. First, the admission of couples without baggage to hotels at late hours . . . and where there is legal evidence that the same woman has been admitted twice in one day as the wife of different men, or that the same room has been rented twice in twenty-four hours.[75]

Members of the research committee also visited dance halls, where, they contended, procurers lured young women into the sex trade. The committee visited seventy-three dance halls in Manhattan and Brooklyn and recorded the comings and goings of young men and women. The investigator briefly interviewed 218 young women, who reported a variety of occupations, including stenographers, clerks, and factory workers. According to the report, the male "spielers," or dancers, usually belonged to gangs or were an "immoral class of young men," and the female spielers were "nearly all immoral."

By the 1910s, female investigators posing as prostitutes had become an integral part of anti-vice investigations. Female agents regularly infiltrated the world of the streetwalkers to gather data on the number of men who solicited them. Female investigators disguised themselves as prostitutes. Unlike the missionary reformer Sara J. Bird, the agents focused on customers as well as the prostitutes. During their visits to dance halls, they documented the number of men who offered to pay for sex.[76] In sum, both male and female investigators working undercover to expose and document prostitution wove in and out of the streets, public leisure spaces, and tenement flats for the sake of social and moral reform. But these men and women were more than observers—in some cases, they were, perhaps, voyeurs. Through their regular presence, albeit "in drag," they added yet another layer to cross-cultural relations, furtively entering the zones already carved out by an ethnically diverse population of working-class locals and middle-class "slummers." The extent to which they actually forged meaningful relationships with their subjects through this kind of subterfuge, however, will likely never be known.

Key to the work of the anti-vice committees was the participation of local residents as agents and as informers. Having Chinese men such as Bing and Wong Aloy use their bilingual skills to assist the police and anti-vice agents in raids on saloons and gambling joints was not an uncommon way to attack rival gangs. It is also not surprising that the committee hired men from these neighborhoods to work as investigators—they were likely to know which buildings housed women plying their trade.

The work of anti-vice reformers met with some skepticism from outside observers who claimed that the reformers overstated the success of their endeavors. For example, in a biting critique of the Chicago anti-vice commission's report on the white slave traffic in 1913, the journalist Walter Lippmann wrote, "Sensational disclosures will often make the public flare up spasmodically. . . . [T]he 'crusade' is looked upon as a melodrama of real life—interesting, but easily forgotten."[77] To be sure, the public cry by civic-minded businessmen and reformers against prostitution, the "white slavery" issue, gambling, and opium use in the cities did gain the public's attention, mainly through the city newspapers, as well as through speeches and sermons given by well-respected and prominent clerics such as Parkhurst.

Under the auspices of zealous anti-vice reformers and the private organizations they established—the Committee of Fifteen, Committee of Fourteen, and Parkhurst's City Vigilance League—prominent and ordinary men and women made a daily practice of anti-vice "slumming" for the moral redemption of the city. In poor and immigrant neighborhoods, residents may never have directly encountered the committee members themselves, but the power of private anti-vice organizations was ever present through the surveillance activities of the agents of the committees and those who staffed day-to-day operations.

Cross-cultural interactions were integral to the work of these organizations. At the same time, local residents did not simply ignore anti-vice activities in their midst. While subjected to surveillance by agents and researchers, people in the area also used the services of the committees when they needed to, whether it was to secure a job with the organizations or to seek assistance in locating their daughters, whom, they often feared, had fallen into the "wrong" element or had been seduced into the sex trade by unscrupulous men. Urban reform in working-class, immigrant neighborhoods thus provided the political and social contexts within which interactions across differences took place.

As the next chapter shows, the urban missionary and settlement house movements provided yet another context for the development of cross-ethnic/racial relations. Moral and religious values often shaped relations between reformers and immigrant and working-class men, women, and children. The activities of clergy and lay reformers, through their work in religious organizations and settlement houses, illustrate the degree to which religious politics shaped perceptions and daily life among reformers and local residents.

5

On (Un)Common Ground

*Religious Politics in Settlements
and Missions*

In a letter to Harry Hopkins shortly before their marriage, Ethel Gross warned him not to be surprised if she decided to "break windows at Christodora House some day."[1] Although Gross's playful threat most likely referred to their desire to break away from the settlement and move on with their life as a couple, her comment also illuminates the multifaceted sides of gender, race, class, and ethnic relations in the urban settlement house and missionary movements, around which religious identity and practices often played a controversial and integral part. As physical and cultural sites of assimilationist ideals, evangelical social settlement houses such as Christodora and the numerous church-sponsored Protestant missions often evoked mixed reactions from neighborhood residents and religious leaders alike.

In many ways, these institutions were like houses of glass, their windows functioning simultaneously as barriers and as sources of physical and spiritual illumination. At the same time that glass provides light and transparency, it is also hard, solid, and fragile, its edges sharp and potentially dangerous. If one stood on Avenue B and looked into the windows of Christodora, for example, one might view the whirlwind of activities the house provided for children and adults in the neighborhood and the daily interactions between the poor and working-class immigrants who participated in the settlement's classes and clubs and the mostly white middle-class social workers and domestic servants who lived and worked there. Within these walls, however, order prevailed.

Standing from within and looking outward, protected from the noise, dirt, grime, and chaos of urban life, one had a clear view of the crowded streets of southern Manhattan—a mix of new and old immigrant laborers, street peddlers, and factory workers. East 9th Street and Avenue B in the northeastern sector of the Lower East Side housed a residential population of mostly first- and second-generation Russian, Austrian, and Hungarian Jews, with a few German Jewish, Irish, Italian, and English households.[2] Christodora's annual report in 1912 counted at least twenty European nationalities in the immediate neighborhood: "Within one block, a casual passer-by heard four languages spoken on the street—German, Russian, Italian, and English."[3]

The evangelical goals, values, and practices of Christian settlement houses and missions exacerbated an already tenuous set of race, class, and ethnic relations. As a result, perceptions of settlements and missions were mixed. For many participants, the English-language and civics classes, Bible study groups, and religious services and celebrations provided a route to skilled jobs and acculturation. Others were more suspicious of the motives and practices of settlements in general, and of evangelical houses in particular, viewing them as intrusive and disruptive influences, particularly in the lives of immigrant children in the neighborhood. Tracing the ways in which religion shaped race, class, gender, and ethnic politics in lower Manhattan from the late nineteenth century through the 1920s does two things. First, it highlights the integral role of religion in identity formation, and second, it gives historians a way to chart changing understandings of race and ethnic difference over time, as expressed in urban social reform and missionary work.

Gross's experience as an insider and outsider at Christodora House illustrates a set of social dynamics that hovered between acceptance and hostility, as well as the limits and opportunities settlements offered to immigrant participants. She had been active at Christodora since age twelve and had come under the tutelage of its founder, Christina Isobel MacColl. Gross's association with MacColl and the settlement had opened doors unavailable to most of the immigrant youngsters who participated in the settlement's activities. Gross had risen within the ranks of the Christodora hierarchy and was one of a small number of female immigrant settlement workers, who numbered about 320 in the city in 1910.[4] The settlement offered a view of the future, of bright possibilities for literally breaking away from the life of struggle and the Lower East Side and achieving the life and status of a middle-class woman. Her vision included Harry, the man with whom she had fallen in love in the winter of 1913. They looked forward to an October wedding and a life together beyond the settlement.

At the same time, the structure of the settlement and the prevailing stereotypes of immigrant groups limited the degree to which Gross could fulfill her potential as a leader, resulting in what feminists in the late twentieth century would describe as the "glass ceiling." As in most settlement houses and Christian missions, the governing structure of Christodora House was hierarchical.[5] Middle- and upper-class white Protestant women made up the governing board. College-educated social workers and Bible teachers taught the classes, while working-class and poor immigrants in the neighborhood worked as servants in the house or participated as "clients" in the various activities the settlement programs offered.[6]

With the backing of wealthy benefactors, MacColl and Sarah Libby Carson had opened Christodora House in 1897 on Avenue B and 9th Street as a "non-sectarian social settlement serving the needy without regard to race or creed."[7] They had originally named their settlement house the Young Women's Settlement. Within a few years, however, they had begun to serve increasing numbers of boys and young men in the neighborhood, which led the Board of Managers to change the name in 1909 to Christodora, a Greek word meaning "Gift of Christ."[8] By changing its name, the board not only eliminated its female focus but also made its evangelical orientation more explicit. Once the settlement was up and running, Carson left to pursue settlement work in Canada, while MacColl remained as Christodora's head worker until her death in 1939.[9]

Christodora House literally was built by industrial "robber barons" of the Gilded Age. The original financial backers were native-born white Protestants who maintained affiliations with the Episcopal or Presbyterian churches in New York City; several had attended elite Northeastern colleges, many were active in the Republican Party, and all were members of the city's elite social clubs. The Board of Managers included women who were married to prominent merchants and industrialists who had accumulated their wealth from the burgeoning industries of the time—oil, railroads, steel—industries that often were at odds with the working classes and labor unions. Their financial resources funded the salaries of workers, new buildings and renovations, and programs.[10]

In some ways, the entrance of MacColl and Carson into the settlement house movement was similar to that of other college-educated female settlement house workers who joined the movement during the late nineteenth century and early twentieth century. Social work had been one of several new professions open to female college graduates. The number of men and women who pursued social work as an occupation had grown significantly between 1900 and 1930. Most were women. By 1920, out of a total of 41,078 social workers in the United States, nearly 27,000 were women, representing a 9.9 percent increase from the previous decade. In New York City, about 1,000 men and more than 3,000 women were classified as "religious, charity and welfare" workers. In 1930, 2,891 women and 687 men were engaged as social welfare workers, and 1,849 women and 602 men were engaged as "religious workers" in New York City.[11]

Missions and settlement houses functioned as what the historian Sarah Deutsch has called "redemptive spaces," safe havens in poor neighborhoods where young women could escape the clutches of pimps and procurers. As Deutsch has demonstrated, female social workers transformed urban spaces for their settlement work activities. One of the earliest collective efforts by female settlement house workers in New York City was the founding of the College Settlement at 95 Rivington Street in 1889.[12] Ten years later, the Council of Jewish Women established the Recreation Rooms and Settlements on Chrystie Street to provide a space for young women to "spend their evenings amid wholesome surroundings."[13] Newly arrived female settlement workers found their work an exciting adventure. For Lillian Wald, a founder of the Nurses' Settlement on Henry Street, her new life as a public health nurse was a world away from her middle-class upbringing in Rochester, New York: "The mere fact of living in the tenement brought undreamed-of opportunities for widening our knowledge and extending our human relationships. That we were Americans was wonderful to our fellow tenants. They were all immigrants—Jews from Russia or Roumania."[14]

Most settlement workers eschewed the evangelical identity that characterized urban reformers earlier in the century to create a more modern, secular, and scientific approach to urban reform. In so doing, they also hoped to erase the image of the urban reformer as patronizing and intrusive proselytizers. So strong was the desire among reformers to reject this image that the National Federation of Settlements, founded in 1911, refused to grant membership to settlements that engaged in overt religious conversion.[15] Modeling their establishments after Toynbee Hall in London, college-educated reformers of the late nineteenth century across the United States emphasized a secular social-service mission. In Chicago, Jane Addams and Ellen Gates Starr opened Hull House on Halsted Street in 1889. In New York City, Stanton Coit established the first settlement house in the city when he opened the Neighborhood Guild on Forsythe Street.[16] Several more soon followed, including the Nurses' Settlement on Henry Street (1895); Madison House (1898), founded by Felix Adler, originally named the Ethical Cultural Society; Hamilton House (1902), established by Pearl Underwood Denison; the Alfred Corning Clark Neighborhood House (1899) on Rivington Street; and the Edward Clark Club House (1905), founded by Mrs. Alfred Corning Clark.[17]

Social settlements varied, but all were linked by a shift in gender roles that encouraged an educated cadre of women to apply new ideas of hygiene, civic improvement, and middle-class domestic values to their work with immigrants and the poor. These new women were not a monolithic group. MacColl and Carson differed from their more visible female colleagues in the movement, such as Florence Kelley and Jane Addams, who had gained national reputations for their participation in large-scale municipal reform that ranged from suffrage and public health to the peace movement and civil rights. MacColl chose not to enter the wider political arena, although she maintained important personal connections with leading activists such as Harriot Stanton Blatch. For the most part, MacColl and Carson were content to work within the classic boundaries defining "proper" men's and women's spheres in public reform activities, leaving the work of reforming city politics to powerful male clerical leaders. Within the settlement, they took the lead as on-site managers, teachers, and spiritual guides.

Both MacColl and Carson had come from religious Christian backgrounds. MacColl was the adopted daughter of a Presbyterian minister.

Born in Canada, MacColl grew up just twenty miles from Rochester, New York, where the historical roots of Protestant religious revivalism ran deep.[18] After graduating from the Emerson School of Oratory (now Emerson College) in Boston in 1893, she moved to Manhattan, where she began her career in the settlement house movement as a secretary for the YWCA.[19]

Carson grew up in a working-class Quaker family in New Jersey and Staten Island, New York. As a young adult, she adopted the more hierarchical structure of the Presbyterian church. Like MacColl, Carson envisioned the creation of a cross-cultural, ecumenical, and evangelical settlement house experience.[20] In a report on the progress of Canadian settlements in 1914, for example, she stated, "If you looked into a Sunday service, where Jew and Gentile and Greek come to hear a message from the Book of books, you would agree that a settlement does meet the city need of the English-speaking person and foreigner alike, and helps the city to solve its problems . . . by standing for all that makes for wholesome recreation, good citizenship and civic righteousness."[21]

The mission of Christodora House claimed roots in both new Progressive reform movements and in mid-nineteenth-century women's evangelical activities. Its constitution was nearly identical to that of the middle-class Ladies' Christian Association of New York City, which stated in 1858, "Any lady who is in good standing of an Evangelical church, may become an active member by paying one dollar annually in advance."[22] Christodora also required officers to be "good standing" members of evangelical churches, automatically excluding Ethel Gross and other non-Christians.[23] In 1930, long after Gross had left the settlement, the Board of Managers loosened this requirement to include persons of "good moral character," but the Christian mission of the house never wavered.[24]

Christodora House's mission to promote "the physical, social, intellectual and spiritual development of the people in the crowded portions of the great cities of the United States and especially the city of New York" fell within the Social Gospel doctrine, which viewed religious duty as perfectly compatible with urban Progressivism.[25] The Social Gospel taught that Christians could improve the lives of the poor and immigrant populations by living among them as "neighbors," as Jesus had done, instituting new ideas of sanitation, hygiene, education, and childrearing and promoting large-scale economic change, the latter of which deviated from earlier evangelical notions of uplifting the individual. In this sense, MacColl and Carson joined an active cadre of male and female reformers such as Vida Scudder, a founder of the College Settlement, and Charles Stelzle, a Presbyterian minister and labor advocate. "Religious fervor," wrote Scudder, "as the past proves, is attended by a vicious danger of spiritual egotism. . . . Everyone knows that religion is undergoing a social revival. Where our fathers agonized over sins of the inner man, we lament our social crimes. Where they analyzed their relation to God, we analyze our relations to our brothers."[26] Stelzle praised Christodora as one of the most successful settlement houses founded "frankly and positively on Christianity."[27] Although, like other social settlements, Christodora House trained female college graduates and other women who sought to work in the settlement house movement, it infused in its social work education "practical methods of Christian work, by means of Bible study, street work, religious meetings, and the various social and educational clubs."[28]

Christodora's close connections to powerful Protestant clergymen in the city illustrated the strength of its evangelical identity. MacColl and Carson held their first meeting at Charles Parkhurst's Madison Square Presbyterian Church. The controversial anti-vice clergyman delivered keynote addresses at the settlement's annual meetings. The connection to Parkhurst and his church was an important one. Not only did Christodora align itself with one of the most controversial anti-vice activists in the city; it also firmly tied itself to leading members of the congregation, especially Harriet and Arthur Curtiss James, major financial backers of Christodora House. Arthur James's father had been a powerful supporter of Parkhurst's pastorate when the young minister first arrived in the city.[29] Josiah Strong provided another link to evangelical leadership in the city. A Congregationalist minister who wrote extensively on the need for the government and social reformers to acculturate immigrants to American civic virtues in his books *Our Country* (1885) and *The Challenge of the City* (1907), Strong served on the Board of Managers and often opened meetings with a prayer.

MacColl's evangelical vision included bridging religious differences by bringing immigrant Jews and Catholics under a Protestant roof. MacColl believed that Christodora House was more successful at attracting

Jews and Catholics than the churches and missions. In fact, the local Jewish and Catholic people on the Lower East Side had resisted Protestant missionaries in their midst. In a letter to a friend, MacColl recalled that a local minister had encouraged her to "locate here and see if you can reach the people," because he observed that most of the immigrants in the neighborhood "will not come near our churches and missions."[30]

Middle-class Christian Protestant values and practices lay at the core of Christodora's identity and its Americanization programs. In addition to offering courses in Bible study and holding regular religious services on Sunday for Christians and Jews, it set up a Christmas tree each year in Tompkins Square, perhaps the most public and visible expression of its Christian identity and mission. Although the conversion of its members was never made explicit, evangelicalism was evident in its annual reports and correspondence. For Christodora House leaders, a shared faith in God was the key to the creation of a pluralistic, international community imbued with American notions of citizenship and civic duty. Northover Camp, Christodora's summer facility, had included an ecumenical Sunday school service: "Most of our family, Jews and Gentiles alike, went to the service held on Sunday in the 'school house' by a minister who came from Northport for the purpose. We felt a pride in adding our number to the rather small congregation, and the hour was a good one for us all."[31] The fact that religious services were held on Sunday as opposed to Friday or Saturday, the usual days of Jewish services, attests to the predominance of Christian Protestant practices at the settlement.

Christodora House leaders, like most settlement house workers adopted prevailing classifications of new European immigrants as distinct races, describing the membership of its first club as "racially and religiously complex."[32] One interviewer quoted MacColl as saying that "people of many different races and backgrounds come to understand one another better" and that Sunday religious services helped build "international good will."[33] The new "races" included Southern and Eastern Europeans, who, in the words of the anthropologist Karen Brodkin, were "not-quite-white" on the black–white continuum and would not "achieve" whiteness until after World War II.[34]

Yet MacColl saw no contradiction in Christodora's explicit Christian bent and its claim to provide a neutral space for immigrant groups:

"All nationalities meet on this common ground, making of the House the social centre for the immediate neighborhood"[35] The creation of an ecumenical religious atmosphere also meant bridging ethnic and cultural differences between working-class children and young adults who participated in Christodora's classes and clubs. She proudly described Christodora House as "an Americanizing force in a neighborhood of Russians, Poles, Germans, Italians, and Irish."[36] Such sentiments were consistent with MacColl's goal to erase differences through common religious devotion: "The settlement ever seeks to emphasize the common grounds, never to emphasize the differences. The common ground of our religious life is the fatherhood and love of God."[37]

MacColl's views, however, did not always match the realities of ethnic organizing within the settlement; nor did she acknowledge real tensions between Christodora and its neighbors. Its clubs, intended to attract a mix of ethnicities, ended up serving as ethnically separate organizations. Moreover, house workers themselves compared ethnic groups. In 1921, one social worker reported that the Irish group exhibited the "best all round spirit" and predicted that it would soon constitute a "strong branch of Christodora." By contrast, the Italians were "petulant" and prone to cliquishness, while the Jewish girls were "easily pleased."[38]

MacColl maintained that Christodora House had never faced "concerted Jewish opposition," although she admitted that intergenerational conflict occurred occasionally between parents and children: "From time to time we have isolated cases where parents oppose the wish of their sons and daughters to come here. . . . When one of our Hebrews accepts Christ no fault is found with Christodora House, though the individual is severely reproached."[39] In other writings, however, MacColl recalled that a rumor about the conversion of several Jewish girls at Christodora House had resulted in an incident between the settlement house and the young women's boyfriends. Howard Crosby Foster, a social worker at Christodora House at the time of the incident, reported that the news had "stirred up the neighborhood a good deal" and "things looked rather stormy." MacColl called on Crosby to stop the fighting on nearby 10th Street and to "soften things down" among the crowd that had gathered in the streets outside the settlement house.[40] The incident illustrated the fragile relations between the settlements and their "neighbors," many of whom remained suspicious of settlement house activities.

Settlement houses, Christodora House included, had come under intense criticism from radicals who had become disillusioned with the liberal benevolent practices of the settlements, as well as from Jewish and Catholic leaders, who accused social workers of proselytizing among the non-Protestant children. Shortly after the Gospel Settlement opened in the fall of 1897, the *New York Times* described it as "Another Experiment in Evangelizing the Jews on the East Side."[41] Like Christodora House, the Gospel Settlement on Clinton Street claimed it did not seek to force conversion, "which may arouse resentment." Rather, Sara J. Bird, founder of the settlement and known as the "Mother of the Bowery," wrote that its goal was to help the children in the neighborhood "meet the temptations of every-day life, to teach them self-control, to make them the right kind of citizens and homemakers."[42] Given these settlements' firm commitment to Christian evangelical teachings, however, they must have hoped their young charges would eventually convert to the doctrines of Christianity. As MacColl wrote in 1903:

> I believe it thoughtfully understood that our object is not to make Protestants out of Catholics or Christians out of Hebrews—but to live out, as best we know, our lives to help all with whom we come into contact to live at their best. . . . This will make the truest Catholics, the most conscientious Hebrews—as they go on further in obedient life many are lead [*sic*] to a knowledge of God's greatest gift, even his son Jesus Christ to be the personal Saviour, the personal friend.[43]

Even though the reported numbers of Jews who joined Protestant churches was relatively low by the turn of the twentieth century, the possibility of conversion was perceived as a danger by many Jewish parents and religious leaders, who may have tolerated and even welcomed the recreational and civic education their children received there but were wary of Christian proselytizing.[44]

A number of Jewish and Catholic leaders leveled scathing attacks on Christian-based settlements. Reverend James B. Curry, the rector at St. James Church at 32 James Street from 1900 to 1916, was one of the most outspoken Catholic priests in New York. Located south of Park Row, St. James parish during the mid-nineteenth century numbered 25,000 and consisted mostly of Irish parishioners.[45] Curry focused his attack on the Jacob A. Riis Neighborhood Settlement House on Henry Street, which was located in his parish. According to Curry, settlement workers "swoop down upon us like a flock of magpies." In one sermon, he warned the children in his congregation not to participate in the house's activities and "took occasion . . . to impress it on their parents." He also spoke directly to parents: "Don't let these strangers influence them [children]. Be careful of the places you let them attend. . . . Do not accept charity that is not prompted by true Christian motives." Curry particularly condemned the female workers at the settlements, who, "with the idle curiosity of their sex, . . . have to put their noses into everything. They are the most annoying, impertinent, and persevering—the pious female sex."[46]

Albert Lucas, secretary of the Union of Orthodox Jewish Congregations and the superintendant of the Jewish Centres Association, concurred with Curry's criticisms. Lucas accused settlement house and Christian charity workers of trying to attract both Catholic and Jewish children and "induce them to become Protestants."[47] He explicitly included Christodora House and the Gospel Settlement in his condemnation of Christian missions.

In 1907, attendees at a convention of the Union of Orthodox Jewish Congregations of the United States and Canada accused Christodora and other settlements of "using every snare and bait" to lure Jewish children into the houses, where the indoctrination of Christianity occurred "gradually and insidiously" by offering them sweets and public displays of brightly lit Christmas trees in public schools. In what may have been a thinly veiled reference to Mary Banta's True Light Mission on Mott Street, the convention's Committee on Schools and Religious Work reported that a mission "in the heart of Chinatown . . . invited the children from the other side of East Broadway to come out of their homes and to cross that thoroughfare and enter the mission house on Mott Street." Once there, the children were given ice cream and sweets.[48] Although Banta is not explicitly named, it was well known that her work focused on children. Underlying much of the opposition to Christian proselytizing was the specter of intermarriage, which members of the convention also publicly condemned.

As much as some Jewish leaders opposed Christian Protestant settlement houses for their covert or overt conversion practices, they engaged in often heated debates about how to handle the problem. One strategy was to establish Jewish settlement houses that held English-language religious classes. In the early 1900s, the Jewish Centres Association, for example, formed a host of organizations that offered Jewish religious education to both sexes. Emanu-el Brotherhood Social House, established in 1903 on East 6th Street, was formed explicitly to counter the Christian missionaries as well as the music halls, both of which the founders considered "pernicious" influences on Jewish youth. The organizers considered the missionaries in particular "a problem too vital to be ignored."[49] Christian proselytizing among Jews and overt anti-Semitism prompted female Jewish leaders to organize on behalf of impoverished immigrant Jews from Southern and Eastern Europe. Although many of these women worked collaboratively with non-Jews and approached assimilationist strategies in similar ways, as Joyce Antler has shown, middle-class Jewish women such as Rebekah Bettelheim Kohut perceived the needs of Jews, despite ethnic, regional, and class differences, as distinct from those of non-Jews. A daughter of Hungarian Jewish immigrants, Kohut was a leading member of the National Council of Jewish Women (NCJW), which was formed in 1894 and established about a dozen Jewish settlement houses.[50]

Not all Jewish leaders supported the alternative settlement idea. Some immigrant rabbis objected as much to the counter-settlement approach as they did to Christian missions, arguing that such establishments, by offering classes in English, were too assimilative and undermined the Hebrew language and Jewish religious practices. Middle-class German Jews, often referred to as the "uptown" Jews, objected to the overt criticism of Christianity, the missions, and the settlements, arguing that such public protests could very well backfire and promote anti-Semitism in the United States.[51] Jacob H. Schiff was one such critic. A German immigrant, Schiff was one of the most powerful bankers in the country and an influential figure in the German Jewish community in New York City. He was also a founding member of the private anti-vice Committee of Fifteen. He and his wife, Therese Loeb Schiff, were well-known benefactors of many Jewish and non-Jewish philanthropic and charitable enterprises in the city.[52]

But the fact that Schiff was Jewish distinguished him from non-Jewish financiers. He often felt the sting of anti-Semitism, such as exclusion from the elite social clubs in Manhattan and anti-Semitic comments from Christian leaders. Thus, even though he opposed Christian missions, his effort to fight anti-Semitism of any kind perhaps accounted for his support of positive interactions between Jews and Christians.[53]

Despite this politically charged atmosphere and the racial, ethnic, and class prejudices that often informed the views of its educated social workers, many adults and youths in the neighborhood found the settlements' activities beneficial, if not invigorating. Ethel Gross's experience underscored both the opportunities and the limitations for advancement in activist work. She was one of the few immigrant "clients" who advanced within Christodora's structure. MacColl hired Gross as a supervisor of kindergarteners at the settlement and then as her personal secretary. As Gross's biographers have pointed out, her work with MacColl also resulted in opportunities beyond the walls of the settlement by introducing her to a wider social and political world. In 1908, through MacColl's introductions, for example, she secured a job as secretary of the newly formed Equal Franchise Society, a local suffrage association under the leadership of the New York socialite Katherine Duer Mackay. Soon after, Gross worked as secretary to Harriot Stanton Blatch, the daughter of the famed suffrage leader Elizabeth Cady Stanton.[54]

Gross was both an insider and an outsider in the world of social reform. As an assistant to elite activist women, she occupied a position within reform organizations that was unavailable to most immigrant women. Consequently, she was the *only* immigrant among the first cohort of officers in the Equal Franchise Society. The majority of the leaders were upper- and middle-class, U.S.-born, white men and women. Not surprisingly, all of the officers except Gross were members of the Board of Trustees.

Perhaps the only member of the governing board who had anything in common with Gross was Maud Nathan, one of the Equal Franchise Society's vice-presidents. Nathan and Gross were the only Jewish officers. But there the similarities ended. Although Nathan and Gross may have shared experiences with anti-Semitism, they came from different class and ethnic backgrounds. Nathan was a member of one of the city's oldest and most prominent Sephardic Jewish families. She and her sister, Annie Nathan Meyer, were leaders in New York reform and philanthropic circles.[55]

By the time Gross joined the Women's Political Union, the suffrage organization under Blatch's leadership, it had come under fire by many activists for turning away from its emphasis on working-class women to an increased reliance on wealthy benefactors.[56] Despite the organization's new approach, Gross welcomed the opportunity for participation and employment the union offered her. In a note to Hopkins, she expressed her excitement at having "joined the 'working class' again" as she prepared for her duties as secretary, equipped with a new rolltop desk and a telephone. Gross felt welcomed by the union's leadership and looked forward to her job, even though "it's work every minute."[57]

At the same time that the settlements' structure offered limited opportunities for immigrant "clients" to rise up within the hierarchy and programs, the settlements themselves provided opportunities for self-expression through the reworking of gender roles. Gross had her feet in both worlds—as a first-generation Jewish immigrant woman who had grown up on the Lower East Side and as an educated young woman who had spent much of her youth at Christodora, working with the immigrant poor as well as with women of wealth and influence.

Gross occupied the margins of conventional understandings of the middle-class, educated, professional, and sexually transgressive new woman and the ghetto girl persona created by single, young, wage-earning Jewish and Italian immigrant women and girls. As Riv-Ellen Prell has suggested, working-class Jewish immigrant girls fashioned their own sense of femininity, defying their immigrant parents' expectations of gender by partaking in American patterns of consumption. With the wages earned in factories and sweatshops, they purchased less expensive versions of fashionable clothing, cosmetics, and other accessories, such as cigarettes, which their parents and non-Jews often deemed "garish" and "vulgar."[58] In the early days of their courtship, Hopkins and Gross enjoyed playful banter about her smoking habits.

Although Gross never quite achieved the same degree of notoriety as other immigrant activists, such as Rose Wieslander Pastor Stokes, Rose Schneiderman, Emma Goldman, and the acclaimed authors Anzia Yezierska and Mary Antin, she shared the social and economic conditions that framed their personal and political choices. All of these women worked within and across ethnic boundaries in the course of their political and intellectual work.

It was also not unusual for radical activists to forge interracial/interethnic friendships and love relationships within their political circles. Pastor, Antin, and Gross had married non-Jewish men. All three marriages ended in divorce, due in part to diverging political interests over time as well as insurmountable personal problems. In *Salome of the Tenements*, Yezierska most directly addressed intermarriage as part of a larger critique of the liberal politics of the settlement house movement. Basing her story on the relationship between her close friend, Pastor, and James Graham Phelps Stokes, the millionaire son of a prominent New York Christian family, Yezierska questioned the depth of commitment to radical beliefs and practices of those from the upper classes who had professed alliances with working-class radicals. In the case of Gross and Hopkins, both sought conventional gender roles within marriage. After she married Hopkins, Gross essentially gave up her career aspirations, settling down to support her husband's career and to rear their three sons.[59] While her husband's career blossomed, his work took him away from the family for long periods of time. She taught art classes, but it was not until after her children were grown that she rekindled her interest in social welfare work. Ultimately, their marriage ended after Hopkins fell in love with another woman.

For Gross and other immigrants, the settlement house experience and the larger reform community offered a path toward assimilation. Gross had come of age when assimilationist theories were being expounded in public discourse, partly as a response to racist, nativist arguments against the new immigration. Writers like Madison Grant had expressed long-held fears among middle- and upper-class Anglo-Saxon Protestants about the danger that Southern and Eastern European and Asian immigrants presented to the future of the nation. As a counterpoint, writers such as the playwright Israel Zangwill proposed the "melting pot" theory—the idea that immigrants, through the adoption of American behavior, values, and ideals, eventually would shed their "Old World" past and emerge as new American citizens. The assumption underlying the early assimilationist rhetoric was that native-born white Americans would come to embrace these "new" Americans, who would now speak English, participate in American cultural practices, and adopt a patriotic civic-mindedness that constituted the ideal American. For immigrant women, assimilation also meant the adoption of middle-class ideas and practices of marriage and motherhood.

In the larger political realm, Gross found excitement, a much needed wage, and another path toward assimilation in the suffrage movement. For those suffragists who still clung to an earlier rhetorical strategy about the natural equality between the sexes, the younger generation of activists who mobilized for the vote near the end of the nineteenth century articulated a new strategy that emphasized the "natural" moral superiority of middle-class educated women, which complemented the work of settlement houses. Both were part of the larger Progressive reform movement that viewed women's suffrage as a way to "clean up" society—by instituting public health programs and garbage collection and combating corruption at all levels of government.[60] Women, they believed, could accomplish these changes as a distinct voting bloc. Gross's participation in the suffrage movement, with its liberal goals of fighting for women's political rights within a democratic framework, and her work in the settlements' Americanization programs were part of a common assimilationist ideal of American womanhood. As Allison Giffen and June Hopkins point out, Gross's presence at the settlement as an acculturated first-generation Jewish immigrant served as a symbol of the success of Christodora's assimilationist efforts.[61]

Contrary to popular belief, however, assimilation is not always a two-way street. As one writer noted, "Journalists named this region the 'melting pot,' for a vast immigrant population was supposedly being made American. Yet the fusion of nationalities was less obvious than their persistently maintained identity, their continuing separateness."[62] Gross may have truly felt Americanized; she acculturated to American society by learning English and the ways of the elite. She engaged in behavior associated with new womanhood, such as smoking, marching in suffrage parades, finding work in the new clerical occupations, and courting a man outside her ethnic group. And she worked diligently alongside middle-class, college-educated reform women who had not grown up in the Lower East Side tenements. But her self-image did not necessarily match the views that others may have held of her. Assimilation occurs when the larger society allows groups into the polity.[63] As Gross negotiated modern conceptions of femininity with her daily life as a Jewish immigrant woman working within a predominantly

Protestant Christian settlement house, native-born middle-class social workers may have perceived her more as a "project" than as a peer. Although she seems to have enjoyed her work immensely, she consistently occupied subordinate positions as secretary and assistant to middle- and upper-class female reformers.

The separateness that Gross experienced at Christodora House was not necessarily one that she had asked for; it resulted from the hierarchies within the settlement structure, which had as much to do with the internalization of racial classifications as with class differences. Within Christodora House, negative images of Jews persisted. During the 1920s, MacColl noted how much had changed over the years—that the current neighbors around the settlement house were Ukrainian immigrants who were "cleaner physically than were the Jews."[64] Moreover, unlike most settlement workers, Gross was not a college graduate. She also did not reside at the house but went home every day to her family's apartment, amid the "neighbors" that Christodora House attempted to serve. These differences alone were constant reminders of her marginalized position at the house and the limits of assimilation.[65]

Not long after Gross and Hopkins left Christodora, the settlement wrestled with what its leaders considered a dangerous threat to its mission and to American society at large. Race, ethnic, and class relations during World War I forced settlement leaders to confront the political life of the Lower East Side's immigrant community. Because of their ties to the industrial elite, Christodora's leaders had long maintained a comfortable distance from radical political movements.[66] An upsurge in labor organizing and the outbreak of World War I in Europe, however, exacerbated already fragile relations between Christian settlement workers and missionaries and their working-class immigrant "neighbors." The Board of Managers had strongly supported the entrance of the United States into World War I and blamed socialists for stirring up antiwar sentiments in the neighborhood.

The Lower East Side was indeed an active site of socialist organizing, dating back to the late nineteenth century. Radicals, many of whom were themselves immigrants, had drawn greater support from the people in the neighborhood than did the middle-class Protestant leaders of the Christodora House settlement. During the early twentieth century, Protestant church leaders blamed the churches as much as the rise of socialism for what Charles Stelzle would later describe as the failure of missionary work in working-class neighborhoods. Stelzle had grown up in the Bowery, and his mother was a sweatshop worker. Driven by Social Gospel principles and the desire to increase church membership, he led the drive to link the churches to efforts to improve conditions in the sweatshops and factories and, in the process, improve relations between working-class people and missionaries. In 1909, for example, in one of numerous speeches he gave on the subject of labor and the churches, he argued that working people needed "unselfish direction" in their struggle for "industrial democracy" through the support of the churches. The war had not helped the churches strengthen the link between the church and "the people." In Stelzle's view, the influence of socialism through labor organizations such as the Industrial Workers of the World (IWW) stymied efforts to forge these links. He once argued that "every existing church was fighting a losing battle" in the effort to reach immigrants in neighborhoods where "Trotsky and his colleagues held forth . . . and I.W.W.ism was exceedingly active."[67]

Concerns about leftist influences in the neighborhood permeated discussions at monthly meetings throughout the war. In October 1917, the annual report issued from Christodora House championed the entrance of the United States into the war and denounced the influence of socialists and pacifists who had campaigned against it. Calling antiwar sentiment "ignorant idealism" fostered by German propaganda, Christodora's leaders apparently believed the socialists had gotten a head start in influencing the local immigrant population: "The trouble is that we have only half-educated our foreign-born population in the American ideals of liberty and democracy, and the Socialists have been the ones to take up the task where we have left it."[68] One report suggested that to investigate Bolshevism was to investigate the housing problem and the labor problem, for "the basis of Bolshevism is discontent and discontent is fostered by unjust conditions."[69]

The board's solution was to intensify its patriotic position through its programs. In 1916, as war raged in Europe, the board adopted Harriet James's recommendation for enhancing the civic-education dimension of Christodora House by creating an internal structure that mirrored the city's government structure. The board created the "City of Christodora," which had a mayor, a board of alderman, and a host of bureaucrats.

The goal of the project was to instill patriotic ideals through participation in a municipal model of government and the application of civic ideals to everyday practice:

> The special way in which Christodora House tries to point out the best kind of living, is in the developing of civic consciousness. To make good citizens,—men and women worthy of their places in the world; able to do their share of the world's work,—is the motive [in] back of all the work and play. The very government of the House is ordered after the manner of the city government. . . . We want our young people, and our older ones too, to learn to think straight, and to realize their responsibility in "doing their bit."[70]

The "City of Christodora" represented one more example of deeply held values among the settlement's leadership about the meaning of "American." For Harriet James and other leading board members, civic responsibility was part of the larger vision of Christian-based settlement work, one that incorporated secular with religious life.

But, the incorporation of relatively new ideas of ecumenicalism into Christodora's commitment to bridging differences and creating international "friendships" among and between Lower East Side immigrants and settlement house workers had mixed results. The effort to bridge cultural differences via the settlement house experience did not necessarily eliminate deeply held prejudices of the settlement house leaders. As a result, the hope that the house would serve as a zone of interethnic community formation did not pan out as smoothly as MacColl and its patrons and participants might have hoped.

If evangelical settlement houses enraged Catholic and Jewish leaders, so did Christian missions, which touted a more overt proselytizing agenda. Not surprisingly, Christian missions also operated as sites of complex dynamics between missionaries and the local population. By the late nineteenth century, immigrant, non–Christian Protestant neighborhoods in the United States had become part of the larger global missionary crusade. The number of missionary women with college educations in foreign mission work had increased by the early twentieth century. "Fifty years ago to be a woman student was exceptional: twenty years ago to be a woman student who was vitally interested in missions was to be truly exceptional," wrote Una M. Saunders, a teacher in Ohio, in 1906.[71] These new women in missionary circles, many of whom were educated in the new missionary training institutes, joined the scores of college-educated female settlement house reformers who descended on immigrant neighborhoods.[72] In 1883, Albert B. Simpson, a Presbyterian minister whose church was located on 13th Street in Manhattan, established the Missionary Training Institute, the first Bible college in the United States, to provide cohesive training to both male and female students in Bible study and evangelism and to send graduates to foreign lands as missionaries.[73]

Protestant religious reformers had been part of urban neighborhoods since the early decades of the nineteenth century as the religious revivalism of the Second Great Awakening swept the Northeast. Clergymen and lay reformers viewed the city as a den of sin and vice that encouraged overindulgence in alcohol and sex among the poor. Under the aegis of the American Tract Society, whose office was located on Nassau Street in southern Manhattan, evangelical men and women armed with Bibles and religious tracts entered poor neighborhoods in droves, knocking on the doors of working-class and poor families.[74] Although both men and women participated in these "home visits," middle-class Protestant women were called on in particular to extend their domestic responsibilities into the public realm of the city streets and often tied their activities to larger reform movements such as temperance and anti-prostitution. In 1850, for example, female members of the New York Ladies' Home Missionary Society held evangelical meetings in the impoverished Five Points district of southern Manhattan.[75]

By the end of the nineteenth century, fueled by U.S. imperialism in places like China, Hawaii, and the Philippines, clerical and lay churchmen and women from a range of denominations looked to expand Christian proselytizing beyond work among Native Americans, which dated back to the eighteenth century, to non-Christian populations outside the United States. For example, American missionaries had been in China since the 1830s, focusing their efforts on converting Chinese women in the hope that they would pass along Christian Protestantism to their children.[76] Infused with Social Gospel ideas and methods, college-trained missionaries sought a more efficient system. Committed to the "science" of missions, they set up formal offices and bureaucracies. Missionary work was now a professional, increasingly global endeavor that focused on proselytizing not only within the geographic boundaries of the United States but also in Asia, Africa, and Latin America.[77]

Many Christian missionaries who chose to remain in the United States focused their proselytizing activities among the new immigrants from East Asia and Southern and Eastern Europe.[78] Others, such as the Chinatown and Bowery Rescue Settlement for Girls, focused on proselytizing among young women in immigrant neighborhoods as a way to "rescue" them from the sex trade. While many joined the social settlement movement, missionaries chose to focus explicitly on conversion. They adopted a variety of approaches to institutionalizing their projects. Some set up missions under the auspices of the City Mission Society, such as the House of Aquila, established in 1890 on Stanton Street, which provided church services, a kindergarten, and recreational facilities to a predominantly Jewish clientele. Others operated directly out of the local church buildings or established missions in storefronts and basements under the supervision of their churches.

The most obvious targets of missionary work were Chinese immigrants, an endeavor that started in the mid-nineteenth century. In New York City, the Five Points House of Industry began to offer classes for local Chinese people in 1865. White missionaries and a handful of Chinese missionaries followed in droves as the years went on as the immigrant Chinese male population increased in lower Manhattan. The work of white missionary women among a predominantly male Chinese immigrant population in the downtown neighborhoods is well known. There is little evidence that the Chinese objected to the work of these women, although Buddhist temples, known by popular white writers as "joss houses," were fixtures in neighborhoods where clusters of Chinese immigrants lived. The first Chinese missionary to administer to the Chinese in the area was Moy Jin Kee. Described as a "Chinese blue blood," Kee was the son of a Methodist minister and part of Canton's elite. His brother was Jin Fuey Moy (also known as Moy Jin Fuey), the Brooklyn-based physician discussed in Chapter 3. Kee established an evening school, first in the Five Points district in 1878 and then at 14 Mott Street the following year for the "religious and intellectual welfare" of the approximately one thousand Chinese men living in the area.[79] Attendance was spotty, at best, at the dozen or so Chinese schools in Manhattan and Brooklyn. The Reverend James Jackson, a former member of the Wesleyan China Mission, noted in 1881 that "it is common for the Chinese to go about from school to school, being registered at different schools as scholars, and permanently attending nowhere."[80]

Like the classes at social settlement houses, the missions offered practical services to Chinese men. According to Jin Fuey Moy, Chinese immigrants cared less about converting or avoiding what reformers considered dangerous vices—prostitution and gambling—than about learning English to succeed in business.[81] The company of young women was undoubtedly also an appealing aspect of the missions for many Chinese men.

The historically based specter of interracial sexuality involving white women and non-white men evoked anxieties among white authorities. Storefront missions invited close scrutiny by the police and urban reformers who feared that interracial sexual liaisons would result from social contact between the missionary women and Chinese men. Stories and drawings depicting marriages between Chinese men and white female Protestant missionaries appeared in popular magazines and dotted the pages of sensational Chinatown stories in "true-to-life" fictional tales of urban life.[82] When the Elsie Sigel murder case broke in 1909, fear of interracial sexuality reached a fever pitch, as police officers embarked on a crusade to "purge" white women from Chinatown as they tried in vain to track down the murderer of the nineteen-year-old missionary, the granddaughter of a Civil War hero.

While many white missionaries targeted the souls of Chinese men, others focused on the potential victims of the predominantly male Chinese community. Several years before the Sigel murder, white Protestant reformers feared for the safety of young white women who had taken up with Chinese men. The missionary sisters Annette and Clemence Boardman established the Chinatown Rescue Settlement and Recreation Room in 1904 on Bayard Street. Within a year, the settlement had changed its name to the Chinatown and Bowery Rescue Settlement for Girls and moved to 10 Mott Street, not coincidentally among the clusters of Chinese–white households at numbers 11, 15, and 17 Mott. By providing a refuge for young white women who had entered the sex trade, the mission attempted to bring "fallen" women into the Christian fold of virtue, even if sexual purity, according to prevailing codes of femininity, was impossible at this point. The Chinatown settlement combined social settlement work and anti-vice activism. Imbued with the popular narratives that portrayed Chinese men as potential seducers of innocent white girls and women, the settlement sought to "save" these women from a life of illicit sex and opium addiction.[83]

Like other religiously based settlement houses, the Chinatown settlement emerged out of the upsurge in anti-vice activism and the Social Gospel movement. Unlike the all-male members and agents of the Committee of Fifteen, the members of the Chinatown and Bowery Rescue Settlement for Girls did not traverse the streets taking the names of prostitutes and their male customers. Rather, like other reform women, they set up home-like quarters for former prostitutes. The Settlement also assessed the effectiveness of police efforts to crack down on interracial households. In the wake of the Sigel case, the mission found that efforts by the local police to expel white women from Chinatown who could not prove they were legally married to the Chinese men with whom they lived had not been completely successful. Rather, the mission workers found that, although the "dives" in Chinatown and the Bowery had been "almost entirely closed," young white women were found on the streets, and many were still living secretly with Chinese men.[84] In the view of these missionaries, interracial relationships were synonymous with prostitution, smoking, and drug addiction. Clemence Boardman outlined the scope of the settlement's work: "Our principal work is done among our young American girls, who make their home in Chinatown and with the Chinese. One, a girl of sixteen . . . drifted into Chinatown, and, unfortunately, became a victim of the cocaine and cigarette habit."[85]

The Chinatown establishment was a product of the phenomena of both the Progressive-era ideas of the Social Gospel and the new woman. The Chinatown and Bowery Rescue Settlement for Girls did not simply support Christian evangelicalism, as Mary Liu suggests; its religious identity was central to its mission and should be viewed within a larger context of missions and settlement house activities in which the Social Gospel played a critical role. The Mott Street establishment was explicit in its Christian orientation and housed female resident workers and a nurse. By 1909, the settlement's advisory board expanded to include

Nellie W. Williams, the wife of a Baptist minister. Clemence Boardman made clear the strong religious values that framed the work: "We
realize that the Power of God has saved in a wonderful manner some
who seemed beyond saving and restored to health and right living those
who apparently were beyond any earthly help."[86] The goal of the organization was similar to that of other rescue mission across the country:
to steer young women away from prostitution, as well as to "rescue"
them from the flourishing urban sex trade. The founders of the Chinatown settlement believed they had situated their home in the heart
of the most morally troubled areas of lower Manhattan, describing the
neighborhood in its annual report for 1907–1908 as a "vortex of sin and
crime." Living conditions in this area, the reformers found, varied, from
"the very worst and most unsanitary houses" to those "girls" who "live
in a sort of oriental luxury."[87] By remaining at the rescue mission after
the Sigel murder, the Boardmans and other white female missionaries at
the settlement legitimized their own presence in the Chinatown neighborhood.

As in the case of settlement house workers, missionary women
founded organizations that gave them access to the public realm, despite
public denunciations of their presence in immigrant neighborhoods.
Unlike Christian-oriented social settlements, Christian missions could
explicitly express their evangelical goals among the poor and immigrant
populations by continuing the older practice of proselytizing in urban
neighborhoods. Mary Ann "Artemesia" Lathbury, Helen F. Clark, and
Mary Elizabeth Banta were three well-known white women who devoted
their lives to missionary work among the Chinese in lower Manhattan.
Lathbury served as secretary of the Chinese Sunday School and then as
superintendent of the Chinese mission when they were located first at
Seventh Avenue and 23rd Street in 1888. She continued her position
as superintendent when the mission and school moved to 30 East 7th
Street, near Tompkins Square Park.[88] Born in Manchester, New York,
in 1841, Lathbury grew up in a ministerial family.[89] She participated
in the Chautauqua Movement, co-founded in 1874 as the New York
Chautauqua Assembly by a Methodist minister to promote training ses-
sions for Sunday school teachers at summer camps at Lake Chautauqua.
Although Lathbury eventually pursued an occupation as a commercial
artist, she was best known in missionary circles for her participation in

the Chinese missionary movement and for the numerous religious songs and poems she wrote.[90]

Clark and Banta worked in the "Chinatown" neighborhood. Clark served as director of the Morning Star Baptist Mission during the early 1890s. After a fire at the mission in 1894, in which Clark sustained serious injuries, she continued her work as director when the mission moved from Doyers Street around the corner to 21 Mott Street. Clark lectured on the need to convert "heathen" populations through "out-door" preaching. She found southern Manhattan a particularly good place to preach, given the "steady stream of foreigners who keep rushing in."[91]

Mary Banta was perhaps the best-known "Chinatown" missionary. As in Lathbury's case, Banta's father was a Methodist minister.[92] Born in 1874, Banta attended a missionary school in Brooklyn—possibly the Union Missionary Training Institute, located a few blocks from her home, established by the Methodist missionary Lucy D. Osborn in 1888 to train an international body of evangelical Christian students for missionary work overseas.[93] Banta spent five months in Garraway, Liberia, but returned to the United States in November 1901 due to ill health.[94]

Banta moved to lower Manhattan in 1904, where she worked as a kindergarten superintendent at the Morning Star Baptist Mission. In an interview conducted in the 1950s, she recalled that she initially had wanted to avoid missionary work in Chinatown but had "promised God that I would enter any door He held open. So I came, and I have stayed."[95] She worked with several missionary organizations in the neighborhood until her death in 1971, including the Presbyterian Board of Foreign Missions and the True Light Lutheran Church.[96]

As part of their missionary work, Clark and Banta supported the antiprostitution movement. Banta assisted newly arrived Chinese immigrant women in a variety of ways, including facilitating immigration into the United States and participating in the crusade to end white slavery.[97] As Peggy Pascoe has shown, the effort to save Chinese women from white slavery was a critical dimension of moral reform across the country, particularly in port cities such as San Francisco and New York.[98] By the 1930s, a cooperative relationship had developed between the U.S. Immigration and Naturalization Service and the local missions. Banta had been instrumental in the readmission of Lung Som Moy discussed in the introduction. After Moy was readmitted as a U.S. citizen in 1935, Chinese Inspector Byron Uhl informed Banta of not only the board's decision but also Moy's intended place of residence in New York and her physical appearance.[99] The brief memo from Uhl to Banta documents what by this time had become a routine procedure. Regular contact with immigration inspectors helped missionary leaders assist newly arrived immigrant women in locating relatives and finding temporary housing. In the process, missionaries could continue to monitor the women's behavior and ensure that they were not entering the country for "immoral" purposes.

Unlike earlier missionaries who focused their work on adult Chinese men, Clark and Banta turned their attention to children. Banta's initial appointment as superintendent of the kindergarten at the mission signaled a demographic change in the Chinese population in lower Manhattan. Although adult men continued to outnumber women and children, the number of Chinese children living in the mainland United States between one month and nine years of age had more than doubled, from 2,181 in 1900 to 5,409 in 1920.[100] An increased focus on childhood as a distinct stage of life among Progressive reformers, educators, and missionaries had resulted in the establishment of classes specifically designed for youngsters. For example, the New York Presbyterian Church established a Sunday school for Chinese children in 1901 at the same time that it opened a Bible school for Chinese women at 11½ Mott Street.[101]

Both women also adopted Chinese girls. Clark did so to prevent them from entering the sex trade, as well as to remove them from what she considered dangerous and unhealthy environments. The power of white Protestant evangelists was evident in the courtrooms, in which Clark argued for taking young Chinese girls away from their parents. In a highly publicized case, she sought to adopt Ah Foon, who lived in "Chinatown" near the mission. Clark testified against the parents, "Mr. and Mrs. Hoe Bow," whom she accused of smoking opium. Joseph C. Thoms, the Chinese physician from Brooklyn, confirmed Clark's testimony, adding that he would not believe anyone who smoked opium. It probably did not help the parents' fight against Clark when Mr. Hoe Bow testified that, in addition to selling cigars for a livelihood, he was an actor and female impersonator.[102]

As in other communities, missionary work in the Chinatown neighborhood met with mixed responses from other reformers, as well as from the Chinese. In 1954, members of Manhattan's Chinese community hosted a celebration in honor of Mary Banta, calling her the "Mother of Chinatown," perhaps in reference to her adoption of several Chinese children during her years in the neighborhood.[103] In a review of her funeral in 1971, the *New York Times* praised Banta for her long missionary career. The laudatory article, however, masked the tensions that sometimes emerged between missionaries and the Chinese families they sought to serve.

In 1922, for example, the Chinese Benevolent Society in New York City established a school for Chinese children at 16 Mott Street.[104] The mission of the Chinese school was to ensure that the children maintained facility in the Chinese language and customs, a strategy similar to that of Jewish settlements. Both functioned in opposition to the evangelical, assimilationist approach of Christian settlements and missions.

White social workers more directly questioned the work of missionaries. Florence Brugger, who was critical of Christian missions in general, critiqued what she viewed as Banta's autocratic style, which, she argued, effectively isolated the mission and the children from the larger non-Chinese community in the area and from other settlements. Brugger criticized Banta (whom she referred to as "Miss M") for preventing the Chinese children under her charge from experiencing life outside the Chinatown neighborhood. Brugger was particularly critical of Banta's practice of using her charges as showpieces: "She has taken children dressed up in their pretty clothes to missionary society meetings and her girl's club has been invited to churches to sing in Chinese. But she does not want them to mix with the Italian and Russian groups and has never encouraged representation from her group on the House Council or other participation in the wider social programs of the very organization that employs her." According to Brugger, Chinese parents often did not attend their children's performances at the mission and, although they respected Banta, "They don't agree with her."[105]

Although it is difficult to ascertain the accuracy of Brugger's observations about Banta's work, the poor and immigrant populations did often find themselves captive audiences of missionaries. While many missionaries during the period were establishing organizations within immigrant and poor neighborhoods, others traversed the wards and rooms of almshouses, hospitals, and orphanages. These institutions had served as sites of Christian evangelism since the eighteenth century. When young Rose Cohen stayed at Presbyterian Hospital during the 1890s, she regularly encountered the missionaries who came through her ward.[106]

Cohen's admission to the hospital was unusual, for most immigrants shunned hospitals. Moreover, the new hospital was located in the Washington Heights neighborhood, far north of the Cherry Street apartment on the Lower East Side, where Cohen resided with her family.[107] Born Rahel Gollup in 1880 in Russia, Cohen was the eldest child in an Orthodox Jewish family. She and her siblings followed her father, a tailor, to the United States in 1892, and she began working in a tailor shop herself. Like other European Jewish immigrants, the Gollups settled in an ethnically mixed but predominantly Jewish neighborhood on Cherry Street.

Cohen had developed a chronic but unspecified illness by age seventeen. Her illness led her to meet Lillian Wald and Mary Brewster at the Henry Street settlement, who advised her to go to the hospital. Separated from friends and family, Cohen spent three months recuperating from her illness and negotiating between Jewish and Christian people and practices. She was at first reluctant to eat the non-kosher food the staff served to her, but she did so with her mother's permission to regain her physical strength. Soon after she arrived, Christian missionaries visited. She remembered one female missionary who came to the ward to lead hymns and talk to the patients about Christ, which, Cohen recalled, made her uncomfortable: "My face began to burn. I saw that she wanted to convert me and I on the other hand thought it a sin even to listen to her. . . . Her lips moved rapidly and gradually a red spot appeared on each cheek, and a tiny white bead of foam worked itself into each corner of her mouth."[108] An elderly man also distributed Bibles in the afternoon. According to Cohen, he seemed less intrusive than the female missionary, which was perhaps why she referred to him as a "religious person" rather than a "missionary." When she informed the man that she was Jewish, he responded by saying that Judaism "is a good religion" and left her alone.[109]

Cohen's encounter with the hospital missionaries, however, did spark a curiosity about Christianity that disconcerted her parents, as well as Wald and Brewster. When Cohen asked Brewster for a copy of the New Testament, Brewster assumed that she was toying with the idea of converting. According to Cohen, her request did not reveal any kind of religious identity crisis; rather, she recalled feeling a strong sense of discomfort when she asked Brewster for more information on Christianity, knowing that to do so would be more of a transgression than eating non-kosher food: "It was hard for a Jewish girl, brought up as I had been, even to utter the words, 'I want to read the New Testament.' The thought of becoming a Christian was nowhere in my mind, but this would be the real step beyond the boundary."

Brewster, recognizing the secular identity of the Henry Street settlement, refused to give the material to her, maintaining that "it would not do for the Settlement."[110] It was at this moment that Cohen learned about the limits of the Henry Street settlement and the lines some workers drew between the secular and the religious. Her exposure to Christianity at the hospital and her subsequent request for a copy of the New Testament forced the settlement to fend off nuances of religious activity. In the end, Cohen maintained a strong Jewish identity throughout her life.[111]

Rose Cohen's experience at the hospital illustrates the tensions and anxieties that sometimes occurred when immigrants encountered Christian proselytizers. Religious institutions also served as sites of conflict and accommodation. The long-standing role of religious organizations and institutions in fulfilling the spiritual, social, and political needs of specific ethnic communities often kept groups from interacting much with one another. Churches and synagogues, for example, provided physical and cultural spaces where unmarried youth could socialize, court, and engage in recreational activities in addition to facilitating culturally specific forms of religious ideology and practice among the faithful.

But conflicts also emerged among co-religionists. For example, dynamics between a predominantly Irish Catholic church leadership in the United States and newly arrived Italian Catholic immigrants, were initially negative, based partly on historically based relations between parish churches and parishioners and Irish–Italian relations in the city. Historians have tended to examine the dynamics between these two groups within the context of the history of Catholicism. As John T. McGreevy has written, a serious linkage between race and religion provides the opportunity to explore the ways in which the Catholic church and, particularly, the local urban parish priests and congregants grappled with racial difference as ethnically diverse groups of European Catholics vied for neighborhood space that centered on a cohesive ethnic Catholic identity.[112] At the same time, historians can also view the dual functioning of race and religion as part of a larger story of urban race and ethnic relations.

The relationship between working-class Italian immigrants and a predominantly Irish Catholic diocese in New York City during the period not only provides a religious institutional framework through which to view these interactions. It also reveals the subtle ways in which assimilation and whiteness functioned simultaneously between two ethnic groups who "achieved" whiteness, and thus Americanization, at different historical moments. Maureen Fitzgerald argues that tense relations between the diocese and Italian Catholics were based mainly on conceptions of "Americans" and "foreigners" at the time rather than whiteness. Yet whiteness was at the core of unspoken assumptions on the part of Irish Catholic priests who administered to Italian immigrant congregants on the Lower East Side.[113] By the time Italians migrated to the United States in large numbers between the 1880s and 1920, the Irish for the most part had established themselves as "white," regardless of whether they were U.S.-born or immigrants.[114] When immigrants from Southern and Eastern Europe, Catholic or not, arrived in the United States near the close of the century, the Irish quite easily could continue to distance themselves from other groups. Southern Italians, like European Jews, would not "achieve" whiteness until the 1930s, despite the fact that census classifications recorded anyone of European ancestry as "white."

So, then, why were Italians treated as a distinct racial/ethnic group? Part of the answer lies in the ways that "Americanness" and "whiteness" functioned simultaneously for people of European ancestry within the context of American nativism. Southern Italians and Jews at the time were what the historian Robert Orsi has described as "inbetween" people, those who occupied the space between black and white on the American racial spectrum. Journalists, social scientists, and other writers at the turn of the twentieth century commonly referred to Italians as "swarthy" and "dark-skinned." Such descriptions of skin tone accompanied negative epithets such as "dago" and stereotypes of innate proclivities toward criminality, low intelligence, and violence.[115] In 1890, Henry Jackson, secretary of the Commissioners of Emigration, considered Southern Italians the "least desirable immigrant[s]."[116]

Irish Catholics initially shared popular negative opinions of Italian immigrants. The clergy in particular expressed frustration with the new Catholic immigrants. One of the foremost complaints was that Italian immigrants did not behave like Irish Catholics, who, by the late nineteenth century and early twentieth century, had set the standards of Catholic religious practices in the United States. Some outlined ethnic distinctions between the Italian and Irish that accounted for different religious practices. Most of the early articulations of difference came from Irish clergymen. In a letter to Archbishop John Murphy Farley of New York in 1917, Father B. J. Reilly, pastor of Nativity Church, described Italians as "not a sensitive people like our own."[117]

Michael Corrigan, archbishop of New York, looked on Italian Catholics as an embarrassment and a serious setback to the assimilation of Catholics into a Protestant nation, a struggle in which Irish and German Catholics had engaged since their migration in mass numbers in the 1840s and 1850s. Thus, one of the goals among city church leaders was to encourage Italians to adopt Irish Catholic religious traditions.[118]

In addition to being distinct in nature from the Irish, according to Reilly, Italians were "callous" toward religion.[119] Reilly's comment stemmed from the frustrations of clerical leaders who found Italian Catholics resistant to providing financial support to sustain the clergy and the church buildings. Their reluctance was based on the historical relationship between parishioners and the church in Italy, where the upkeep of church buildings had been paid for by the state.[120] In the United States, where the separation of church and state prevailed, Catholic parishes often struggled financially, relying on tithes and donations from parishioners. In urban areas such as New York City, parishioners were most often working class or poor. In a more sympathetic vein, Bernard J. Lynch, writing for *Catholic World*, confirmed the notion that the Italians and Irish were culturally distinct, "almost of a different civilization." Yet Lynch held out hope for Italian Catholic children if parents followed the Irish lead: "They must tag after the Irish, and little by little their children will do great things for God in America."[121]

Differing religious practices, poverty, and a dearth of Italian priests also contributed to relations that at times were tense between the Irish clergy and Italian immigrants. At best, the Irish church leaders ignored the needs of newly arrived Italian Catholics, who for years pleaded for the establishment of their own parish. At worst, Irish priests and nuns expressed explicit disdain for Italian people and their religious customs. Since the early twentieth century, historians of Catholic church history have written about the "Italian Problem."[122] Italian immigrants, they claimed, clung to religious practices that "dangerously bordered on superstition" and "overemphasized" a devotion to particular saints.[123] In his massive two-volume history of the Catholic archdiocese in New York, Reverend John Talbot Smith noted that Italian immigrants generally ignored the laws of the church, did not attend mass regularly, neglected the sacraments, and failed to provide their children with religious training.

According to Smith, the few Italian priests who had immigrated to the United States were of little help during the early years of Italian migration. By 1902, as the number of Italian clergy and the assistance of the New York archdiocese increased, the religious life of Italian Catholics in the city improved significantly. Of particular importance in Smith's view were the Jesuits who had set up a mission for Italians on Elizabeth Street. For example, the Reverend John F. Kearney, rector of St. Patrick's Church on Mott Street made the Italians of the parish his "special care."[124] Reverend John V. Tolino, a second-generation Italian, also credited the Irish Catholic clergy with assimilating their Italian co-religionists into a more "American" way of Catholicism. As a result, Italian parishioners became more willing to structure their parishes along "ordinary" parish lines.[125]

The growth of political power among Irish Catholic men in New York City's religious and secular politics by the late nineteenth century helped facilitate the push for the assimilation of Italian Catholics by way of Irish Catholicism. Beginning in 1865 under the leadership of Archbishop John McCloskey, for example, charities sponsored by the Catholic church, and dominated by Irish lay and church leaders, increased significantly in the city. Many of these organizations would eventually become part of the Catholic Charities of the Archdiocese of New York, a federation of charitable agencies overseen by the Catholic church. In the secular realm, the political presence of Irish Catholics in city politics contributed to the election of John Kelly as the first Irish Catholic boss in Tammany Hall in 1872 and of John Purroy Mitchel as the city's first Irish Catholic mayor. Italians would not gain this kind of political solidarity for several more decades.[126]

By the 1930s, perceptions of Italians as a different race and a frustrating population of Catholic congregants had subsided within Catholic parishes and in the country at large. As one contributor for the *Ecclesiatical Review* wrote in 1938, the Italians, despite suffering from "racial and religious prejudices" earlier in the century, were now treated and accepted as "regular Americans."[127]

Like the urban anti-vice crusade, the settlement house and missionary movements brought reformers and working-class women, men, and children into regular and sometime uneasy contact with one another. As much as reformers, missionaries, and the clergy provided important services to the poor—health care, recreational facilities, child care, and language classes—their presence could also heighten tensions in the neighborhood between themselves and the groups they hoped to serve. Oppositional representations of reformers as obnoxious "do-gooders" and as unselfish heroes who sought to achieve harmony through "simple friendliness" have often overshadowed a more complicated set of relations and differential power relations between institutions and the working-class and poor immigrant populations.

Religion played a strong and often controversial role in race, ethnic, gender, and class relations in the social settlement house and missionary movements during a period when shifting notions of gender and race threatened the social order. Some, such as Ethel Gross, made the most of the services and opportunities for advancement and acculturation that settlements provided while at the same time encountering the proverbial glass ceiling as an outsider in a predominantly middle-class Christian Protestant community of activists.

Collective opposition to Protestant evangelism and the often tense dynamics between Irish and Italian Catholics also reveal the fragile relationship between race and religion during this period. Catholic and Jewish leaders together decried the proselytizing efforts of Christian-based settlements and missions and faced strong anti-Catholicism and anti-Semitism throughout the country. But definitions of whiteness as much as religious differences placed them in a slightly different position in the national racial discourse and the national polity. Although anti-

Catholicism would persist well into the 1960s, Catholics of Northern and Central European ancestry could, by the early twentieth century, lay a stronger claim to whiteness than could Jews and immigrants from Southern Europe, who would occupy the "not-quite-white" or "inbetween" position for several more decades. Discourses of assimilation and whiteness, as understood by reformers, the clergy, and local residents, circulated through sustained activities that held religious devotion at its core, whether through the Social Gospel movement among Protestants, Jewish settlement houses, or parish development among Catholic priests.

Conclusion

This book offers a social history of southern Manhattan that challenges conventional notions of this area of New York as either a hotbed of interracial sex and violence or a cluster of isolated ethnic communities. Romanticized notions of New York history, rooted in ethnic and racial stereotypes, as well as in memories of family and community, belie and oversimplify the complexity of urban social relations that simmered below the surface during the late nineteenth century and in the early decades of the twentieth century. Although interracial sex and criminality were certainly a part of daily realities in working-class neighborhoods, more mundane, unglamorous relations also developed as people struggled to form and sustain families, create communal networks, and earn decent livelihoods. Working-class and immigrant people who lived and labored in lower Manhattan created a range of social, political, and economic relationships both within and across ethnic communities.

In a larger sense, this study explores the processes of urban community formation among working-class and immigrant peoples during a time when Jim Crow segregation and xenophobia maintained an uneasy and often contradictory co-existence with Progressive ideals of democracy and social reform. National ideologies of "difference" shaped public discourses about "assimilation" and the meaning of "American" and "whiteness." These ideas flourished among both Progressive-era reformers, who sought to change individuals by improving the urban environment, and exclusionists, who rallied to prevent the new immigrants from weakening the body politic. An intersectional approach allows us to view the ways in which concepts of "isolation," "integration," "assimilation," "American," and "whiteness" played out daily through interactions across lines of race, ethnicity, class, and gender.

Between 1880 and 1930, New York State followed federal immigration and citizenship laws by limiting access to certain occupations to those deemed eligible for citizenship. At the municipal level, police cracked down on interracial sex and marriage, and wealthy male leaders initiated the formation of private anti-vice organizations to combat corruption and vice. But instead of separating people, such policies and practices actually facilitated social, economic, and political relations within and between ethnic groups. The development of co-ethnic and interracial/interethnic networks of family, friends, neighbors, fellow workers, and community leaders was essential to meeting the basic needs and desires of the men, women, and children in urban neighborhoods who were establishing families, birthing babies, caring for the sick, burying the dead, conducting business, and finding employment.

Personal desire was sometimes strong enough to resist social taboos. As Chapter 1 illustrates, condemnation from the larger society and within co-ethnic communities did not prevent people from marrying across ethnic and racial boundaries and establishing mixed families within safe niches. This is evident in the residential patterns of mixed-race couples in the "Chinatown" neighborhood over time. But as the stories of Bert Eutemey and Louise Holmes and Ethel Gross and Harry Hopkins illustrate, such unions sometimes exacerbated existing tensions around both family expectations and larger societal conceptions about difference.

The collective historical experience of Asian immigrants, in particular, is instructive regarding the residual effects of formal and informal discrimination in the paid labor force. In the case of Chinese New Yorkers, such restrictions resulted in reliance on outsiders for many essential services and, at the same time, facilitated a mutually dependent set of economic relations with non-Chinese businessmen from the neighborhood, as well as from those from other parts of the city. At the same time, Chinese and other immigrant small-business owners in the city maintained economic and social connections that extended beyond the neighborhoods, crossing local, state, and national borders to maintain a flow of goods and capital to stock their stores and their eating and drinking establishments. Thus, rather than functioning as isolated entities, immigrant communities were in fact active participants in a growing transnational commercial world.

The very presence of vibrant urban working-class immigrant communities, however, provoked anxiety among reformers and municipal leaders. The nationwide effort to control or eliminate illicit behavior manifested itself in cities across the country and focused to a great extent on poor and immigrant neighborhoods. As illustrated by the activities of the Committee of Fifteen and Committee of Fourteen in New York City, wealthy civic leaders, industrialists, ministers, and social scientists sought to stamp out prostitution, gambling, illegal drugs, and corruption in the police and municipal government. At the level of neighborhood politics, interactions between anti-vice reformers and the men and women who lived in these areas were not whole antagonistic or cooperative. Rather, while many resisted the presence of agents in their midst, others saw anti-vice organizations as an opportunity for employment or as a resource.

In part, the effort to institute control over the behavior of the poor and working classes was a response to larger changes in gender roles and identities, both of which were rooted in shifting understandings of what it meant to be a "modern" and "American" woman. Both middle-class and working-class women and girls carved out their own versions of new womanhood, signaling a proactive fashioning of femininity. Just as young, unmarried white men sought new jobs in the burgeoning clerical and white-collar sectors of industry, young, mainly white women found new opportunities in higher education and the professions. These shifts in gender roles and identities also carried expanding notions of "whiteness" and the increasing rigidity of who belonged in this category and who did not. The drive to assimilate the new immigrants to "American" values and practices found expression in the settlement house movement, a resurgence of the Social Gospel among mainly white Protestant evangelical reformers, and among Catholic priests. The settlements presented a double-edged sword for immigrant participants. Some, like Ethel Gross, found opportunities in the settlements while at the same time encountering barriers because of immigrant, working-class backgrounds. Others opposed the settlements for their evangelical and assimilationist practices.

Individuals and families—Ah Fung, Lung Som Moy, Johanna Hurley, Ethel Gross, Harry Hopkins, Christina MacColl, the Naughtons, the Buonocores, the Eutemeys, the Wongs, and all the rest—carried historical legacies of racism, sexism, and classism that undergirded the limits and opportunities for family and community formation at specific moments in time. Their stories, however uneven, fragmented, and contradictory, illustrate the multiple and shifting meanings of "community"—a concept that is at once firmly rooted in geography, kinships, and friendships and unstable and fluid—shaped by changing personal desires as much as by structural forces.

Race and ethnic relations as practiced in daily life both within and across class divides and between men and women were part of the process of community formation that would continue after the 1930s. Restaurants, shops, and drinking establishments would continue to serve diverse clienteles. Prostitution, the drug trade, and municipal corruption continued despite efforts by anti-vice organizations to crack down on illegal activities. After World War II, a shift in cultural attitudes resulted in a set of different approaches to eradicate social ills. Gone were the private anti-vice organizations and the sensationalist public acts by clerical leaders. The New Deal had introduced a larger role for government in solving social problems. By the 1960s, social welfare workers, the clergy, and municipal government sought different approaches, under new guidelines from the federal government, to eliminate wide-scale problems such as poverty, crime, and addiction.

Settlement houses and missions, which had come under intense scrutiny and criticism by Jewish and Catholic leaders, some reformers, and local populations, would find a place in changing times. Many continued to operate in what would remain working-class neighborhoods into the late twentieth century, weathering the hardships brought on by national and international crises, while others eventually disbanded. By the 1960s, a number of settlements had moved out of southern Manhattan to other parts of the city. Christodora House, for example, began renting space in its building during the Great Depression to sustain itself financially. The settlement eventually moved to East 53rd Street in midtown Manhattan. The original building lay abandoned until the

1980s, when it became a symbol for gentrification in the area as a high-rise luxury condominium. The Jacob Riis Neighborhood Settlement House relocated to Queens after World War II. For some settlements, such as Christodora House, the evangelical mission by the 1960s would seem anachronistic in an increasingly secular urban renewal movement. Many would become known more for their recreational and civic programs than for proselytizing among non-Protestants.

Systems of inclusion and exclusion did not completely determine people's futures, but they did they present specific kinds of obstacles around which working-class people negotiated to survive and, in some cases, prosper. Ethnic "isolation," therefore, was a partial reality, and nowhere was this more evident than in the daily lives of people who lived, worked, and played in southern Manhattan during the early decades of the twentieth century. As people wove in and out of each other's lives in public and private spaces, interactions could result in fleeting or lasting friendships and solidarity as much as competition, social distancing, and outright hostility.

Momentous forces at the national and international levels that seemed to be out of the hands of most middle- and working-class people—the Great Depression, World War II, postwar demobilization—would also result in a different set of social, economic, and political conditions that would render the "not-quite-white" as "white ethnics" and facilitate geographic mobility out of the poorest sections of New York City to suburbs and farms in northern New Jersey, where second- and third-generation Poles and Italians hoped to prosper. The demographic makeup of southern Manhattan would change in the process. A mix of Chinese, most of whom had come from southern China, and a diverse population of immigrants from Southern and Eastern Europe resided there in the first three decades of the twentieth century. After World War II, new ethnic groups from Taiwan, Korea, Hong Kong, and Latin America began settling in lower Manhattan to begin the process of negotiating cultural and physical space within and across ethnic communities, finding common and uncommon ground again and again. Within this process of change, however, discourses of race, ethnicity, gender, and sexuality have continued to frame the ways in which ordinary people form individual and group identities and construct families and communities.

Notes

INTRODUCTION

1. *New York World*, 2 February 1877; *New York Times*, 29 January 1877 and 1 February 1877.

2. *New York World*, 1 February 1877.

3. For a full account of the riots that deteriorated into a racial conflict, see Iver Bernstein, *The New York City Draft Riots: Their Significance for American Society and Politics in the Age of the Civil War* (New York: Oxford University Press, 1990).

4. John Kuo Wei Tchen, *New York before Chinatown: Orientalism and the Shaping of American Culture, 1776–1882* (Baltimore: Johns Hopkins University Press, 1999), 82–83; *New York Times*, 29 January 1877, 8.

5. After the murder, Tung Ha, Theresa, and their infant son, Thomas, moved and by 1880 were living on Mulberry Street, where they continued to manufacture cigars: *Tenth Census of the United States, 1880, Population*, Borough of Manhattan.

6. Elizabeth Ewen, *Immigrant Women in the Land of Dollars: Life and Culture on the Lower East Side* (New York: Monthly Review Press, 1985), 113–115.

7. *New York World*, 2 February 1877. Kennedy died in 1892. *New York Times*, 26 October 1892, 8. See also Ewen, *Immigrant Women in the Land of Dollars*, 113; Daniel Soyer, *Jewish Immigrant Associations and American Identity in New York, 1880–1939* (Cambridge, Mass.: Harvard University Press, 1997).

8. Arthur Bonner, *Alas! What Brought Thee Hither? The Chinese in New York, 1800–1950* (Madison, N.J.: Fairleigh Dickinson University Press, 1997), 38; *New York World*, 2 February 1877, 2.

9. Jeff Kisseloff, *You Must Remember This: An Oral History of Manhattan from the 1890s to World War II* (New York: Harcourt Brace Jovanovich, 1989), 27; U.S. Bureau of the Census, *Manuscript Schedules of the Population Census*, 1880, 1920, Borough of Manhattan.

10. U.S. Department of Labor, Immigration and Naturalization Services, Chinese Exclusion Act Case Files, box 177, case no. 25/422.0, National Archives and Records Administration, Northeast Region, New York.

11. Selma Berrol, *The Empire City: New York and Its People, 1624–1996* (Westport, Conn.: Praeger, 1997), 84; Frederick M. Binder and David M. Reimers, *All the Nations under Heaven: An Ethnic and Racial History of New York City* (New York: Columbia University Press, 1995), 97–112; Arthur M. Schlesinger, *The Rise of the City, 1878–1898* (New York: Macmillan, 1933), 83.

12. For a more extensive analysis of Italian immigrant residential patterns in New York, see Donna R. Gabaccia, *From Sicily to Elizabeth Street: Housing and Social Change among Italian Immigrants, 1880–1930* (Albany: State University of New York Press, 1984).

13. Lillian W. Betts, "The Italian in New York," *University Settlement Studies and the Eighteenth Annual Report of the University Settlement Society of New York, 1904* (March 1905), 90; Lloyd Morris, *Incredible New York: High Life and Low Life of the Last Hundred Years* (New York: Random House, 1951), 274.

14. Edwin G. Burrows and Mike Wallace, *Gotham: A History of New York City to 1898* (New York: Oxford University Press, 1999), 1117; Joyce Mendelsohn, *The Lower East Side Remembered and Revisited: History and Guide to a Legendary New York Neighborhood* (New York: Lower East Side Press, 2001), 1.

15. David Wickers and Charlotte Atkins, *Essential New York* (Lincolnwood, Ill.: Passport Books, 1994), 12.

16. Israel Zangwill, a London-born writer and activist, used the term "melting pot" to describe the assimilation of European immigrants, in particular, to American society: Maxwell F. Marcuse, *This Was New York! A Nostalgic Picture of Gotham in the Gaslight Era* (New York: LIM Press, 1969), 15.

17. The Page Act was named for Horace F. Page, a Republican Congressman from California, who sponsored the bill. Page was a strong proponent of Chinese exclusion and supported the Chinese Exclusion Act of 1882: Page Act of 1875, Public Law, 43rd Cong., 2nd sess. (3 March 1875); George Anthony Peffer, *If They Don't Bring Their Women Here: Chinese Female Immigration before Exclusion* (Urbana: University of Illinois Press, 1999), 36.

18. *New York Times*, 25 July 1904.

19. Betts, "The Italian in New York," 90; Madison Grant, *The Passing of the Great Race* (New York: C. Scribner's Sons, 1916), 16.

20. Hasia R. Diner, "Introduction to the Transaction Edition," in Louis Wirth, *The Ghetto* (New Brunswick, N.J.: Transaction, 1998), l.

21. Henry Yu, *Thinking Orientals: Migration, Contact, and Exoticism in Modern*

America (New York: Oxford University Press, 2001), 133–134; see Paul C. P. Siu, *The Chinese Laundryman: A Study of Social Isolation* (New York: New York University Press, 1987); Erika Lee, *At America's Gates: Chinese Immigration during the Exclusion Era, 1882–1943* (Chapel Hill: University of North Carolina Press, 2003).

22. Diner, "Introduction," xxxii–xxxvii; John Kuo Wei Tchen, "Editor's Introduction," in Siu, *The Chinese Laundryman,* xxviii–xxx, xxxiv.

23. Yu, *Thinking Orientals,* 203; Pei-Yao Chen, "The 'Isolation' of New York City Chinatown: A Geo-Historical Approach to a Chinese Community in the U.S.," Ph.D. diss., City University of New York, 2003. See also Nayan Shah, *Contagious Divides: Epidemics and Race in San Francisco's Chinatown* (Berkeley: University of California Press, 2001).

24. *Oxford English Dictionary,* 2nd ed. (New York: Clarendon Press, 1989).

25. See Peggy Pascoe, *What Comes Naturally: Miscegenation Law and the Making of Race in America* (New York: Oxford University Press, 2008).

26. Rudolph J. Vecoli, "An Inter-Ethnic Perspective on American Immigration History," *Mid-America* 75 (April–July 1993): 224–225; Susan A. Glenn, *Daughters of the Shtetl: Life and Labor in the Immigrant Generation* (Ithaca, N.Y.: Cornell University Press, 1990), 56.

27. As in other cities in the Northeast, New York's non-white population remained small compared to the population of those with European ancestry. In 1900, Boston's white population numbered 548,083, compared with 11,591 "Negroes," three Indians, and 1,215 Chinese, usually described as "Mongolians." In the same year, 5,069 "Mongolians" resided in the boroughs of Manhattan and the Bronx combined and 1,777 lived in Philadelphia. In 1920, Boston's Chinese population numbered 1,075, while nearly 3,862 resided in Manhattan: U.S. Census, 1900, Population, Boston and Borough of Manhattan.

28. See Glenn, *Daughters of the Shtetl;* Riv-Ellen Prell, "The Ghetto Girl and the Erasure of Memory," in *Remembering the Lower East Side,* ed. Hasia R. Diner, Jeffrey Shandler, and Beth S. Wenger (Bloomington: Indiana University Press, 2000), 86–112; Kathy Peiss, *Cheap Amusements: Working Women and Leisure in Turn-of-the-Century New York* (Philadelphia: Temple University Press, 1986); Kathie Friedman-Kasaba, *Memories of Migration: Gender, Ethnicity, and Work in the Lives of Jewish and Italian Women in New York, 1870–1924* (Albany: State University of New York Press, 1996), chap. 5.

29. See Shah, *Contagious Divides;* George Chauncey, *Gay New York: Gender, Urban Culture, and the Making of the Gay Male World, 1890–1940* (New York: Basic Books, 1994).

30. Ted Merwin, "The Performance of Jewish Ethnicity in Anne Nichols' *Abie's Irish Rose," Journal of American Ethnic History* 20 (Winter 2001): 3–37.

31. *New York Times,* 17 September 1897, 3.

32. William Norr, *Stories of Chinatown: Sketches From the Life in the Chinese Colony on Mott, Pell and Doyers Streets* (New York: W. Norr, 1892), 1. See also Jinhua Emma Teng, "Miscegenation and the Critique of Patriarchy in Turn-of-

the-Century Fiction," in *Asian American Studies: A Reader*, ed. Jean Yu-Wen Shen Wu and Min Song (New Brunswick, N.J.: Rutgers University Press, 2000), 107.

33. Marilyn Halter, *Shopping for Identity: The Marketing of Ethnicity* (New York: Schocken Books, 2000), 37–40.

34. See Mary Ting Yi Liu, *The Chinatown Trunk Mystery: Murder, Miscegenation, and Other Dangerous Encounters in Turn-of-the-Century New York City* (Princeton, N.J.: Princeton University Press, 2005).

35. The term "Lower East Side" came into popular usage after World War II: see Moses Rischin, "Toward the Onomastics of the Great New York Ghetto: How the Lower East Side Got Its Name," in Diner et al., *Remembering the Lower East Side*, 15–18, 22–23.

36. Gold was born Irwin or Isaac M. Granich in 1893 to Bessarabian Jewish immigrants: *New York Times*, 16 May 1967; California Death Index, 1967; Michael Gold, *Jews without Money* (1930), 3rd repr. ed. (New York: Carroll and Graf, 1990), 33, 164.

37. *New York Times*, 29 August 1902; 31 August 1902. Rose Cohen, *Out of the Shadows: A Russian Girlhood on the Lower East Side* (Ithaca, N.Y.: Cornell University Press, 1995), 104–105.

38. Kisseloff, *You Must Remember This*, 49.

39. See Donald Tricarico, "Influence of the Irish on Italian Communal Adaptation in Greenwich Village," *Journal of Ethnic Studies* 13 (Fall 1985): 127–137; James R. Barrett and David R. Roediger, "The Irish and the 'Americanization' of the 'New Immigrants' in the Streets and the Churches of the Urban United States, 1900–1930," *Journal of American Ethnic History* 8 (Summer 2005): 3–33.

40. See Kevin J. Mumford, *Interzones: Black and White Sex Districts in Chicago and New York in the Early Twentieth Century* (New York: Columbia University Press, 1997).

41. Kimberlé Williams Crenshaw, "Mapping the Margins: Intersectionality, Identity Politics, and Violence against Women of Color," *Stanford Law Review* 43 (1991): 1241–1299; Margaret L. Anderson and Patricia Hill Collins, eds., *Race, Class, and Gender: An Anthology* (New York: Wadsworth, 2004), 7.

42. Robert W. De Forest and Lawrence Veiller, eds., *The Tenement House Problem: Including the Report of the New York State Tenement House Commission of 1900 by Various Writers*, 2 vols. (New York: Macmillan, 1903), 1:386–387, 392.

43. See Teal Kristen Rothschild, "Alliances across Skill, Gender, and Ethnicity: A Structural and Identity-Based Analysis of Two Strikes in the New York City Garment Industry, 1885–1921," Ph.D. diss., New School for Social Research, New York, 2001; Daniel Letwin, "Interracial Unionism, Gender, and 'Social Equality' on the Alabama Coalfields, 1878–1908," *Journal of Southern History* 61 (August 1995): 519–554.

44. Matthew Frye Jacobson, *Whiteness of a Different Color: European Immigrants and the Alchemy of Race* (Cambridge, Mass.: Harvard University Press,

1998), 6–11; Noel Ignatiev, *How the Irish Became White* (New York: Routledge, 1995); David R. Roediger, *The Wages of Whiteness: Race and the Making of the American Working Class* (London: Verso, 1991); Karen Brodkin, *How Jews Became White Folks and What That Says about Race in America* (New Brunswick, N.J.: Rutgers University Press, 1998).

45. The *Report of the U.S. Immigration Commission* of 1911 is often referred to simply as the Dillingham report.

46. *Report of the U.S. Immigration Commission*, vol. 2 (1911), 720; *Report of the U.S. Immigration Commission*, vol. 1 (1911), 17–19.

47. *Fourteenth Census of the United States, Population, 1920*, 10.

48. Jacobson, Whiteness of a Different Color, 6.

49. See Gabaccia, *From Sicily to Elizabeth Street*.

50. The Century Dictionary and Cyclopedia with a new Atlas of the World (New York: Century, 1913), 4926.

51. See Peggy Pascoe, "Miscegenation Law, Court Cases, and Ideologies of 'Race' in Twentieth Century America," *Journal of American History* 83 (June 1996): 44–69.

52. See William Z. Ripley, *Races of Europe: A Sociological Study* (London: Kegan Paul, Tench, Trübner, 1899).

53. See Daniel Scott Smith, "The Meanings of Family and Household: Change and Continuity in the Mirror of the American Census," *Population and Development Review* 18 (September 1992): 437.

CHAPTER 1

1. *Fifteenth Census of the United States, 1930, Population*, Borough of Brooklyn.

2. Elizabeth S. Alexander, "For Better or Worse: Marriages across Boundaries," *Journal of Women's History* 19 (Fall 2007): 214; Henry Yu, "Mixing Bodies and Cultures: The Meaning of America's Fascination with Sex between 'Orientals' and 'Whites,'" in *Sex, Love, and Race: Crossing Boundaries in North American History*, ed. Martha Hodes (New York: New York University Press, 1999), 446–447.

3. John Kuo Wei Tchen offers an extensive description of marriages between Irish women and Chinese men in lower Manhattan during the early nineteenth century: see John Kuo Wei Tchen, *New York before Chinatown* (Baltimore: Johns Hopkins University Press, 1999), 77–80. For an analysis of nineteenth-century black–white marriages, see Jane Dabel, "'A Superior Colored Man . . . and a Scotch Woman': Interracial Marriages in New York City, 1850–1870," *International Social Science Review* 80 (Fall–Winter 2005): 87–102.

4. The *New York Times* sometimes spelled the name "Zeigler."

5. See Julius Drachsler, *Intermarriage in New York City: A Statistical Study of the Amalgamation of European Peoples* (New York: Columbia University Press, 1921).

6. Paul C. P. Siu, *The Chinese Laundryman: A Study of Social Isolation* (New York: New York University Press, 1987), 263.

7. Shepard Schwartz, "Mate Selection among New York City's Chinese Males, 1931–38," *American Journal of Sociology* 56 (May 1951): 563.

8. John R. McKivigan and Thomas J. Robertson, "The Irish American Worker in Transition, 1877–1914: New York as a Test Case," in *The New York Irish,* ed. Ronald H. Bayor and Timothy J. Meagher (Baltimore: Johns Hopkins University Press, 1996), 303.

9. Kathleen Sullivan, "Beneath the Surface of Chinatown," unpublished ms., Chinatown History Museum, New York. For a short history of the tenement reform movement and the development of housing codes, see Richard Plunz, *A History of Housing in New York City: Dwelling Type and Social Change in the American Metropolis* (New York: Columbia University Press, 1990), chap. 2.

10. James D. McCabe, Jr., *Lights and Shadows of New York Life; or Sights and Sensations of the Great City* (Philadelphia: National Publishing, 1872), 734; Tchen, *New York before Chinatown,* 83, 227–228.

11. U.S. Census, 1880, Borough of Manhattan.

12. Ibid., 1900.

13. *New York Times,* 19 July 1901, 5; U.S. Census, 1900.

14. *Compendium of the Tenth Census of the United States,* 1880, Population, 3; U.S. Census, 1910, 225, 1920, 676. See also Robert G. Lee, *Orientals: Asian Americans in Popular Culture* (Philadelphia: Temple University Press, 1999), 140–141; Roger Daniels, *Asian America: Chinese and Japanese in the United States since 1850* (Seattle: University of Washington Press, 1988; Paul R. Spickard, *Japanese Americans: The Formation and Transformation of an Ethnic Group* (New York: Twayne, 1996), 49.

15. Arthur E. Wilson to Committee of Fifteen, 1 March 1901, Committee of Fifteen Records, University of Washington, Seattle.

16. U.S. Census, 1900, 1910, 1920, Borough of Manhattan.

17. Arthur Bonner, *Alas! What Brought Thee Hither? The Chinese in New York, 1800–1950* (Madison, N.J.: Fairleigh Dickinson University Press, 1997), 139.

18. Mary Ting Yi Liu, *The Chinatown Trunk Mystery: Murder, Miscegenation, and Other Dangerous Encounters in Turn-of-the-Century New York City* (Princeton, N.J.: Princeton University Press, 2005), 33.

19. U.S. Census, 1930, Borough of Manhattan.

20. See Tchen, *New York before Chinatown,* chap. 5.

21. William Norr, *Stories of Chinatown* (New York: William Norr, 1892), 4.

22. Jacob Riis, *How the Other Half Lives: A Study among the Tenements of New York* (1890), repr. ed. (New York: Dover, 1971), 78.

23. George Washington Walling, *Recollections of a New York Chief of Police* (New York: Caxton Book Concern, 1887), 428.

24. Alfred T. Trumble, *The Mott Street Poker Club: The Secretary's Minutes* (New York: White and Allen, 1888), 45.

25. Liu, *The Chinatown Trunk Mystery*, 47, *New York Times*, 25 August 1909, 9.

26. U.S. Census, 1910, Borough of Manhattan, 1930, Borough of Brooklyn; certificate and record of birth, Maggie Hart, 22 July 1900, State of New York.

27. According to the 1900 federal census, Dominick Franko, an Italian immigrant laborer, and his Scots wife, Annie, constituted the only ethnically mixed household on Cherry Street.

28. Nancy F. Cott, *Public Vows: A History of Marriage and the Nation* (Cambridge, Mass.: Harvard University Press, 2000), 165.

29. *Congressional Record*, 47th Cong., 1st sess., 1882, 13, pt. 3: 2967–2974, 3588; Shawn Obitz, "Tracing Early Chinese Immigration into the U.S.: The Use of INS Documents," *Amerasia Journal* 14 (1988): 39–43. Several offices administered the exclusion law between its passage and the early twentieth century. The administration of the laws first came under the jurisdiction of the Customs Office, then the Office of the Superintendent of Immigration in the Department of the Treasury, which later became the present Immigration and Naturalization Service. During the exclusion period, a Chinese Division was established within the INS to handle the Chinese Exclusion Act cases.

30. See Kitty Calavita, "The Paradoxes of Race, Class, Identity, and 'Passing': Enforcing the Chinese Exclusion Acts, 1882–1910," *Law and Social Inquiry* 24 (1999): 1–40.

31. Gilbert may have been the "Harry Gilbert" listed in the 1920 Census as a manager of a grocery store: U.S. Census, 1920, Borough of Manhattan.

32. Albert B. Wiley to F. S. Pierce, Inspector in Charge, 17 February 1921, Chinese Exclusion Act Case Files, box 184, case no. 25/710, National Archives and Records Administration, Northeast Region, New York.

33. U.S. Census, 1900, 1910, Nassau County, N.Y.

34. Gail Bouknight-Davis "Chinese Economic Development and Ethnic Identity Formation in Jamaica," in *The Chinese in the Caribbean*, ed. Andrew R. Wilson (Princeton, N.J.: Markus Wiener, 2004), 72.

35. Calvin B. Holder, "The Causes and Composition of West Indian Immigration to New York City, 1900–1952," Afro-Americans in New York Life and History (January 1987): 8; Andrew W. Lind, "Adjustment Patterns among the Jamaican Chinese," *Social and Economic Studies* 7 (June 1958): 152; U.S. Census, 1930, Borough of Brooklyn.

36. See Matthew Pratt Guterl, "After Slavery: Asian Labor, the American South, and the Age of Emancipation," *Journal of World History* 14 (June 2003): 209–241; Lucy M. Cohen, "Entry of the Chinese to the Lower South, 1865 to 1870: Policy Dilemmas," *Southern Studies* 2 (Fall–Winter 1991): 281–313; "The Shopkeepers: Commemorating 150 of the Chinese in Jamaica," *Jamaica Journal* 28 (December 2004): 68.

37. See Li Anshan, "Survival, Adaptation and Integration: Origins and Evolution of the Chinese Community in Jamaica: Origins and Evolution of the

Chinese Community in Jamaica (1854–1962), in Wilson, *The Chinese in the Caribbean*, 41–68; Bouknight-Davis, "Chinese Economic Development and Ethnic Identity Formation in Jamaica," 41–71.

38. Lind, "Adjustment Patterns among the Jamaican Chinese," 152; Bouknight-Davis, "Chinese Economic Development and Ethnic Identity Formation in Jamaica," 83.

39. Ching Chieh Chang, "The Chinese in Latin America: A Preliminary Geographical Survey with Special Reference to Cuba and Jamaica," Ph.D. diss., University of Maryland, College Park, 1956, 129–130.

40. U.S. Census, 1930, Borough of Brooklyn; Loring P. Eutemey to the author, 29 March 2005; Lind, "Adjustment Patterns among the Jamaican Chinese," 151; Samuel J. Hurwitz and Edith F. Hurwitz, *Jamaica: A Historical Portrait* (New York: Praeger, 1971), 162. See also Walton Look Lai, *Indentured Labor, Caribbean Sugar: Chinese and Indian Migrants to the British West Indies, 1838–1918* (Baltimore: Johns Hopkins University Press, 1993).

41. Patrick Bryan, *The Jamaican People, 1880–1902: Race, Class, and Social Control* (London: Macmillan, 1991), 83; Mervyn C. Alleyne, *The Construction and Representation of Race and Ethnicity in the Caribbean and the World* (Kingston, Jamaica: University of the West Indies Press, 2002), 205, 214; Lind, "Adjustment Patterns among the Jamaican Chinese," 151, 155–161; Lee Tom Yin, *The Chinese in Jamaica*, 2nd ed. (Kingston, Jamaica: Chung Sun News, 1963), 45.

42. Lee, *The Chinese in Jamaica*, 24.

43. Alleyne, *The Construction and Representation of Race and Ethnicity*, 7.

44. Available online at http://www.ancestry.com (accessed 5 January 2007).

45. Craig Steven Wilder, *A Covenant with Color: Race and Social Power in Brooklyn* (New York: Columbia University Press, 2000), 124–125.

46. Draft registration card for Bert Val Eutemey, available online at http://www.ancestry.com (accessed 5 January 2007).

47. The number of blacks in Brooklyn had increased during the early twentieth century but remained small compared with the white population. For example, in 1920 the "Negro" population in the borough numbered 31,912, a third of Manhattan's black population yet the second largest of all five boroughs. By 1930, the number of blacks in Brooklyn had more than doubled. The native-born and foreign-born white populations were much more numerous in Brooklyn: 1.3 million and 659,287, respectively. Black churches served as an important locus for social and political networks: see Clarence Taylor, *The Black Churches of Brooklyn* (New York: Columbia University Press, 1994).

48. U.S. Census, 1880, 1910, 1920, 1930, Borough of Brooklyn.

49. *Fifteenth Census of the United States, 1930, Population,* Borough of Brooklyn.

50. The Manhattan Bridge began construction in 1901 and opened in 1909, connecting western Brooklyn with Manhattan.

51. Elliot Willensky, *When Brooklyn Was the World, 1920–1957* (New York: Harmony Books, 1986), 63.

52. See Ralph Foster Weld, *Brooklyn Is America* (New York: Columbia University Press, 1950), 2–3, 93–94; Edwin G. Burrows and Mike Wallace, *Gotham: A History of New York City to 1898* (New York: Oxford University Press, 1999), 1228.

53. By 1930, ten years after Margaret's marriage, her father, Dominick, his second wife, Margaret, and two remaining daughters had moved from Third Avenue in Manhattan to Brooklyn.

54. Allison Giffen and June Hopkins, eds., *Jewish First Wife, Divorced: The Correspondence of Ethel Gross and Harry Hopkins* (Lanham, Md.: Lexington Books, 2002), 3–4.

55. June Hopkins, *Harry Hopkins: Sudden Hero, Brash Reformer* (New York: St. Martin's Press, 1999), 11–15. See also Eleanor J. Stebner, "More than Maternal Feminists and Good Samaritans: Women and the Social Gospel in Canada," in *Gender and the Social Gospel,* ed. Wendy J. Deichmann Edwards and Carolyn DeSwarte Gifford (Urbana: University of Illinois Press, 2003), 53–67.

56. "Grinnell College History," available online at http://www.grinnell.edu (accessed 6 July 2005).

57. U.S. Census, 1900, Chicago; *New York Times,* 30 January 1946, 19.

58. The Ethical Culture Movement was one of several religious movements that emerged out of growing criticism of Protestantism during the late nineteenth century. Adler and other Social Gospelites argued that "true" religion should not be confined to the intellectual sphere, but that Protestantism should take an active role in addressing social problems: see Charles Howard Hopkins, *The Rise of the Social Gospel in American Protestantism, 1865–1915* (New Haven, Conn.: Yale University Press, 1940), 57–58.

59. For an early analysis of interethnic marriages of white ethnics, see Drachsler, *Intermarriage in New York City;* Riv-Ellen Prell, *Fighting to Become Americans: Jews, Gender, and the Anxiety of Assimilation* (Boston: Beacon, 1999), 67–73.

60. David Blaustein, *Memoirs of David Blaustein: Educator and Communal Worker* (New York: McBride, Nast, 1913), 3, 221.

61. Prell, *Fighting to Become Americans,* 73–77; Bayor and Meagher, *The New York Irish,* 7; Charles Musser, "Ethnicity, Role Playing, and American Film Comedy: From Chinese Laundry to Whoopee, 1894–1930," in *Unspeakable Images: Ethnicity and the American Cinema,* ed. Lester Friedman (Urbana: University of Illinois Press, 1991), 58.

62. Harry Hopkins to Ethel Gross, 26 March 1913, as cited in Giffen and Hopkins, *Jewish First Wife, Divorced,* 58.

63. Ethel Gross to Harry Hopkins, 17 March 1913, as cited in ibid., 49.

64. Ethel Gross to Harry Hopkins, 12 March 1913, as cited in ibid., 49–50.

65. Harry Hopkins to Ethel Gross, postmarked 22 April 1913, as cited in ibid., 82.

66. Ethel Gross to Harry Hopkins, postmarked 7 May 1913, as cited in ibid., 90.

67. Harry Hopkins to Ethel Gross, March 1913, as cited in ibid., 44, 54, 60.

68. Ibid., 19; Hopkins, *Harry Hopkins,* 146.

CHAPTER 2

1. Arthur Bonner, *Alas! What Brought Thee Hither? The Chinese in New York, 1800–1950* (Madison, N.J.: Fairleigh Dickinson University Press, 1997), 71.

2. Chinese Exclusion Act Case Files, box 25, case no. 697.1, National Archives and Records Administration, Northeast Region, New York.

3. Edwin G. Burrows and Mike Wallace, *Gotham: A History of New York City to 1898* (New York: Oxford University Press, 1999), 478; Tyler Anbinder, *Five Points: The Nineteenth-Century New York City Neighborhood That Invented Tap Dance, Stole Elections, and Became the World's Most Notorious Slum* (New York: Penguin, 2001), 436–437; Mary Ting Yi Liu, *The Chinatown Trunk Mystery: Murder, Miscegenation, and Other Dangerous Encounters in Turn-of-the-Century New York City* (Princeton, N.J.: Princeton University Press, 2005), 46–48; John Kuo Wei Tchen, *New York before Chinatown* (Baltimore: Johns Hopkins University Press, 1999), 77–79; Timothy J. Gilfoyle, *City of Eros: New York City, Prostitution, and the Commercialization of Sex, 1790–1920* (New York: W. W. Norton, 1992), 218–219.

4. See Madelon Powers, *Faces along the Bar: Lore and Order in the Workingman's Saloon, 1870–1920* (Chicago: University of Chicago Press, 1998.

5. Mansel G. Blackford, *A History of Small Business in America*, 2nd ed. (Chapel Hill: University of North Carolina Press, 2003), 71.

6. Ivan H. Light, *Ethnic Enterprise in America: Business and Welfare among Chinese, Japanese, and Blacks* (Berkeley: University of California Press, 1972), 15–16. Rose Hum Lee cites the limited occupational opportunities open to the Chinese as one factor that led to the decline of Chinese communities in cities that contained native populations of fewer than 50,000 and relied on single industries for survival: Rose Hum Lee, "The Decline of Chinatowns in the United States," *American Journal of Sociology* 54 (March 1949): 425. Proprietors of Chinese restaurants took the lead in promoting the tourist industry in Chinatowns throughout the United States, which involved a collective effort to curb vice trafficking in opium and sex: see Ivan H. Light, "From Vice District to Tourist Attraction: The Moral Career of American Chinatowns, 1880–1940," *Pacific Historical Review* 43 (1974): 367–394; Marlene Pitkow, "A Temple for Tourists in New York's Chinatown," *Journal of American Culture* 10 (Summer 1987): 112; S. W. Kung, *The Chinese in American Life: Some Aspects of Their History, Status, Problems, and Contributions* (Westport, Conn.: Greenwood Press, 1962), 57.

7. Yong Chen, *Chinese San Francisco: A Trans-Pacific Community, 1850–1943* (Stanford, Calif.: Stanford University Press, 2000), 197–198; Donna R. Gabaccia,

We Are What We Eat: Ethnic Food and the Making of Americans (Cambridge, Mass.: Harvard University Press, 1998), 66–67.

8. U.S. Census, 1900, Borough of Manhattan.

9. Tchen, *New York before Chinatown*, 82–83.

10. Peter Kwong, *Chinatown Labor and Politics, 1880–1930* (New York: New Press, 2001), 83–84.

11. U.S. Census, 1930, Borough of Manhattan; see also Shepard Schwartz, "Mate-Selection among New York City's Chinese Males, 1931–38," *American Journal of Sociology* 56 (May 1951): 563.

12. Evelyn Nakano Glenn, *Unequal Freedom: How Race and Gender Shaped Citizenship and Labor* (Cambridge, Mass.: Harvard University Press, 2002), 20.

13. The term "merchant" was used quite loosely after the passage of the Chinese Exclusion Act, which restricted the admission of male "laborers" into the United States. "Merchant" basically included any man who was not classified as a "laborer" and who usually had entered into a business partnership with other Chinese men through the Chinese Consolidated Benevolent Association. Louis Beck counted seven Chinese farms in the New York City areas of Flatbush and Astoria (Queens Borough): see Louis J. Beck, *New York's Chinatown: An Historical Presentation of Its People and Places* (New York: Bohemia Publishing, 1898), 86; Jesse Lynch Williams, *New York Sketches* (New York: C. Scribner's Sons, 1902), 122–123; "Chinese Farm to Give Way to a Golf Course," *Newtown (N.Y.) Register*, 3 August 1916, 3; see also Mary Beth Burke, *Queens County Agriculture of the Nineteenth Century: Kitchen and Herb Gardens, Chinese Truck Farms* (New York: City University of New York, 1993), 34–37; Chen Hsiang-Shui and John Kuo Wei Tchen, "A History of the Chinese in Queens," *Queens Tribune*, 25 June 1992, 47.

14. Light, *Ethnic Enterprise in America*, 7–8; Kung, *The Chinese in American Life*, 182.

15. Michael and Anne Batterberry, *On the Town in New York from 1776 to the Present* (New York: Charles Scribner's Sons, 1973), 72; Richard McDermott, "The Oldest Building in New York City Known to Have Once House a Black-Owned Business," *New York Journal of American History* 66 (2005): 72–73; John H. Hewitt, "Mr. Downing and His Oyster House: The Life and Good Works of an African-American Entrepreneur," *New York History* (July 1993): 229, 233.

16. Gabaccia, *We Are What We Eat*, 102.

17. Anbinder, *Five Points*, 357.

18. Port Arthur and the Chinese Tuxedo both opened in 1897: Jacob Riis, *How the Other Half Lives: A Study among the Tenements of New York* (1890), repr. ed. (New York: Dover, 1971), 60–61; Daniel Ostrow, *Manhattan's Chinatown* (New York: Arcadia, 2008), 11, 59; Bonner, *Alas!* 152.

19. It was not uncommon for Caucasian women to work in Chinese restaurants. Margaret Hart Wong worked as a cashier in her husband's restaurant on Doyers Street during the 1920s: telephone conversations with James Wong, 1997–2000, and Chinese Exclusion Act Case Files, box 71, case no. 12/1048.

20. Allan Forman, "Celestial Gotham," *Arena* 7 (April 1893): 622.

21. Negative images of Chinese cuisine had permeated American culture since the early nineteenth century in such venues as minstrel shows, newspaper articles and cartoons, and film. For scholarship that focuses specifically on this theme, see Robert G. Lee, *Orientals: Asian Americans in Popular Culture* (Philadelphia: Temple University Press, 1999), 38–39, 41; Hasia R. Diner, *Hungering for America: Italian, Irish, and Jewish Foodways in the Age of Migration* (Cambridge, Mass.: Harvard University Press, 2001), 205.

22. Stephen Graham, *New York Nights* (New York: George Doran, 1927), 179.

23. Kung, *The Chinese in American Life*, 181–182.

24. Beck, *New York City's Chinatown*, 326.

25. George Hanson Towne, *This New York of Mine* (New York: Cosmopolitan Book, 1931), 266.

26. *New York Tribune*, 3 February 1901, illustrated supp.

27. *Evening Post*, 29 December 1900.

28. James Weldon Johnson, *Autobiography of an Ex-Coloured Man* (1912; repr., New York: Avon, 1965), 446.

29. Jenna Weissman Joselit, *The Wonders of America: Reinventing Jewish Culture, 1880–1950* (New York: Hill and Wang, 1994), 214; Gabaccia, *We Are What We Eat*, 104.

30. Gaye Tuchman and Harry Gene Levine, "New York Jews and Chinese Food: The Social Construction of an Ethnic Pattern," in *The Taste of American Place: A Reader on Regional and Ethnic Foods*, ed. Barbara G. Shortridge and James R. Shortridge (New York: Rowman and Littlefield, 1998), 168–172.

31. Elliot Willensky, *When Brooklyn Was the World, 1920–1957* (New York: Harmony Books, 1986), 194–195.

32. *New York Tribune*, 3 February 1901.

33. James W. Loewen, *The Mississippi Chinese: Between White and Black* (Cambridge, Mass.: Harvard University Press, 1971), 60; Robert Seto Quan, *Lotus among the Magnolias: The Mississippi Chinese* (Jackson: University Press of Mississippi, 1982), 53.

34. Louis H. Chu, "The Chinese Restaurant," master's thesis, New York University, 1939, 54–55.

35. Beck, *New York's Chinatown*, 86, 325; *Evening Post*, 29 December 1900.

36. Paul Louie Fletcher, "The Chinese Wholesale Shirt Laundries of New York," *Management Research News* 25 (2002): 19.

37. Application for naturalization, 16 October 1878, available online at http://www.ancestry.com (accessed 12 June 2003).

38. *City Directory of New York, 1890*, available online at http://www.ancestry.com; U.S. Census, 1900, Borough of Manhattan.

39. *Tenth and Twelfth Census of the United States, 1880–1900, Occupations*; see also Carol Pernicone Groneman, "'The Bloody Ould Sixth': A Social Analysis of a Mid-Nineteenth Century Working Class Community," Ph.D. diss., University of Rochester, 1986, 114–115.

40. U.S. Census, 1880, 1900, Boroughs of Manhattan and the Bronx.

41. Chinese Exclusion Act Case Files, box 174, case no. 25/254.1, box 165, case no. 2/128.

42. Federal Writers' Project, *The Italians of New York: A Survey* (New York: Random House, 1938), 73; Donna R. Gabaccia, *From Sicily to Elizabeth Street: Housing and Social Change among Italian Immigrants, 1880–1930* (Albany: State University of New York Press, 1984), 66–67.

43. Chinese Exclusion Act Case Files, 1922; U.S. Census, Population, 1920, 1930, Borough of Manhattan. Although Frank Anthony Buonocore Jr. opened his own store selling "fine groceries and rare fruit" on Seventh Avenue in the early 1920s, by 1930 he had left the grocery business and moved his family uptown to West 115th Street: *New York Times*, 15 November 1921, 39.

44. In 1902, Spaduzzi served as a witness on behalf of Coppola when the latter applied for naturalization. U.S. Census, 1920, Borough of Manhattan, 1900, Borough of Brooklyn; application for naturalization, 18 April 1902, available online at http://www.ancestry.com (accessed 30 March 2011).

45. Chinese Exclusion Act Case Files, box 165, case no. 24/1393; U.S. Census, 1910, 1930, Borough of Manhattan.

46. Light, *Ethnic Enterprise in America*, 10–12, 15–16; idem, "From Vice Districts to Tourist Attraction," 385.

47. See Ernest R. May and John K. Fairbank, eds., *America's China Trade in Historical Perspective: The Chinese and American Performance* (Cambridge, Mass.: Harvard University Press, 1986).

48. Adam Gimbel began his department store enterprise in the Midwest. By 1910, he had established a store in New York City. In 1923, he purchased Saks: *New York Times*, 9 June 1920. See also Jan Whitaker, *Service and Style: How the American Department Store Fashioned the Middle Class* (New York: St. Martin's Press, 2006); Mari Yoshihara, *Embracing the East: White Women and American Orientalism* (New York: Oxford University Press, 2003), 31–33; Leon Harris, *Merchant Princes* (New York: Harper and Row, 1979), 71–72, 74–75.

49. See Timothy B. Spears, *One Hundred Years on the Road: The Traveling Salesman in American Culture* (New Haven, Conn.: Yale University Press, 1995).

50. Meyer resided in Manhattan, first on Henry Street and, by 1920, uptown on 125th Street, both predominantly Jewish neighborhoods: Chinese Exclusion Act Case Files, box 169/306; U.S. Census, 1880, 1920, Population, Borough of Manhattan; Chinese Exclusion Act Case Files, box 192, case no. 25/1117.1, 1921–1922.

51. See Thomas Kessner, *The Golden Door: Italian and Jewish Immigrant Mobility in New York City, 1880–1915* (New York: Oxford University Press, 1977).

52. Ibid., 15; "Statistics of Occupations," U.S. Census, 1900, Boroughs of Manhattan and the Bronx.

53. U.S. Census, 1900, Borough of Manhattan.

54. John Stewart Burgess, "A Study of the Characteristics of the Cantonese Merchants in Chinatown, New York, as Shown by Their Use of Leisure Time," master's thesis, Columbia University, New York, 1909, 2.

55. *Fourteenth Census of the United States, 1924, State Compendium, New York.*

56. By "preference," Storey referred to the practice of Chinese inspectors who gave women children priority in terms of considering their cases, not preference regarding actual admission, where Chinese women were scrutinized closely out of fear that they were entering the country for "immoral" purposes: James V. Storey to Chin You Jung, New York City, 10 July 1923, Chinese Exclusion Act Case Files, box 74, case no. 12/1180.

57. Julie R. Winch, *A Gentleman of Color: The Life of James Forten* (New York: Oxford University Press, 2002), 75–76, 84–85, 298; idem, "'A Person of Good Character and Considerable Property': James Forten and the Issue of Race in Philadelphia's Antebellum Business Community," *Business History Review* 75 (Summer 2001): 275.

58. Out of a total of 20,071 deliverymen, 13,017 were native-born white and 6,505 were foreign-born white: *State Compendium, New York*, U.S. Census, 1920 (1924), 90–91; Chinese Exclusion Act Case Files, Bartels–1922, box 38, case no. 6/1772; *Twelfth Census, Special Reports, Occupations*, 642; the occupation of "commercial broker" appeared in the 1920 New York State Census reports. Among insurance agents, 11,815 were native-born white and 4,652 were foreign-born white out of a total of 16, 510: U.S. Census, 1920, Borough of Manhattan.

59. In 1930, nearly 45 percent of employed Chinese men worked in some form of restaurant job: see Schwartz, "Mate Selection among New York City's Chinese Males," 563.

60. Shih-Shan Henry Tsai, *The Chinese Experience in America* (Bloomington: Indiana University Press, 1986), 105; Paul C. P. Siu, *The Chinese Laundryman: A Study of Social Isolation* (New York: New York University Press, 1987), 41–42, 84.

61. *Murphy's New York City Business Directory* (New York: National Directory, 1888), 249–251; *New York Times*, 21 April 1888, 8.

62. *New York Times*, 9 January 1884.

63. Renqiu Yu, *To Save China, to Save Ourselves: The Chinese Hand Laundry Alliance of New York* (Philadelphia: Temple University Press, 1992), 34.

64. Siu, *The Chinese Laundryman*, 10–13; Ronald T. Takaki, *Strangers from a Different Shore: A History of Asian Americans* (New York: Penguin, 1989), 241; John Haddad, "The Laundry Man's Got a Knife!" in *Chinese America: History and Perspectives* (2001): para. 18–19.

65. Siu, *The Chinese Laundryman*, 84–85, 265–271, 280.

66. Bonner, *Alas!* 105; Yu, *To Save China*, 119–122; Kwong, *Chinatown*, 87.

67. Batterberry and Batterberry, *On the Town in New York*, 148–149.

68. See Roger E. Kislingbury, *Saloons, Bars, Cigar Stores: Historical Interior Photographs* (Pasadena, Calif.: Waldo and Van Winkle, 1999).

69. "Statistics of Occupations," U.S. Census, 1890, Population, New York, 704–705, 1900, Population, Boroughs of Manhattan and the Bronx, 642–643.

70. Batterberry and Batterberry, *On the Town in New York*, 149–150.

71. Raymond Calkins, *Substitutes for the Saloon* (New York: Houghton Mifflin, 1901), 2, 5.

72. *Twelfth and Thirteen Censuses of the United States, 1900, 1910, Population*, Borough of Manhattan. See Jeremy P. Felt, "Vice Reform as a Political Technique: The Committee of Fifteen in New York, 1900–1901," *New York History* 54 (January 1973): 24–51.

73. Sharon V. Salinger, *Taverns and Drinking in Early America* (Baltimore: Johns Hopkins University Press, 2002), 132, 226–227; George Chauncey, *Gay New York: Gender, Urban Culture, and the Making of the Gay Male World, 1890–1940* (New York: Basic Books, 1994).

74. Graham Hodges, "'Desirable Companions and Lovers': Irish and African Americans in the Sixth Ward, 1830–1870," in *The New York Irish*, ed. Ronald H. Bayor and Timothy J. Meagher (Baltimore: Johns Hopkins University Press, 1996), 109.

75. Powers, *Faces along the Bar*, 145; see also Luc Sante, *Low Life: Lures and Snares of Old New York* (New York: Farrar, Straus, and Giroux, 1991), chap. 2.

CHAPTER 3

1. In 1900, the census lumped midwives and nurses into one category. In that year, the census counted 1,835 Irish, 1,109 German, 62 Italian, 33 Polish, and 155 Russian women as "midwives and nurses" in Manhattan and the Bronx; U.S. Census, 1900, Boroughs of Manhattan and the Bronx; Lawrence G. Miller, "Pain, Parturition, and the Profession: Twilight Sleep in America," in *Health Care in America*, ed. Susan Reverby and David Rosner (Philadelphia: Temple University Press, 1979), 29; Francis Kobrin, "American Midwifery Controversy: A Crisis of Professionalization," *Bulletin of the History of Medicine* 40 (1966): 350–363; Regina Markell Morantz-Sanchez, *Sympathy and Science: Women Physicians in American Medicine* (New York: Oxford University Press, 1985), 297.

2. Lena Dufton, *History of Nursing at the New York Post-Graduate Medical School and Hospital* (New York: Alumni Association, 1944), Jane E. Mottus, *New York Nightingales: The Emergence of the Nursing Profession at Bellevue and New York Hospital, 1850–1920* (Ann Arbor: Research Press, 1981), 96–97, 163.

3. M. Elizabeth Carnegie, *The Path We Tread: Blacks in Nursing Worldwide, 1854–1994*, 3rd ed. (New York: National League for Nursing Press, 1995), 24; Susan Reverby, *Ordered to Care: The Dilemma of American Nursing, 1850–1945* (Cambridge: Cambridge University Press, 1987), 80; Sharon Sachs, ed., *Sentimental Women Need Not Apply*, documentary film, Direct Cinema, Santa Monica, Calif., 1990; Darlene Clark Hine, *Black Women in White: Racial Confict and Cooperation in the Nursing Profession, 1890–1950* (Bloomington: Indiana University Press, 1989), 147–150.

4. P. Berman, "Mary Maud Brewster," *American Journal of Nursing* 110 (August 2010): 62–63.

5. Mary Adelaide Nutting served as superintendent of murses at Johns Hopkins University and then at Columbia University: *Thirteenth Census of the United States, 1900, Population*, Baltimore; Karen Buhler-Wilkerson, *No Place like Home: A History of Nursing and Home Care in the United States* (Baltimore: Johns Hopkins University Press, 2001), 106–107.

6. Alan M. Kraut, *Silent Travelers: Germs, Genes, and the "Immigrant Menace"* (New York: Basic Books, 1994), 107.

7. Buhler-Wilkerson, *No Place like Home*, 107–108.

8. In the boroughs of Manhattan and the Bronx combined, there were 3,151 of this group, compared with 1,418 foreign white men and 48 "colored" men, of whom 27 were "Negroes." The remaining 21 "colored" physicians were listed as "Japanese or Chinese." The Chinese in this group would have included only native-born men of Chinese descent, given the state citizenship laws restricting medical licenses to citizens: Milton R. Konvitz, *The Alien and The Asiatic in American Law* (Ithaca, N.Y.: Cornell University Press, 1946), 178, 196–197, 203.

9. Moses Rischin spells James's name Harrie Abijah James, but in the U.S. manuscript census, his name appears as Harry James: Moses Rischin, *The Promised City: New York's Jews, 1870–1914* (Cambridge, Mass.: Harvard University Press, 1962), 71.

10. *Hunt's New York City Directory* (New York: Hunt Publishing, 1890); *New York Times*, 7 August 1892, 17; *New York Herald*, 13 March 1892, 12. Edson was called on to handle the typhus epidemic, which mainly targeted Russian Jewish immigrants who had arrived in New York City on the *S.S. Massilia* in January 1892: Howard Markel, *Quarantine! Eastern European Jewish Immigrants and the New York City Epidemics of 1892* (Baltimore: Johns Hopkins University Press, 1997), 44.

11. Out of 9,449 physicians and surgeons in New York City, 2,932 were men of foreign white or mixed parentage and 3,025 were immigrant whites: U.S. Census, 1920, Population, Occupations by State, 1160.

12. Rischin, *The Promised City*, 72–73.

13. U.S. Census, 1910, 1930, Borough of Manhattan (1910), 1920, Borough of the Bronx. According to witness testimony for the readmission of Lung Som Moy, Schlansky had attended Moy's birth: Chinese Exclusion Act Case Files, box 177, case no. 25/422, National Archives and Records Administration, Northeast Region, New York; World War I draft registration card for Harry Philip Schlansky, 1917–1918; U.S. Census, 1900, 1910, Population, Borough of Manhattan.

14. *New York Times*, 29 December 1890, 1.

15. Ibid., 20 May 1929, 23.

16. Louis J. Beck, *New York's Chinatown: An Historical Presentation of Its People and Places* (New York: Bohemia Publishing, 1898), 206–208; Arthur Bonner, *Alas! What Brought Thee Hither? The Chinese in New York, 1800–1950* (Madison, N.J.: Fairleigh Dickinson University Press, 1997), 124; E. Clowes Chorley, *The Centennial History of Saint Bartholomew's Church in the City of New York* (New York: Episcopalian Church, 1935), 221.

17. *Jin Fuey Moy v. United States*, 254 U.S. 189 (1920). David F. Musto, *The American Disease: Origins of Narcotic Control* (New York: Oxford University Press, 1987), 129–130; Arthur W. Hafner, ed., *Directory of Deceased American Physicians, 1804–1929: A Geneaological Guide to over 149,000 Medical Practitioners*, vol 2 (Chicago: American Medical Association, 1993), 1120.

18. See John C. Burnham, *Bad Habits: Drinking, Smoking, Taking Drugs, Gambling, Sexual Misbehavior, and Swearing in American History* (New York: New York University Press, 1993).

19. Gregory Yee Mark, "Opium in America and the Chinese," *Chinese America: History and Perspectives* (1997): 62.

20. *Jin Fuey Moy v. United States*.

21. Kraut, *Silent Travelers*, 222.

22. Beck, *New York's Chinatown*, 64–65.

23. For a more extensive examination of the role of Chinese herbalists in the United States, see Haiming Liu, "Chinese Herbalists in the United States," in *Chinese American Transnationalism*, ed. Sucheng Chan (Philadelphia: Temple University Press, 2006), 136–155.

24. Judy Yung, *Chinese Women of America: A Pictorial History* (Seattle: University of Washington Press, 1986), 120.

25. Undated report, Lillian Wald Papers, New York Public Library.

26. *New York Times*, 31 May 1896, 24.

27. Ibid., 9 December 1906, 6.

28. Ibid.

29. Ibid., 16 July 1882, 8; James Joseph Walsh, *History of Medicine in New York: Three Centuries of Medical Progress*, vol. 3 (New York: National Americana Society, 1919), 786.

30. Daniel Soyer, *Jewish Immigrant Associations and American Identity in New York, 1880–1939* (Cambridge, Mass.: Harvard University Press, 1997), 150–151.

31. In 1912, Italian Hospital moved farther north along the East River to 83rd and 84th streets: Mary Louise Sullivan, "Mother Cabrini: Missionary to Italian Immigrants," *U.S. Catholic Historian* 6 (Fall 1987): 265–279; Walsh, *History of Medicine*, 787, 791–792.

32. *Twelfth Census of the United States, 1900*; Sullivan, "Mother Cabrini," 270.

33. Robert Coit Chapin, *The Standard of Living among Workingmen's Families in New York City* (New York: Charities Publication, 1909), 191–194.

34. Louise Boland More, *Wage Earners' Budgets: A Study of Standards and Costs of Living in New York City* (New York: Henry Holt, 1907), 144–145; *New York Times*, 8 March 1903; George Enrico Pozzetta, "The Italians of New York City, 1880–1914," Ph.D. diss., Duke University, Durham, N.C., 1971, 244.

35. House Committee on Public Works and Transportation, Hearings before the Subcommittee on Public Buildings and Grounds, *The Foley Square Construction Project and the Historic African Burial Ground, New York, N.Y.*, 102nd Cong., 2nd

sess., 27 July 1992 and 24 September 1992. See also Leslie M. Harris, *In the Shadows of Slavery: African Americans in New York City, 1626–1863* (Chicago: University of Chicago Press, 2003), 1–2. I borrow the term "absent presence" from Caroline Chung Simpson, *An Absent Presence: Japanese Americans in Postwar American Culture, 1945–1960* (Durham, N.C.: Duke University Press, 2001).

36. Slave men who were able to learn carpentry skills provided coffins for plantation households, including the slave quarters. Such skills were a valuable asset to the community in the North: *Freedom's Journal* (September 1828). Juliet E. K. Walker, *The History of Black Business in America: Capitalism, Race, Entrepreneurship*, vol. 1 (Chapel Hill: University of North Carolina Press, 2009), 148; Charlton D. McIlwain, *Death in Black and White: Death, Ritual, and Family Ecology* (Cresskill, N.J.: Hampton Press, 2003), 37–42.

37. Rhoda Golden Freeman, *The Free Negro in New York City in the Era before the Civil War* (New York: Garland, 1994), 337.

38. This imbalance continued into the late twentieth century: see Karla F. C. Holloway, *Passed On: African American Mourning Stories* (Durham, N.C.: Duke University Press, 2002), 17, 38–40.

39. For example, R. C. Scott and A. D. Price serviced the large African American population in Richmond, Virginia, in the early twentieth century: see Michael A. Plater, *African-American Entrepreneurship in Richmond, 1890–1940: The Story of R. C. Scott* (New York: Garland, 1996).

40. Out of an aggregate number of 2,986 undertakers in the State of New York in 1900, 16 were classified as "colored," compared with 1,282 native-born white (with native-born parents), 1,208 native-born white (with foreign-born parents), and 480 foreign-born white. No women were listed in any of these ethnic/racial categories: U.S. Census, 1920, Special Reports, 64. The official definition of "colored" remained in subsequent census reports: see *Abstract of the Fourteenth Census of the United States, 1920* (Washington, D.C.: U.S. Government Printing Office, 1923), 14.

41. Holloway, *Passed On*, 21.

42. The participation of blacks during the yellow fever crisis brought mixed responses from whites in the city. At first, the free black community received praise for its work, and some slaves who provided assistance gained their freedom as a result. Tensions, however, soon followed. Some white Philadelphians, such as the reformer Matthew Carey, accused Jones and Allen of profiting from the venture and overcharging for their services. In a published address to the people of Philadelphia, Jones and Allen defended their actions, claiming that they had actually gone into debt by the time the crisis was over. Violence and threats of violence by whites against blacks who attempted to remove corpses also occurred: Richard Allen and Absalom Jones, *A Narrative of the Proceedings of the Black People, during the Late and Awful Calamity in Philadelphia, in the Year 1793, and a Refutation of Some Censures, Thrown upon Them in Some Late Publications* (Philadelphia: Rhistoric Publications, 1969), 20.

43. *Census of the United States, 1880, Population, New York*; Maxwell F. Marcuse, *This Was New York! A Nostalgic Picture of Gotham in the Gaslight Era* (New York: LIM Press, 1969), 146, Robert Ernst, *Immigrant Life in New York City, 1825–1863* (New York: King's Crown Press, 1949), 38, 46; W. Carlos Martyn, *William E. Dodge: The Christian Merchant* (New York: Funk and Wagnalls, 1894), 53–59, *New York Mercantile Union Business Directory, 1850–51* (New York: French and Plat, Henshaw, 1850), 391; Ronald H. Bayor and Timothy J. Meagher, eds., *The New York Irish* (Baltimore: Johns Hopkins University Press, 1996), 21.

44. *New York Times*, 1 May 1854, 24.

45. *New York World*, 3 February 1877, 5.

46. *New York Times*, 26 October 1881, 8; 18 September 1892, 4.

47. A. W. Loomis, "Chinese 'Funeral Baked Meats,'" *Overland Monthly* (July 1869): 22, 24. In imperial China, the women of the household were required to announce the death of a loved one by wailing loudly in high-pitched tones: see James L. Watson, "The Structure of Chinese Funerary Rites," in *Death Ritual in Late Imperial and Modern China*, ed. James L. Watson and Evelyn S. Rawski (Berkeley: University of California Press, 1988), 12. I thank Madeleine Dong for pointing me to this last reference

48. I thank Christopher Gerteis for providing me with insight into the role of women in funerary practices in China.

49. The author may have been Alfred T. Trumble. The publisher, Richard Kyle Fox, published another of Trumble's short stories, "The Mott Street Poker Club: The Secretary's Minutes": see A. T. (An Old Californian), *The "Heathen Chinee" at Home and Abroad* (New York: Richard K. Fox, 1882), 75.

50. Frank Moss, *The American Metropolis from Knickerbocker Days to the Present Time: New York City Life in All Its Various Phases*, vol. 2 (New York: Peter Fenelon Collier, 1897), 425–426.

51. Qingsong Zhang, "The Origins of the Chinese Americanization Movement: Wong Chin Foo and the Chinese Equal Rights League," in *Claiming America: Constructing Chinese American Identities during the Exclusion Era*, ed. K. Scott Wong and Sucheng Chan (Philadelphia: Temple University Press, 1998), 42–43; Wong Chin Foo, "The Chinese in New York," *Cosmopolitan* 5 (1888): 25.

52. *New York World*, 3 February 1877, 5.

53. Kung, *The Chinese in American Life*, 77.

54. *Irish American*, 16 November 1861. By November 1865, Kennedy was the sole proprietor of the business, dropping Malone from the advertisement.

55. Other ethnic groups represented in this group of undertakers with at least one foreign-born parent included 213, Germany; 48, Great Britain; 26, Italy; 19, Austria-Hungary; 8, English Canada; 8, Russia; 6, Scandinavia, 3, Poland; 1,French Canada; and 14, "other": U.S. Census, 1900, Special Reports, 643; see also Bayor and Meagher, *The New York Irish*, 22.

56. According to the 1910 federal census, James Naughton, sixty-two; his wife, Ann, sixty-one; and their five children resided at 611 Lexington Avenue in Manhattan: U.S. Census, 1910, Borough of Manhattan.

57. *New York Times*, 30 October 1888.

58. U.S. Census, 1900, Borough of Brooklyn. For the only scholarly work on the history of female undertakers, see Georgeanne Rundblad, "Exhuming Women's Premarket Duties in the Care of the Dead," *Gender and Society* 9 (April 1995): 173–192; idem, "From 'Shrouding Women' to Lady Assistant: An Analysis of Occupational Sex Typing in the Funeral Industry," Ph.D. diss., University of Illinois, Urbana, 1993.

59. Church sextons, whose tasks included taking care of church cemeteries and digging graves, sometimes expanded their death-care services. Cabinet and furniture makers often included caskets in their list of products: *Irish American*, 9 May 1857 and 1 October 1864; Robert W. Habenstein and William M. Lamers, *The History of American Funeral Directing* (Milwaukee: Bulfin, 1962), 226–227; Michael J. Steiner, *A Study of the Intellectual and Material Culture of Death in Nineteenth Century America* (Lewiston, N.Y.: Edwin Mellen, 2003), 84–85.

60. Bayor and Meagher, *The New York Irish*, 20; Graham Hodges, "'Desirable Companions and Lovers': Irish and African Americans in the Sixth Ward, 1830–1870," in Bayor and Meagher, *The New York Irish*, 109, 117.

61. Cypress Hills Cemetery opened in November 1848: see Bayor and Meagher, *The New York Irish*, 77; Alter F. Landesman, *A History of New Lots, Brooklyn* (Port Washington, N.Y.: Kennikat Press, 1977), 153.

62. William Sadlier Dinger, telephone conversation with the author, 26 September 2005.

63. Like other trades, the undertaking business, despite its roots in women's midwifery, would remain predominantly a men's occupation well into the twentieth century. In 1870, of 1,996 undertakers listed, 20 were female. In 1930, although the total number of undertakers was more than 30,000 nationally, the number of female undertakers remained comparatively low at 1,940. New York City reflected this trend. City business directories for New York City list several undertaking business owned or operated by women, even if in name only. In 1890, one city directory listed only four female undertakers in its list of 237 such businesses: H. Dewey Anderson and Percy E. Davidson, *Occupation Trends in the United States* (Palo Alto, Calif.: Stanford University Press, 1940), 436–437, 463–465; U.S. Census, 1920, Bulletin, 10; *Fifteenth Census of the United States, 1930, Population*, vol. 5, *General Report on Occupations*, 1933, 19; *Hunt's New York City Business Director*, 680–682.

64. Lawrence Naughton Sr. and his family resided on East 94th Street in 1930. He continued the business after a stint in real estate. He is listed as an undertaker, but it is unclear where the business was located: U.S. Census, 1930, Borough of Manhattan.

65. U.S. Census, 1900, Occupations.

66. *Bulletins of the Twelfth Census of the United States, 1901, Census of the United States, State Compendium*, New York (1923), 43.

67. In the 1870s, one Chinese undertaking business, Main Fook Undertaker, was operating in San Francisco: Yong Chen, *Chinese San Francisco: A Trans-Pacific Community, 1850–1943* (Stanford, Calif.: Stanford University Press, 2000), 64; *Twelfth Census, Special Reports, Occupations*, cxlv; *Abstract of the Fourteenth Census*, 493; *Fourteenth Census of the United States, State Compendium*, New York, 91.

68. For a general overview of the modernization of funerals in the United States, see James J. Farrell, *Inventing the American Way of Death, 1830–1920* (Philadelphia: Temple University Press, 1980), esp. chap. 5.

69. The three Chinese men, one of whom claimed to be a cousin of the victim, were released a week later: *New York Times*, 9 January 1884 and 18 January 1884.

70. Bonner, *Alas!* 149.

71. *New York Times*, 5 February 1915; Bonner, *Alas!* 149.

72. At Chinese funerals, mourners typically placed artificial money in the casket with the deceased: Bonner, *Alas!* 104–105.

73. Paul C. P. Siu, *The Chinese Laundryman: A Study of Social Isolation* (New York: New York University Press, 1987), 135, Adam McKeown, *Chinese Migration Networks and Cultural Change: Peru, Chicago, Hawaii, 1900–1936* (Chicago: University of Chicago Press, 2001),132; Chen, *Chinese San Francisco*, 105, 127, John Kuo Wei Tchen, *New York before Chinatown* (Baltimore: Johns Hopkins University Press, 1999), 239–240; Watson, "The Structure of Chinese Funerary Rites," 16–17.

74. Bonner, *Alas!* 77; Jay P. Dolan, *The Immigrant Church: New York's Irish and German Catholics, 1815–1865* (Baltimore: Johns Hopkins University Press, 1975), 61–62.

75. As was typical of most testimony by white witnesses in these cases, Naughton testified that Lau was not a laborer and had never worked in a laundry or restaurant: Chinese Exclusion Act Case Files, 1908.

76. Mary Ann Jung, "Big Apple Greeter: A Guide to Chinatown," available online at http://bigapplegreeter.org (accessed 4 April 2011).

77. Dinger, telephone conversation.

78. Donna R. Gabaccia, *From Sicily to Elizabeth Street: Housing and Social Change among Italian Immigrants, 1880–1930* (Albany: State University of New York Press, 1984), chaps. 5–6.

79. *Phillips' Standard Buyer and Business Directory of the Principal Cities of New York State* (New York: Phillips' Standard Buyer, 1926), 1103–1106; *Hunt's New York City Business Directory*, 680–682.

80. Perazzo, who had married Charles's sister Caroline, continued the business. By 1920, Eugene Baciagalupo had left the funeral home business. While his brother-in-law ran Baciagalupo's, Perazzo ran his own funeral parlor at 199

Bleecker Street: see *Hunt's New York City Business Directory*, 680; U.S. Census, 1920, 1930, Borough of Manhattan; Mary Elizabeth Brown, *From Italian Villages to Greenwich Village: Our Lady of Pompeii, 1892–1992* (New York: Center for Migration Studies, 1992), 29, 47, 49; *Phillips' Standard Buyer and Business Directory of the Principal Cities of New York State*, 1105.

81. R. J. Werblowsky and Geoffrey Wisoder, eds., *Oxford Dictionary of the Jewish Religion* (New York: Oxford University Press, 1997), 143.

82. U.S. Census, 1910, 1920, Borough of Manhattan; *Philips' Standard Buyer and Business Directory of the Principal Cities of New York State*, 1104; *Murphy's New York City Business Directory* (New York: National Directory, 1890), 416.

83. U.S. Census, 1900, Borough of Manhattan. See Gabaccia, *From Sicily to Elizabeth Street*.

84. *The Jewish Communal Register of New York City, 1917–1918* (New York: Kelillah of New York City, 1918), 1121.

85. Jenna Weissman Joselit, *The Wonders of America: Reinventing Jewish Culture, 1880–1950* (New York: Hill and Wang, 1994), 270; Soyer, *Jewish Immigrant Associations*, 61.

86. *The Jewish Communal Register of New York City*, 334-338; Soyer, *Jewish Immigrant Associations*, 87–89.

87. Calavita, "The Paradoxes of Race, Class, Identity, and 'Passing': Enforcing the Chinese Exclusion Acts, 1882–1910," *Law and Social Inquiry* 25 (Winter 2000): 1–3. Bonner, *Alas!* 159. *New York Times*, 31 October 1924; 1 August 1933; 24 February 1945; 25 February 1945, 11. See also "Consolidated Laws," art. 14, sec. 293, *Thompson's Laws of New York*, pt. 2 (New York: Edward Thompson, 1939), 78.

88. Steven Kurutz, "The Street of No Return," *New York Times*, 29 August 2004, 5.

89. The term "electrical worker" included everything from the often disparaged "mechanical bell hangers" to the elite of an increasingly specialized trade, the electrical engineer. Although many worked in power plants and factories, others started small independent enterprises of their own: American Institute of Electrical Engineers conference, 1892, as cited in A. Michal McMahon, *The Making of a Profession: A Century of Electrical Engineering in America* (New York: Institute of Electrical and Electronics Engineering, 1984), 37.

90. *Census of the United States, 1900, Occupations*, New York, 642, 648; *Census of the United States, 1920*, vol. 4, *Occupations by State*, 1158.

91. Chinese Exclusion Act Case Files, box 172, no. 176.2.

92. Stephen R. Prothero, *Purified by Fire: A History of Cremation in America* (Berkeley: University of California Press, 2001), 47.

93. Lawrence Veiller, "Housing as a Factor in Health Progress in the Past Fifty Years," in Mazÿck P. Ravenel, *A Half Century of Public Health: Jubilee Historical Volume of the American Health Association* (New York: American Public Health Association, 1921), 331.

CHAPTER 4

1. *New York Times*, 9 February 1901, 2; 9 April 1901, 5; 29 June 1933, 19.

2. Ibid., 2 July 1901, 1.

3. See Mary Ting Yi Liu, *The Chinatown Trunk Mystery: Murder, Miscegenation, and Other Dangerous Encounters in Turn-of-the-Century New York City* (Princeton, N.J.: Princeton University Press, 2005); Jennifer Fronc, "'I Led Him On': Undercover Investigation and the Politics of Social Reform in New York, 1900–1918," Ph.D. diss., Columbia University, 2005, chap. 5.

4. Charles Benedict Davenport, *Heredity in Relation to Eugenics* (New York: Henry Holt, 1911), 219; Lynne M. Getz, "Biological Determinism in the Making of Immigration Policy in the 1920s," *International Social Science Review* 70 (1995): 27. See also Elazar Barkan, "Reevaluating Progressive Eugenics: Herbert Spencer Jennings and the 1925 Immigration Legislation," *Journal of the History of Biology* 24 (Spring 1991): 91–112; Michael Mezzanno, "The Progressive Origins of Eugenics Critics: Raymond Pearl, Herbert S. Jennings, and the Defense of Scientific Inquiry," *Journal of the Gilded Age and Progressive Era* 4 (January 2005): 83–98.

5. Nancy Ordover, *American Eugenics: Race, Queer Anatomy, and the Science of Nationalism* (Minneapolis: University of Minnesota Press, 2003), 14.

6. B. O. Flowers, "Wellsprings and Feeders of Immorality," *Arena* 11 (December 1894): 58–59.

7. Robert W. DeForest and Lawrence Veiller, eds., *The Tenement House Problem: Including the Report of the New York State Tenement House Commission of 1900 by Various Writers*, vol. 1 (New York: Macmillan, 1903), 10, 51.

8. Nathaniel Hawthorne, "My Kinsman, Major Molineaux," in *Heath Anthology of American Literature*, vol. 1, ed. Paul Lauter (Lexington, Mass.: D. C. Heath, 1994), 2121.

9. See Timothy J. Gilfoyle, *City of Eros: New York City, Prostitution, and the Commercialization of Sex, 1790–1920* (New York: W. W. Norton, 1992); Christine Stansell, *City of Women: Sex and Class in New York, 1789–1860* (Urbana: University of Illinois Press, 1987), 172–192; G. G. Foster, *New York by Gas-Light with Here and There a Streak of Sunshine* (New York: Dewitt and Davenport, 1850), 7; Patricia Cline Cohen, *The Murder of Helen Jewett* (New York: Vintage, 1998), 108–115.

10. See Gilfoyle, *City of Eros*.

11. For discussions of prostitution in U.S. cities during the nineteenth century, see Christine Stansell, *City of Women*; Barbara Berg, *The Remembered Gate: Origins of American Feminism—The Woman and the City, 1800–60* (New York: Oxford University Press, 1978).

12. Shirley J. Yee, *Black Women Abolitionists: A Study in Activism, 1828–1860* (Knoxville: University of Tennessee Press, 1992), 82; Gilfoyle, *City of Eros*, 183.

13. Ruth Rosen, *The Lost Sisterhood: Prostitution in America, 1900–1918* (Baltimore: Johns Hopkins University Press, 1982), 9; William W. Sanger, *The*

History of Prostitution: Its Extent, Causes, and Effects throughout the World (New York: Harper and Brothers, 1859).

14. *New York Times Illustrated Weekly Magazine*, 27 June 1897, 14.

15. Gilfoyle, *City of Eros*, 188–189.

16. See Charles W. Gardner, *The Doctor and the Devil, or Midnight Adventures of Dr. Parkhurst* (New York: Gardner, 1894); Warren Sloat, *A Battle for the Soul of New York: Tammany Hall, Police Corruption, Vice and Reverent Charles Parkhurst's Crusade against Them, 1892–1895* (New York: Cooper Square, 2002).

17. Rosen, *The Lost Sisterhood*, 72–73; Jesse T. Todd Jr., "Battling Satan in the City: Charles Henry Parkhurst and Municipal Redemption in Gilded Age New York," *American Presbyterians* 71 (Winter 1993): 245.

18. Erving was a member of Parkhurst's congregation and taught Sunday school at the Madison Square Presbyterian Church. He later served as vice president of the City Vigilance League. Erving came from a wealthy New York family, the son of Cornelia Van Rensselaer Erving and John Erving, an attorney: *New York Times*, 14 August 1895, 1.

19. *New York Times*, 6 May 1892, 8; Gardner, *The Doctor and the Devil*, 14–15, 17–20, 22, 32–40.

20. *New York Times*, 7 May 1892, 8; 11 May 1892, 8. *New York Sun*, 7 April 1892, 1–2.

21. A Hattie Adams is listed as an inmate on Blackwell's Island in 1900, although it is unclear whether she was incarcerated for the crime with which she was charged in 1892 or for another crime: U.S. Census, 1900, Population, Borough of Manhattan; *New York Times*, 11 May 1892, 8.

22. *New York Times*, 21 November 1893, 2; 12 December 1894, 9. See also Edward Robb Ellis, *The Epic of New York City* (New York: Coward-McCann, 1966), 425.

23. Arthur Bonner, *Alas! What Brought Thee Hither? The Chinese in New York, 1800–1950* (Madison, N.J.: Fairleigh Dickinson University Press, 1997), 139–141.

24. George Haven Putnam, *Memories of a Publisher, 1865–1915* (New York: Putnam's Sons, 1915), 345–351.

25. *New York Times*, 29 March 1931; Jeremy P. Felt, "Vice Reform as a Political Technique: The Committee of Fifteen in New York, 1900–1901," *New York History* 54 (January 1973): 37; *New York Times*, 14 February 1934. See also Sloat, *A Battle for the Soul of New York*.

26. William Abbott to William Baldwin, 2 December 1900, Committee of Fifteen Records, University of Washington, Seattle.

27. Gilfoyle, *City of Eros*, 189; George Morgan to William Baldwin, 9 January 1901, Committee of Fifteen Records; James F. Richardson, *The New York Police: Colonial Times to 1901* (New York: Oxford University Press, 1970), 237–238, 258, 274; U.S. Census, 1870, 1880, 1890, Population, Borough of Manhattan.

28. *New York Times*, 20 May 1901, 8.

29. Ibid., 3 December 1900, 3; 17 December 1900, 22.

30. Gilfoyle, *City of Eros*, 182–196. See Hasia R. Diner, *Erin's Daughters: Irish Immigrant Women in the Nineteenth Century* (Baltimore: Johns Hopkins University Press, 1983). Felt, "Vice Reform as a Political Technique," 33. See also Egal Feldman, "Prostitution, the Alien Woman, and the Progressive Imagination, 1910–1915," *American Quarterly* 19 (Summer 1967): 192–206.

31. John Burke to George Morgan, 21 March 1901, and Dr. C. Botkin to William Baldwin, 1 March 1901, Committee of Fifteen Records, 1900–1901.

32. Robert Paddock to George Morgan, 28 May 1901, Committee of Fifteen Records.

33. O. Edward Janney to William Baldwin, January 1901, Baltimore, Committee of Fifteen Records.

34. Major M.J.H. Ferris to William Baldwin, 11 December 1900, Committee of Fifteen Records.

35. Anna M. Jackson to Charles Sprague, January 1901, New York, Committee of Fifteen Records; U.S. Census, Population, 1900, Borough of Manhattan. The Penington House was established in 1897 by New York City Quakers: see Maxwell F. Marcuse, *This Was New York! A Nostalgic Picture of Gotham in the Gaslight Era* (New York: LIM Press, 1969); Hugh Barbour, Christopher Densmore, Elizabeth H. Moger, Nancy C. Sorel, Alson D. Van Wagner, eds., *Quaker Cross Currents: Three Hundred Years of Friends in the New York Yearly Meetings* (New York: New York Yearly Meeting of Friends, 1995); *New York Times*, 11 March 1915, 11.

36. George Morgan to Josephine Shaw Lowell, 6 March 1901, Committee of Fifteen Records; U.S. Census, 1900, 1920, Population, Borough of Manhattan. Rossiter Johnson, *The Twentieth Century Biographical Dictionary of Notable Americans*, vol. 7 (Boston: Biographical Society, 1904), n.p.

37. Felt, "Vice Reform as a Political Technique," 41.

38. Morgan to Baldwin, 9 January 1901, Committee of Fifteen Records.

39. Citizens of Mott Street to Committee of Fifteen, n.d., Committee of Fifteen Records.

40. Unsigned letter to William Baldwin, 22 October 1901, Committee of Fifteen Records.

41. Carlotta Russell Lowell to Committee of Fifteen, 21 December 1900, Committee of Fifteen Records.

42. Morgan to Baldwin, 9 January 1901.

43. W. C. Steele Jr. to Committee of Fifteen, 26 July 1901; H. S. Conklin to Committee of Fifteen, 26 July 1901, both in Committee of Fifteen Records.

44. U.S. Census, 1900, Population, Boroughs of Manhattan and Brooklyn.

45. *New York Times*, 3 September 1901; U.S. Census, 1900, 1910, 1930, Population, Borough of Manhattan.

46. Isaac Silverman to the Committee of Fifteen, 13 July 1901; Max Moskowitz to the Committee of Fifteen, 15 July 1901, both in Committee of Fifteen Records.

47. Unknown author, 29 March 1901, Committee of Fifteen Records.

48. Wong Aloy to A. E. Wilson, 6 April 1901, Committee of Fifteen Records.

49. Bonner, *Alas!* 88. Quan Yick Nam had taken Arthur Wilson to this address to observe illegal gambling: Committee of Fifteen Records.

50. Committee of Fifteen Records, n.d.

51. It is unclear whether this particular organization was an official branch of the Young Men's Christian Association (YMCA). According the Rose Hum Lee, Chinese branches of the YMCA and the YWCA had emerged in large cities in the United States: Rose Hum Lee, *The Chinese in the United States of America* (Hong Kong: Oxford University Press, 1960), 182, 434.

52. Lillian D. Wald to George Morgan, 9 January 1901, New York, Committee of Fifteen Records.

53. Mary E. Odem, *Delinquent Daughters: Protecting and Policing Adolescent Female Sexuality in the United States, 1885–1920* (Chapel Hill: University of North Carolina Press, 1995).

54. See also Gunther Peck, "White Slavery and Whiteness: A Transnational View of the Sources of Working-Class Radicalism and Racism," *Labor: Studies in Working Class History* 1 (Summer 2004): 41–42; Peggy Pascoe, *Relations of Rescue: The Search for Female Moral Authority in the American West, 1874–1939* (New York: Oxford University Press, 1990). For an excellent discussion of how the white slavery scare helped create racial hierarchies, see Brian Donovan, *White Slave Crusades: Race, Gender, and Anti-Vice Activism, 1887–1917* (Urbana: University of Illinois Press, 2006), chaps. 1–2.

55. Christopher Diffee, "Sex and the City: The White Slavery Scare and Social Governance in the Progressive Era," *American Quarterly* 57 (June 2005): 411–412.

56. George Morgan to Edwin R. A. Seligman, 4 April 1901, Committee of Fifteen Records. A "demonstrator" was typically a woman who sold items from department store counters. See Susan Porter Benson, *Counter Cultures: Saleswomen, Managers, and Customers in American Department Stores, 1890–1940* (Urbana: University of Illinois Press, 1986).

57. Clara de Hirsch Home for Working Girls, "Excerpts: Certificate of Incorporation, 1905"; Edwin R. A. Seligman to Rose Sommerfeld, 4 April 1901, both in Committee of Fifteen Records.

58. Rose Sommerfeld to George Morgan, 5 April 1901, Committee of Fifteen Records.

59. Undercover investigation also took place among Progressive reformers who sought to understand the life of seasonal male workers: see Frank Tobias Higbie, *Indispensable Outcasts: Hobo Workers and Community in the American Midwest, 1880–1930* (Urbana: University of Illinois Press, 2003).

60. Charles Stelzle, *Christianity's Storm Center* (New York: Fleming H. Revel, 1907), 101.

61. The Raines Law, passed in 1896, made it illegal for saloons but not hotels to sell liquor on Sundays: Mara L. Keire, "The Committee of Fourteen and

Saloon Reform in New York City, 1905–1920," *Business and Economic History* 27 (Winter 1997): 574–575.

62. The clergymen on the committee included Rabbi H. Pereira Mendes, the Catholic priest William J. B. Daly, and the Reverend Lee W. Beattie, a New York–born Presbyterian minister who had recently moved from Minnesota to take up a pastorate in Brooklyn.

63. Veiller was one of the main organizers of the Committee of Fourteen but later left the committee in opposition to its support of an amendment in 1924 that would have punished the male customers in prostitution raids. Veiller argued that such a law was unenforceable because the men would simply deny that they paid the women for sex: Thomas C. Mackey, *Pursuing Johns: Criminal Law, Defending Character, and New York City's Committee of Fourteen, 1920–1930* (Columbus: Ohio State University Press, 2005), 2, 118–119.

64. Scheiffelin was also a founder of the New York College of Pharmacy and served on the Board of Trustees at Columbia University.

65. Mary Kingsbury Simkhovitch, *Neighborhood: My Story of Greenwich House* (New York: W. W. Norton, 1938), 87; *One Hundred Fifty Years Service to American Health* (New York: Schieffelin, 1944).

66. Ruth Baldwin was born in 1865 in Springfield, Massachusetts, to Samuel and Mary Sanford Dwight Bowles: U.S. Census, 1870, 1880, Population, Springfield, Mass.

67. *New York Times*, 15 December 1934; Barbara Miller Solomon, *In the Company of Educated Women: A History Women and Higher Education in America* (New Haven, Conn.: Yale University Press, 1985), 48.

68. For an extensive analysis of Scudder's work at Denison House, see Sarah Deutsch, *Women and the City: Gender, Space, and Power in Boston, 1870–1940* (New York: Oxford University Press, 2000). Balch (1867–1961) was the daughter of the lawyer Francis V. Balch and Ellen Noyes Balch. In 1946, she was awarded the Nobel Peace Prize: see Mercedes M. Randall, *Improper Bostonian: Emily Greene Balch, Nobel Peace Laureate, 1946* (New York: Twayne, 1964); idem, ed., *Beyond Nationalism: The Social Thought of Emily Greene Balch* (New York: Twayne, 1972).

69. Simkhovitch, *Neighborhood*, 46, 87; Domenica M. Barbuto, *American Settlement House and Progressive Social Reform: An Encyclopedia of the American Settlement Movement* (Phoenix: Oryx Press, 1999), 190; U.S. Census, 1870, Newton, Mass., 1910, Hunterdon County, N.J.

70. Ellen Fitzpatrick, *Endless Crusade: Women Social Scientists and Progressive Reform* (New York: Oxford University Press, 1990), 17–19; Barbuto, *American Settlement House and Progressive Social Reform*, 112.

71. Darlene Clark Hine, ed. *Black Women in America: An Historical Encyclopedia*, vol. 2 (New York: Carson, 1993), 759–760.

72. Lucy Maynard Salmon (1853–1927) was the first history professor at Vassar College: see Lucy Maynard Salmon, *Domestic Service* (New York: Macmillan, 1897); David M. Katzman, *Seven Days a Week: Women and Domestic Service in Industrializing America* (Urbana: University of Illinois Press, 1981).

73. Frances A. Kellor, *Experimental Sociology* (New York: Macmillan, 1901), 30–31.

74. *The Social Evil in New York City: A Study of Law Enforcement* (New York: Andrew H. Kellogg, 1910), 17–18.

75. Ibid., 42.

76. George J. Kneeland, *Commercialized Prostitution in New York City* (1913), repr. ed. (Montclair, N.J.: Patterson Smith, 1969), 67–68.

77. Walter Lippman, *A Preface to Politics* (New York: Macmillan, 1913), 70. See also Gretchen Soderlund, "Covering Urban Vice: *The New York Times*, 'White Slavery,' and the Construction of Journalistic Knowledge," *Critical Studies in Media Communications* 19 (December 2002): 439.

CHAPTER 5

1. Ethel Gross to Harry Hopkins, 10 March 1913, as cited in Allison Giffen and June Hopkins, eds., *Jewish First Wife, Divorced: The Correspondence of Ethel Gross and Harry Hopkins* (Lanham, Md.: Lexington Books, 2002), 10, 42.

2. See Elizabeth Lasch-Quinn, *Black Neighbors: Race and the Limits of Reform in the American Settlement House Movement, 1890–1945* (Chapel Hill: University of North Carolina Press, 1993); *Thirteenth Census of the United States, 1910, Population*, Borough of Manhattan.

3. Annual Report, 1912. Christodora House Papers (hereafter, CHP).

4. U.S. Census, 1910, New York.

5. One exception was the Hudson Guild in the Chelsea neighborhood, which attempted a more democratic structure by including people in the neighborhood on its governing board: Jeff Kisseloff, *You Must Remember This: An Oral History of Manhattan from the 1890s to World War II* (New York: Harcourt Brace Jovanovich, 1989), 503–504.

6. There are a number of fine studies of the history of the settlement house movement, including Allen F. Davis, *Spearheads for Reform: The Social Settlements and the Progressive Movement, 1890–1914* (New York: Oxford University Press, 1967); Dapne Spain, *How Women Saved the City* (Minneapolis: University of Minnesota Press, 2001). Judith Trolander's analysis compares the social settlement house movement in the 1980s to the earlier movement in the 1880s in Judith Trolander, *Professionalism and Social Change: From the Settlement House Movement to Neighborhood Centers, 1886 to the Present* (New York: Columbia University Press, 1987). For particular attention to gender and the settlement house movement, see Sarah Deutsch, *Women and the City: Gender, Space, and Power in Boston, 1870–1940* (New York: Oxford University Press, 2000).

7. Christodora House constitution and bylaws, 1897, CHP.

8. Christodora's records reveal that its clientele did not include Asians. Sunday schools on Doyers and Bayard streets directly targeted the Chinese in their midst: see Arthur Bonner, *Alas! What Brought Thee Hither? The Chinese*

in New York, 1800–1950 (Madison, N.J.: Fairleigh Dickinson University Press, 1997), 48–49.

9. In 1902, Carson relocated to Toronto, where she helped establish Evangelia House, located in one of the poorest immigrant neighborhoods in the city.

10. The board included Harriet James; Caroline Sellew (Caroline Barker Goldsmith), the wife of a wealthy furniture dealer; Caroline Slade (Caroline McCormick), the wife of a lumber merchant; and Florence Gibb Pratt, the daughter of a wealthy Brooklyn merchant and the wife of Herbert Lee Pratt, vice president of Standard Oil.

11. Until the 1930s, this profession was included within the occupational category "religious, charity, and welfare workers." By 1930, the U.S. government had created separate categories for religious workers and social settlement house workers. Influenced by the dire circumstances brought on by the Great Depression, that number had jumped by 1940 to a total of 9,053, out of which 5,693 were women: Joseph A. Hill, *Women in Gainful Occupations, 1870–1920* (Washington, D.C.: Bureau of the Census, U.S. Department of Commerce, 1929), 56; U.S. Census, 1920, 1930, 1940, Occupations, New York.

12. Davis, *Spearheads for Reform*, 11; Robert A. Woods and Albert J. Kennedy, eds., *Handbook of Settlements* (New York: Charities Publication Committee, 1911), 193.

13. Woods and Kennedy, *Handbook of Settlements*, 220.

14. Lillian D. Wald, *The House on Henry Street* (New York: Henry Holt, 1915), 13.

15. Trolander, *Professionalism and Social Change*, 3.

16. Toynbee Hall was established in 1884 in memory of the social reformer Arnold Toynbee. Located in London's East End, Toynbee Hall was Great Britain's first university settlement and was run by Samuel Augustus Bennett, the canon of St. Jude's Church. The Neighborhood Guild in New York City, one of many modeled after Toynbee Hall, was later reorganized into the University Settlement: see Stanton Coit, *Neighborhood Guilds: An Instrument of Social Reform* (London: Swan Sonnenschein, 1891); Charles B. Stover, "The Neighborhood Guild in New York," in "Arnold Toynbee," by F. C. Montague, *Johns Hopkins University Studies in Historical and Political Science* 7 (1889): 65–70.

17. Harry P. Krause, *The Settlement House Movement in New York City* (New York: Arno Press, 1980), 121.

18. MacColl grew up as the adopted daughter of her "cousin," the Reverend Dugald D. MacColl, and his wife, Rebecca. MacColl was a Presbyterian clergyman who held pastorates in the farming villages of Monroe and Genessee counties between 1860 and 1880. According to MacColl, her birth father was a physician. Born in Scotland, he had immigrated to Canada during the early nineteenth century: Charles Wachsman, address, 10 December 1939, CHP, Rare Books and Manuscripts, Columbia University, New York. *Thirteenth Census of the United States, 1910, Population,* Borough of Manhattan; *Eighth Census of*

the United States, 1860, Population, Monroe County, N.Y.; *Tenth Census of the United States, 1880, Population*, Bergen, Genessee County, N.Y.; *Gazetteer and Business Directory of Monroe County, N.Y., for1869–70* (Syracuse: Hamilton Child, 1869), 282; Christina I. MacColl to Anna Hempstead Branch, ca. 1923, Anna Hempstead Branch Papers, Smith College, Northampton, Mass.

19. "Student Directory, Emerson College of Oratory, 1892–93," application for admission and transcripts, courtesy of Emerson College Archives, Boston.

20. Sara Libby Carson, born in 1861, was the daughter of Elizabeth and Charles Carson, a blacksmith: U.S. Census, 1870, Population, New York, 1880, Population, New Jersey; Robert F. Harney, ed., *Gathering Places: Peoples and Neighborhoods of Toronto, 1834–1946* (Toronto: Multicultural History Society of Ontario, 1995), 17; Robert F. Harney and Harold Troper, *Immigrants: A Portrait of the Urban Experience, 1890–1930* (Toronto: Van Nostrand Reinhold, 1975), 1–3.

21. Sara Libby Carson, "The Social Settlement," Social Service Congress, Ottawa, Canada, 1914, *Reports and Proceedings*, 138.

22. Elizabeth Wilson, *Fifty Years of Association Work among Young Women, 1866–1916* (1916), repr. ed. (New York: Garland, 1987), 23, as cited in Spain, *How Women Saved the City*, 255; CHP.

23. Christodora House bylaws, art. 3, CHP.

24. The Great Depression was a turning point in the history of Christodora House, when, like other settlements, it suffered financial setbacks. During this period, the board began renting out rooms and apartments in its new high-rise building on Ninth Avenue to people who were not associated with Christodora House. The board eventually sold the building to the city, and the settlement moved into low-income housing. In 1986, the sixteen-story building was converted into luxury condominium: Helen Hall, *Unfinished Business in Neighborhood and Nation* (New York: Macmillan, 1971), 82; *Village Voice*, 1 June 2004.

25. "Board Meeting," 16 June 1927, CHP.

26. Vida Scudder, *The Church and the Hour: Reflections of a Socialist Churchwoman* (New York: E.P. Dutton, 1917), as cited in Douglas M. Strong, *They Walked in the Spirit* (Westminster: John Knox Press, 1997), 74.

27. Charles Stelzle, *Christianity's Storm Center* (New York: Fleming H. Revel, 1907), 140.

28. Christadora House Constitution and Bylaws, art. 2, CHP; Woods and Kennedy, *Handbook of Settlements*, 235; Christodora House, minutes, 4 April 1899, CHP.

29. Charles H. Parkhurst, *My Forty Years in New York* (New York: Macmillan, 1923), 72–73.

30. C. I. MacColl to Miss Sewall, 18 May 1903, CHP.

31. *Annual Report, 1905–1906*, CHP.

32. "Christodora House Clubs: A Chronological Study," CHP. See also William P. Dillingham, *Dictionary of Races and Peoples*, U.S. Immigration

Commission, vol. 5 (Washington, D.C.: U.S. Government Printing Office, 1911).

33. "Histories, 1926–1980," CHP.

34. See Karen Brodkin, *How Jews Became White Folks and What That Says about Race in America* (New Brunswick, N.J.: Rutgers University Press, 1998), chap. 4.

35. *Annual Report, 1905–1906.*

36. C. I. MacColl to Josephine T. Emerson, n.d., CHP.

37. Ibid., n.d., CHP.

38. Christodora House, minutes, 4 January 1921, CHP.

39. MacColl to Miss Sewall, 18 May 1903.

40. Howard Crosby Foster to Josephine T. Emerson, New York, 31 January 1939, CHP.

41. *New York Times,* 14 November 1897; 26 December 1897.

42. Woods and Kennedy, *Handbook of Settlements,* 236.

43. MacColl to Miss Sewall, 18 May 1903.

44. Yaakov Ariel, *Evangelizing the Chosen People: Missions to the Jews in America, 1880–2000* (Chapel Hill: University of North Carolina Press, 2000), 39.

45. Jay P. Dolan, *The Immigrant Church: New York's Irish and German Catholics, 1815–1865* (Baltimore: Johns Hopkins University Press, 1975), 19; U.S. Census, 1910, Borough of Manhattan.

46. *New York Times,* 13 April 1908, 1; 14 April 1908, 5.

47. Ibid., 14 April 1908, 5.

48. Ibid., 10 June 1907, 7.

49. Woods and Kennedy, *Handbook of Settlements,* 236.

50. Joyce Antler, *The Journey Home: Jewish Women and the American Century* (New York: Free Press, 1997), 46–51.

51. Jeffrey S. Gurock, "Jewish Communal Divisiveness in response to Christian Influences on the Lower East Side," in Todd Endelmann, *Jewish Apostasy in the Modern World* (Teaneck, N.J.: Holmes and Meier, 1987), 264–265.

52. Jacob Henry Schiff (1847–1920) formed the brokerage firm Budge, Schiff, and Company. He later joined the private banking firm Kuhn, Loeb, and Company and served as president of the New York, Lake Erie, and Western and Louisville and Nashville railroads. In 1875, he married Therese Loeb, eldest daughter of Bettie and Solomon Loeb, German Jewish immigrants who had immigrated to the United States in the 1850s. Henry Hall, *America's Successful Men of Affairs: An Encyclopedia of Contemporaneous Biography,* vol. 1 (New York: New York Tribune, 1895–96), 577; *Tenth Census of the United States, 1880, Population,* New York; Naomi W. Cohen, *Jacob H. Schiff: A Study in American Jewish Leadership* (Hanover, N.H.: Brandeis University Press, 1999), 91–92; Karen Buhler-Wilkerson, *No Place like Home: A History of Nursing and Home Care in the United States* (Baltimore: Johns Hopkins University Press, 2001), 100;

Marjorie N. Feld, "An Actual Working out of Internationalism: Russian Politics, Zionism, and Lillian Wald's Ethnic Progressivism," *Journal of the Gilded Age and Progressive Era* 2 (April 2003): 121–122.

53. Cohen, *Jacob H. Schiff*, 20–21, 60–61.

54. *New York Times*, 24 December 1908; 6 October 1913; 22 October 1913, 9.

55. Annie Nathan Meyer was a founder of Barnard College, a controversial proponent of education reform for women, and an anti-suffragist: see Lynn D. Gordon, "Annie Nathan Meyer and Barnard College: Mission and Identity in Women's Higher Education, 1889–1950," *History of Education Quarterly* 26 (Winter 1986): 503–522.

56. Ellen Carol Dubois, *Harriot Stanton Blatch and the Winning of Woman Suffrage* (New Haven, Conn.: Yale University Press, 1997), 119–120.

57. Giffen and Hopkins, *Jewish First Wife, Divorced*, 48–49.

58. Riv-Ellen Prell, "The Ghetto Girl and the Erasure of Memory," in *Remembering the Lower East Side: American Jewish Reflections*, ed. Hasia Diner, Jeffrey Shandler, and Beth S. Wenger (Bloomington: Indiana University Press, 2000), 87.

59. June Hopkins, *Harry Hopkins: Sudden Hero, Brash Reformer* (New York: St. Martin's Press, 1999), 144–146.

60. See Nancy F. Cott, *The Grounding of Modern Feminism* (New Haven, Conn.: Yale University Press, 1987).

61. Giffen and Hopkins, *Jewish First Wife, Divorced*, 7.

62. Lloyd Morris, *Incredible New York: High Life and Low Life of the Last Hundred Years* (New York: Random House, 1951), 274.

63. Judy Yung, *Unbound Feet: A Social History of Chinese Women in San Francisco* (Berkeley: University of California Press, 1995), 107; Robert G. Lee, *Orientals: Asian Americans in Popular Culture* (Philadelphia: Temple University Press, 1999), 158–159; Brodkin, *How Jews Became White Folks*, 178.

64. "Histories, 1926–1980 CHP."

65. Giffen and Hopkins, *Jewish First Wife, Divorced*, 7–8.

66. Herbert Lee Pratt's father, Charles Pratt, was an early associate of John D. Rockefeller and founder of Charles Pratt and Company, which Rockefeller purchased in 1874. Pratt was later a partner in the Atlantic Refining Company.

67. *New York Times*, 11 July 1909, 6; 21 February 1921, 10. Strong, *They Walked in the Spirit*, 49–50.

68. *Annual Report, 1917*, CHP.

69. Annual Meeting, *Minutes*, 2 April 1919, CHP.

70. *Annual Report, 1916*, CHP.

71. Una M. Saunders, "The Missionary Possibilities of the Women Students of the World," in *Students and the Modern Missionary Crusade* (New York: Student Volunteer Movement for Foreign Missions, 1906), 75.

72. Patricia R. Hill, *The World Their Household: The American Foreign Mission*

Movement and Cultural Transformation, 1870–1920 (Ann Arbor: University of Michigan Press, 1985), 4.

73. Dana L. Robert, *American Women in Mission: A Social History of Their Thought and Practice* (Macon, Ga.: Mercer University Press, 1996), 199.

74. The American Tract Society traces its origins to the New England Tract Society, established in 1814 by a diverse group of evangelical publicists.

75. Christine Stansell, *City of Women: Sex and Class in New York, 1789–1860* (Urbana: University of Illinois Press, 1982), 64–75; Wade Crawford Barclay, *The Methodist Episcopal Church, 1845–1939, Volume 3, Part 2: History of Methodist Missions* (New York: Board of Missions of the Methodist Church, 1949), 223. See also Carroll Smith-Rosenberg, *Religion and the Rise of the American City: The New York City Mission Movement, 1812–1870* (Ithaca, N.Y.: Cornell University Press, 1971).

76. Sasha Su-Ling Welland, *A Thousand Miles of Dreams: The Journeys of Two Chinese Sisters* (New York: Rowman Littlefield, 2006), 81–82.

77. For a more comprehensive study of women's participation in the foreign missionary movement, see Hill, *The World Their Household.*

78. Spain, *How Women Saved the City*, xii.

79. Mary Ting Yi Liu, *The Chinatown Trunk Mystery: Murder, Miscegenation, and Other Dangerous Encounters in Turn-of-the-Century New York City* (Princeton, N.J.: Princeton University Press, 2005), 118; John Kuo Wei Tchen, *New York before Chinatown* (Baltimore: Johns Hopkins University Press, 1999), 69. Bonner, *Alas!* 113; Barclay, *The Methodist Episcopal Church*, 290; Tyler Anbinder, *Five Points: The Nineteenth-Century New York City Neighborhood That Invented Tap Dance, Stole Elections, and Became the World's Most Notorious Slum* (New York: Penguin, 2001), 418; *New York Times*, 5 May 1879.

80. Barclay, *The Methodist Episcopal Church*, 290.

81. Louis J. Beck, *New York's Chinatown: An Historical Presentation of Its People and Places* (New York: Bohemia Publishing, 1898), 235–236.

82. Bonner, *Alas!* 117–118.

83. Liu, *The Chinatown Trunk Mystery*, 103.

84. Chinatown and Bowery Rescue Settlement for Girls, *Fifth Annual Report*, 1908–1909, 5.

85. Idem, *Fourth Annual Report*, 1908.

86. Ibid.

87. Idem, *Sixth Annual Report, 1910.*

88. *Ninth Census of the United States, 1870, Population*, Carmel, Putnam County, N.Y.; Barclay, *The Methodist Episcopal Church*, 290.

89. *Ninth Census of the United States, 1870, Population*, Ohio. *New York Times*, 2 March 1937, 21; 12 November 1939, 48.

90. Lathbury died in East Orange, New Jersey, in 1913; see the website at http://www.cyberhymnal.org (accessed 28 April 2008).

91. *New York Times*, 16 January 1900, 14.

92. *Ninth Census of the United States, 1970, Population*, Jeffersonville, Sullivan County, N.Y.

93. Banta's actual place of birth is unclear. The U.S. federal census of 1880 lists her birthplace as Ohio, but the census of 1900 lists her place of birth as New York. The 1900 census describes her occupation as "missionary student." In 1917, the National Bible Institute took over the Union Missionary Training Institute: *New York Times*, 8 November 1895, 9; *Missionary Review of the World*, vol. 30, 1917, 713.

94. "Missionary Notes," *Gospel in All Lands* (December 1901): 571.

95. Mae C. Berger, comp., *Meyer Berger's New York* (New York: Random House, 1960), 84.

96. *New York Times*, 10 May 1954, 25.

97. Ann Marie Nicolosi, "We Do Not Want Our Girls to Marry Foreigners," *NWSA Journal* 13 (Fall 2001): 11.

98. See Peggy Pascoe, *Relations of Rescue: The Search for Female Moral Authority in the American West, 1874–1939* (New York: Oxford University Press, 1990).

99. Byron Uhl to Mary Banta, care of Presbyterian Board of Foreign Missions, 22 July 1935, Chinese Exclusion Act Case Files, box 177, case no. 25/422.0, National Archives and Records Administration, Northeast Region, New York.

100. U.S. Census, 1900, 1920, Population.

101. *New York Times*, 2 November 1901, 10.

102. Ibid., 12 November 1898, 3.

103. Ibid., 25 May 1954. It is unclear whether Banta legally adopted these children.

104. Ibid., 29 May 1922, 17.

105. Florence Brugger, "The Chinese American Girl: A Study of Cultural Conflicts," master's thesis, New York University, 1935, 72–73; Bonner, *Alas!* 164.

106. The hospital merged with Columbia Hospital in 1928 and was renamed Columbia-Presbyterian (Hospital) Medical Center.

107. Presbyterian Hospital opened in October 1872 under the auspices of the Society for the Presbyterian Hospital, founded by James Lennox, a philanthropist and president of the American Bible Society whose charitable contributions supported the work of the Presbyterian church. The new building occupied the block of 70th and 71st streets and Madison and Fourth avenues: *New York Times*, 26 February 1870 and 7 October 1872.

108. Rose Cohen, *Out of the Shadows: A Russian Girlhood on the Lower East Side* (Ithaca, N.Y.: Cornell University Press, 1995), 242–243.

109. Ibid., 244.

110. Ibid., 248–249.

111. Only one reference exists to document her death at age forty-five, a notation at the MacDowell Colony in New Hampshire: ibid., xixn2.

112. John T. McGreevy, *Parish Boundaries: The Catholic Encounter with Race in the Twentieth-Century Urban North* (Chicago: University of Chicago Press, 1996), 3–5.

113. Maureen Fitzgerald, *Habits of Compassion: Irish Catholic Nuns and the Origins of New York's Welfare System, 1830–1920* (Urbana: University of Illinois Press, 2006), 277n22.

114. See Noel Ignatiev, *How the Irish Became White* (New York: Routledge, 1995); David Roediger, *The Wages of Whiteness: Race and the Making of the American Working Class* (London: Verso, 1991); Brodkin, *How Jews Became white Folks.*

115. Robert Orsi, "The Religious Boundaries of an Inbetween People: Street *Feste* and the Problem of the Dark-Skinned Other in Italian Harlem, 1920–1990," *American Quarterly* 44 (September 1992): 313–318; Matthew Frye Jacobson, *Whiteness of a Different Color: European Immigrants and the Alchemy of Race* (Cambridge, Mass.: Harvard University Press, 1998), 56; John Higham, *Strangers in the Land: Patterns of American Nativism, 1860–1925* (New York: Atheneum, 1970), 65–66.

116. *New York Times*, 10 April 1890, 8.

117. John Murphy Farley, later Cardinal John Farley (1842–1918), was the fourth archbishop and the seventh bishop of the Roman Catholic Diocese of New York: Reverend B. J. Reilly to Cardinal Farley, New York, 4 March 1917, as cited in Silvano M.Tomasi, *Piety and Power: The Role of Italian Parishes in the New York Metropolitan Area, 1880-1930* (New York: Center for Migration Studies, 1975), 45.

118. Silvano M. Tomasi, *The Role of the Italian Parishes in the New York Metropolitan Area, 1880–1930* (New York: Center for Migration Studies, 1975), 44.

119. Reverend B. J. Reilly to Cardinal John Farley, as cited in Tomasi, *Piety and Power*, 45. See also McGreevy, *Parish Boundaries*, 11–13.

120. Silvano M. Tomasi, "Scalabrinians and the Pastoral Care of Immigrants in the United States, 1887–1987," *U.S. Catholic Historian* 6(4) (1987): 255–256.

121. Bernard J. Lynch, "The Italians of New York," *Catholic World* 67 (April 1888): 72; Mary Elizabeth Brown, "The Making of Italian-American Catholics: Jesuit Work on the Lower East Side, 1890's–1950's," *Catholic Historical Review* (April 1987): 195–208.

122. Mary Elizabeth Brown, *Churches, Communities, and Children: Italian Immigrants in the Archdiocese of New York, 1880–1945* (New York: Center for Migration Studies, 1993), 27–47.

123. John V. Tolino, "Solving the Italian Problem," *Ecclesiastical Review* (1938): 247, 249.

124. John Talbot Smith, *The Catholic Church in New York: A History of the New York Diocese from Its Establishment in 1808 to the Present Time*, vol. 2 (New York: Hall and Locke, 1905), 448–449.

125. Tolino, "Solving the Italian Problem," 252.

126. Dorothy Brown and Elizabeth McKeown, *The Poor Belong to Us: Catholic Charities and American Welfare* (Cambridge, Mass.: Harvard University Press, 1997), 18–19; John F. McClymer, "Of 'Mornin' Glories' and 'Fine Old Oaks': John Purroy Mitchel, Al Smith, and Reform as an Expression of Irish-American Aspiration," in *The New York Irish*, ed. Ronald H. Bayor and Timothy J. Meagher (Baltimore: Johns Hopkins University Press, 1996), 374, 377–379.

127. Tolino, "Solving the Italian Problem," 246.

Bibliography

MANUSCRIPT COLLECTIONS

Anna Hempstead Branch Papers, Smith College, Northampton, Mass.

Christodora House Papers, Rare Books and Manuscripts, Columbia University, New York

Committee of Fifteen Records, 1900–1901, University of Washington, Seattle

Edwin Seligman Papers, Rare Books and Manuscripts, Columbia University Library, New York

Emerson College Archives, Emerson College, Boston

Lillian Wald Papers, New York Public Library

Society for the Prevention of Crime, Rare Books and Manuscripts, Columbia University, New York

GOVERNMENT DOCUMENTS

Chinese Exclusion Act Case Files, National Archives and Records Administration, Northeast Region, New York

Dillingham, William P. *Dictionary of Races and Peoples*. U.S. Immigration Commission, vol. 5. Washington, D.C.: U.S. Government Printing Office, 1911.

Hill, Joseph A. *Women in Gainful Occupations, 1870–1920*. Washington, D.C.: Bureau of the Census, U.S. Department of Commerce, 1929.

House Committee on Public Works and Transportation. Hearings before the Subcommittee on Public Buildings and Grounds. *The Foley Square Construction Project and the Historic African Burial Ground, New York, N.Y.* 102nd Cong., 2nd sess., 27 July 1992.

U.S. Census, 1789–1945, Historical Statistics of the United States.

U.S. Census, 1900, Special Reports, Occupations.
U.S. Census, 1900, 1910, 1920, 1930, Population, New York.
U.S. Census, 1900, 1920. Abstracts.
U.S. Census, 1910–1920, Mortality Rates.
U.S. Census, 1920, Bulletin.
U.S. Census, 1920, State Compendium, New York.
U.S. Census, 1930, Population, Volume 5: General Report on Occupations.

AUTOBIOGRAPHIES AND MEMOIRS

Blaustein, David. *Memoirs of David Blaustein: Educator and Communal Worker.* New York: McBride, Nast, 1913.

Cohen, Rose. *Out of the Shadows: A Russian Girlhood on the Lower East Side.* Ithaca, N.Y.: Cornell University Press, 1995.

Johnson, James Weldon. *Autobiography of an Ex-Coloured Man* (1912), repr. ed. New York: Avon, 1965.

Parkhurst, Charles H. *My Forty Years in New York.* New York: Macmillan, 1923.
———. *Our Fight with Tammany.* New York: Charles Scribner's Sons, 1895.

Putnam, George Haven. *Memories of a Publisher, 1865–1915.* New York: Putnam's Sons, 1915.

Simkhovitch, Mary Kingsbury. *Neighborhood: My Story of Greenwich House.* New York: W. W. Norton, 1938.

Towne, George Hanson. *This New York of Mine.* New York: Cosmopolitan Book, 1931.

Wald, Lillian D. *The House on Henry Street.* New York: Henry Holt, 1915.

Walling, George Washington. *Recollections of a New York Chief of Police.* New York: Caxton Book Concern, 1887.

NEWSPAPERS AND MAGAZINES

Chicago Defender
Cosmopolitan
Daily Mail and Empire (Toronto)
Evening Post
Freedom's Journal
Gospel in All Lands
Irish American
Missionary Review of the World
National Police Gazette
Newtown (N.Y.) Register
New York Age
New York Herald
New York Sun

New York Times
New York Tribune
New York World
Overland Monthly
Queens Tribune
Village Voice

ORGANIZATIONAL REPORTS

Annual reports, Chinatown and Bowery Rescue Settlement for Girls, 1908–1910, Museum of Chinese in America, New York.

Annual reports, Christodora House, 1900–1939, Columbia University, New York.

Committee of Fourteen, *The Social Evil in New York City: A Study of Law Enforcement.* New York: Andrew H. Kellogg, 1910.

DeForest, Robert W., and Lawrence Veiller, eds. *The Tenement House Problem: Including the Report of the New York State Tenement House Commission of 1900 by Various Writers,* 2 vols. New York: Macmillan, 1903.

Reports and Proceedings of the Senate Committee Appointed to Investigate the Police Department of the City of New York. 5 vols. Albany: James B. Lyon, 1895.

Seligman, Edwin R. A., ed. *The Social Evil, with Special Reference to Conditions Existing in the City of New York.* New York: G. P. Putnam's Sons, 1912.

THESES AND DISSERTATIONS

Brugger, Florence. "The Chinese American Girl: A Study in Cultural Conflicts." Master's thesis, New York University, 1935.

Burgess, John Stewart. "A Study of the Characteristics of the Cantonese Merchants in Chinatown, New York." Master's thesis, Columbia University, New York, 1909.

Chen, Pei-Yao. "The 'Isolation' of New York City Chinatown: A Geo-historical Approach to a Chinese Community in the U.S." Ph.D. diss., City University of New York, 2003.

Ching Chieh Chang. "The Chinese in Latin America: A Preliminary Geographical Survey with Special Reference to Cuba and Jamaica." Ph.D. diss., University of Maryland, College Park, 1956.

Chu, Louis H. "The Chinese Restaurant." Master's thesis, New York University, 1939.

Fronc, Jennifer. "'I Led Him On': Undercover Investigation and the Politics of Social Reform in New York, 1900–1918." Ph.D. diss., Columbia University, New York, 2005.

Groneman, Carol Pernicone. "'The Bloody Ould Sixth': A Social Analysis of a Mid-Nineteenth Century Working Class Community." Ph.D. diss., University of Rochester, 1986.

Pozzetta, George Enrico. "The Italians of New York City, 1880–1914." Ph.D. diss., Duke University, Durham, N.C., 1971.

Rothschild, Teal Kristen. "Alliances across Skill, Gender, and Ethnicity: A Structural and Identity-Based Analysis of Two Strikes in the New York City Garment Industry, 1885–1921," Ph.d. diss., New School for Social Research, New York, 2001.

Rundblad, Georgeanne. "From 'Shrouding Women' to Lady Assistant: An Analysis of Occupational Sex Typing in the Funeral Industry." Ph.D. diss., University of Illinois, Urbana, 1993.

NOVELS AND PLAYS

Nichols, Anne. *Abie's Irish Rose*. New York: Samuel French, 1937.

Norr, William. *Stories of Chinatown: Sketches from the Life in the Chinese Colony on Mott, Pell and Doyers Streets*. New York: W. Norr, 1892.

Trumble, Alfred T. *The Mott Street Poker Club: The Secretary's Minutes*. New York: White and Allen 1889.

DIRECTORIES

The American Jewish Year Book, vol 21. Philadelphia: Jewish Publication Society of America, 1919.

Gazetteer and Business Directory of Monroe County, N.Y., 1869–70. Syracuse, N.Y.: Hamilton Child, 1869.

Hafner, Arthur W., ed. *Directory of Deceased American Physicians, 1804–1929: A Geanological Guide to over 149,000 Medical Practitioners*. Chicago: American Medical Association, 1993.

Hunt's New York City Business Directory. New York: Hunt Publishing, 1890.

The Jewish Communal Register of New York City, 1917–1918. New York: Kehilla of New York City, 1918.

Murphy's New York City Business Directory. New York: National Directory, 1888.

New York City Directory, 1890. Online database, Ancestry.com. Provo, Utah: Generations Network, 1999.

New York Mercantile Union Business Directory, 1850–51. New York: French and Plat, Henshaw, 1850.

Phillips' Standard Buyer and Business Directory of the Principal Cities of New York State. New York: Phillips' Standard Buyer, 1926.

BOOKS AND ARTICLES

Adler, Cyrus. *Jacob H. Schiff: His Life and Letters*, 2 vols. New York: Doubleday, Doran, 1928.

Alexander, Elizabeth S. "For Better or Worse: Marriages across Boundaries." *Journal of Women's History* 19 (Fall 2007): 213–221.

Allen, Richard, and Absalom Jones. *A Narrative of the Proceedings of the Black People, during the Late and Awful Calamity in Philadelphia, in the Year 1793, and a Refutation of Some Censures, Thrown upon Them in Some Late Publications.* Philadelphia: Rhistoric Publications, 1969.

Alleyne, Mervyn C. *The Construction and Representation of Race and Ethnicity in the Caribbean and the World.* Kingston, Jamaica: University of the West Indies Press, 2002.

Anbinder, Tyler. *Five Points: The Nineteenth-Century New York City Neighborhood That Invented Tap Dance, Stole Elections, and Became the World's Most Notorious Slum.* New York: Penguin, 2001.

Anderson, H. Dewey, and Percy E. Davidson. *Occupation Trends in the United States.* Palo Alto, Calif.: Stanford University Press, 1940.

Anderson, Margaret L., and Patricia Hill Collins, eds. *Race, Class and Gender: An Anthology.* New York: Wadsworth, 2004.

Antler, Joyce. *The Journey Home: Jewish Women and the New Century.* New York: Free Press, 1997.

Ariel, Yaakov. *Evangelizing the Chosen People: Missions to the Jews in America, 1880–2000.* Chapel Hill: University of North Carolina Press, 2000.

A. T. (An Old Californian). *The "Heathen Chinee" at Home and Abroad.* New York: Richard K. Fox, 1882.

Aubitz, Shawn. "Tracing Early Chinese Immigration into the United States: The Use of INS Documents." *Amerasia Journal* 14 (1988): 37–46.

Bao, Xiaolan. "When Women Arrived: The Transformation of New York's Chinatown." In *Not June Cleaver: Women and Gender in Postwar America, 1945–1960,* ed. Joanne Meyerowitz, 19–36. Philadelphia: Temple University Press, 1994.

Barbour, Hugh, Christopher Densmore, Elizabeth H. Moger, Nancy C. Sorel, Alson D. Van Wagner, and Arthur J. Worrall, eds. *Quaker Cross Currents: Three Hundred Years of Friends in the New York Yearly Meetings.* New York: New York Yearly Meeting of Friends, 1995.

Barbuto, Domenica M. *American Settlement Houses and Progressive Social Reform: An Encyclopedia of the American Settlement Movement.* Phoenix: Oryx Press, 1999.

Barclay, Wade Crawford. *The Methodist Episcopal Church, 1845–1939, Volume 3, Part 2: History of Methodists Missions.* New York: Board of Missions of the Methodist Church, 1949.

Barkan, Elazar. "Reevaluating Progressive Eugenics: Herbert Spencer Jennings and the 1925 Immigration Legislation." *Journal of the History of Biology* 24 (Spring 1991): 91–112.

Barrett, James R., and David R. Roediger. "The Irish and the 'Americanization' of the 'New Immigrants' in the Streets and the Churches of the Urban United States, 1900–1930." *Journal of American Ethnic History* 8 (Summer 2005): 3–33.

Barrows, Esther G. *Neighbors All: A Settlement Notebook.* Boston: Houghton Mifflin, 1929.

Batterberry, Michael, and Anne Batterberry. *On the Town in New York from 1776 to the Present.* New York: Charles Scribner's Sons, 1973.

Bayor, Ronald H., and Timothy J. Meagher, eds. *The New York Irish.* Baltimore: Johns Hopkins University Press, 1996.

Beck, Louis J. *New York's Chinatown: An Historical Presentation of Its People and Places.* New York: Bohemia Publishing, 1898.

Bender, Thomas. *Community and Social Change in America.* New Brunswick, N.J.: Rutgers University Press, 1978.

Benson, Susan Porter. *Counter Cultures: Saleswomen, Managers, and Customers in American Department Stores, 1890–1940.* Urbana: University of Illinois Press, 1986.

Berg, Barbara. *The Remembered Gate: Origins of American Feminism—The Woman and the City, 1800–60.* New York: Oxford University Press, 1978.

Berger, Mae C., comp. *Meyer Berger's New York.* New York: Random House, 1960

Berman, P. "Mary Maud Brewster." *American Journal of Nursing* 110 (August 2010): 62–63.

Berrol, Selma. *The Empire City: New York and Its People, 1624–1996.* Westport, Conn.: Praeger, 1997.

Betts, Lillian W. "The Italian in New York." *University Settlement Studies and the Eighteenth Report of the University Settlement of New York, 1904* (March 1905): 90–105.

Binder, Frederick M., and David M. Reimers. *All the Nations under Heaven: An Ethnic and Racial History of New York City.* New York: Columbia University Press, 1995.

Black, Doris. "The Black Chinese." *Sepia* (December 1975): 19–24.

Blackford, Mansel G. *A History of Small Business in America,* 2nd ed. Chapel Hill: University of North Carolina Press, 2003.

Bodnar, John. *The Transplanted: A History of Immigration in Urban America.* Bloomington: Indana University Press, 1985.

Bonner, Arthur. *Alas! What Brought Thee Hither? The Chinese in New York, 1800–1950.* Madison, N.J.: Fairleigh Dickinson University Press, 1997.

Boyer, Paul. *Urban Masses and Moral Order in America, 1820–1920.* Cambridge, Mass.: Harvard University Press, 1978.

Brodkin, Karen. *How Jews Became White Folks and What That Says about Race in America.* New Brunswick, N.J.: Rutgers University Press, 1998.

Brown, Dorothy, and Elizabeth McKeown. *The Poor Belong to Us: Catholic Charities and American Welfare.* Cambridge, Mass.: Harvard University Press, 1997.

Brown, Mary Elizabeth. *Churches, Communities, and Children: Italian Immigrants in the Archdiocese of New York, 1880–1945.* New York: Center for Migration Studies, 1993.

———. *From Italian Villages to Greenwich Village: Our Lady of Pompeii, 1892–1992.* New York: Center for Migration Studies, 1992.

———. "The Making of Italian-American Catholics: Jesuit Work on the Lower East Side, 1890's–1950's." *Catholic Historical Review* (April 1987): 195–210.

Bryan, Patrick. *The Jamaican People, 1880–1902: Race, Class, and Social Control.* London: Macmillan, 1991.

Buhler-Wilkerson, Karen. *No Place like Home: A History of Nursing and Home Care in the United States.* Baltimore: Johns Hopkins University Press, 2001.

Burke, Mary Beth. *Queens County Agriculture of the Nineteenth Century: Kitchen and Herb Gardens, Chinese Truck Farms.* New York: City University of New York, 1993.

Burnham, John C. *Bad Habits: Drinking, Smoking, Taking Drugs, Gambling, Sexual Misbehavior, and Swearing in American History.* New York: New York University Press, 1993.

Burrows, Edwin G., and Mike Wallace. *Gotham: A History of New York City to 1898.* New York: Oxford University Press, 1999.

Calavita, Kitty. "The Paradoxes of Race, Class, Identity, and 'Passing': Enforcing the Chinese Exclusion Acts, 1882–1910." *Law and Social Inquiry* 25 (2000): 1–40.

Calkins, Raymond. *Substitutes for the Saloon.* New York: Houghton Mifflin, 1901.

Carnegie, Elizabeth. *The Path We Tread: Blacks in Nursing Worldwide, 1854–1994,* 3rd ed. New York: National League for Nursing Press, 1995.

Carson, Mina. *Settlement Folk: Social Thought and the American Settlement Movement, 1885–1930.* Chicago: University of Chicago Press, 1990.

Chapin, Robert Coit. *The Standard of Living among Workingmen's Families in New York City.* New York: Charities Publication, 1909.

Chauncey, George. *Gay New York: Gender, Urban Culture, and the Making of the Gay Male World, 1890–1940.* New York: Basic Books, 1994.

Chen, Yong. *Chinese San Francisco: A Trans-Pacific Community, 1850–1943.* Stanford, Calif.: Stanford University Press, 2000.

Chorley, E. Clowes. *The Centennial History of Saint Bartholomew's Church in the City of New York.* New York: Episcopalian Church, 1935.

Choy, Philip P., Lorraine Dong, and Marlon K. Hom. *Coming Man: 19th Century American Perceptions of the Chinese.* Seattle: University of Washington Press, 1994.

Christoff, Peggy Spitzer. "An Archival Resource: INS Case Files on Chinese Women in the American Midwest." *Journal of Women's History* 10 (Fall 1998): 155–170.

Cohen, Lucy M. "Entry of the Chinese to the Lower South, 1865 to 1870: Policy Dilemmas." *Southern Studies* 2 (Fall–Winter 1991): 281–313.

Cohen, Naomi W. *Jacob Schiff: A Study in American Jewish Leadership.* Hanover, N.H.: Brandeis University Press, 1999.

Cohen, Patricia Cline. *The Murder of Helen Jewett.* New York: Vintage, 1998.

Coit, Stanton. *Neighborhood Guilds: An Instrument of Social Reform.* London: Swan Sonnenschein, 1891.

Coolidge, Mary Roberts. *Chinese Immigration.* New York: Henry Holt, 1909.

Cott, Nancy F. *The Grounding of Modern Feminism.* New Haven, Conn.: Yale University Press, 1987.

———. *Public Vows: A History of Marriage and the Nation.* Cambridge, Mass.: Harvard University Press, 2000.

Crenshaw, Kimberlé Williams. "Mapping the Margins: Intersectionality, Identity Politics, and Violence against Women of Color." *Stanford Law Review* 43 (1991): 1241–1299.

Dabel, Jane. "'A Superior Colored Man . . . and a Scotch Woman': Interracial Marriages in New York City, 1850–1870." *International Social Science Review* 80 (Fall–Winter 2005): 87–102.

Daniels, Roger. *Asian America: Chinese and Japanese in the United States since 1850.* Seattle: University of Washington Press, 1988.

Davenport, Charles Benedict. *Heredity in Relation to Eugenics.* New York: Henry Holt, 1911.

Davis, Allen F. *Spearheads for Reform: The Social Settlements and the Progressive Movement, 1890–1914.* New York: Oxford University Press, 1967.

Deutsch, Sarah. *Women and the City: Gender, Space, and Power in Boston, 1870–1940.* New York: Oxford University Press, 2000.

Diffee, Christopher. "Sex and the City: The White Slavery Scare and Social Governance in the Progressive Era." *American Quarterly* 57 (June 2005): 411–438.

Diner, Hasia R. *Erin's Daughters: Irish Immigrant Women in the Nineteenth Century.* Baltimore: Johns Hopkins University Press, 1983.

———. *Hungering for America: Italian, Irish, and Jewish Foodways in the Age of Migration.* Cambridge, Mass.: Harvard University Press, 2001.

———. "Introduction to the Transaction Edition." In Louis Wirth, *The Ghetto,* 1–10. New Brunswick, N.J.: Transaction, 1998.

———. *Lower East Side Memories: A Jewish Place in America.* Princeton, N.J.: Princeton University Press, 2000.

Diner, Hasia, Jeffrey Shandler, and Beth S. Wenger, eds. *Remembering the Lower East Side: American Jewish Reflections.* Bloomington: Indiana University Press, 2000.

Disturnell, John. *New York as It Was and Is.* New York: D. Van Nostrand, 1876.

Dolan, Jay P. *The Immigrant Church: New York's Irish and German Catholics, 1815–1865.* Baltimore: Johns Hopkins University Press, 1975.

Donovan, Brian. *White Slave Crusades: Race, Gender, and Anti-vice Activism, 1887–1917.* Urbana: University of Illinois Press, 2006.

Drachsler, Julius. *Intermarriage in New York City: A Statistical Study of the Amalgamation of European Peoples.* New York, 1921.

Dubois, Ellen Carol. *Harriot Stanton Blatch and the Winning of Woman Suffrage.* New Haven, Conn.: Yale University Press, 1997.

Duffy, John. *The Sanitarians: A History of American Public Health.* Urbana: University of Illinois Press, 1990.

Dufton, Lena. *History of Nursing at the New York Post-Graduate Medical School and Hospital*. New York: Alumni Association, 1944.

Edwards, Wendy Deichmann, and Carolyn De Swarte Gifford, eds. *Gender and the Social Gospel*. Urbana: University of Illinois Press, 2003.

Ellis, Edward Robb. *The Epic of New York City*. New York: Coward-McCann, 1966.

Endelmann, Todd, ed. *Jewish Apostasy in the Modern World*. New York: Holmes and Meier, 1987.

Ernst, Robert. *Immigrant Life in New York City, 1825–1863*. New York: King's Crown Press, 1949.

Ewen, Elizabeth. *Immigrant Women in the Land of Dollars: Life and Culture on the Lower East Side*. New York: Monthly Review Press, 1985.

Farrell, James J. *Inventing the American Way of Death, 1830–1920*. Philadelphia: Temple University Press, 1980.

Federal Writers' Project. *The Italians of New York: A Survey*. New York: Random House, 1938.

Feld, Marjorie N. "An Actual Working Out of Internationalism: Russian Politics, Zionism, and Lillian Wald's Ethnic Progressivism." *Journal of the Gilded Age and Progressive Era* 2 (April 2003): 119–149.

———. *Lillian Wald: A Biography*. Chapel Hill: University of North Carolina Press, 2008.

Feldman, Egal. "Prostitution, the Alien Woman and the Progressive Imagination, 1910–1915." *American Quarterly* 19 (Summer 1967): 192–206.

Felt, Jeremy P. "Vice Reform as a Political Technique: The Committee of Fifteen in New York, 1900–1901." *New York History* 54 (January 1973): 24–51.

Fitzgerald, Maureen. *Habits of Compassion: Irish Catholic Nuns and the Origins of New York's Welfare System, 1830–1920*. Urbana: University of Illinois Press, 2006.

Fitzpatrick, Ellen. *Endless Crusade: Women Social Scientists and Progressive Reform*. New York: Oxford University Press, 1990.

Fletcher, Paul Louie. "The Chinese Wholesale Shirt Laundries of New York." *Management Research News* 25 (2002): 1–63.

Flowers, B. O. "Wellsprings and Feeders of Immorality," *Arena* 11 (December 1894): 58–59.

Forman, Allan. "Celestial Gotham." *Arena* 7 (April 1893): 620–628.

Foster, G. G. *New York by Gas-Light with Here and There a Streak of Sunshine*. New York: Dewitt and Davenport, 1850.

Frankel, Noralee, and Nancy S. Dye, eds. *Gender, Class, Race, and Reform in the Progressive Era*. Lexington: University of Kentucky Press, 1991.

Freeman, Rhoda Golden. *The Free Negro in New York City in the Era before the Civil War*. New York: Garland, 1994.

Friedman-Kasaba, Kathie. *Memories of Migration: Gender, Ethnicity, and Work in the Lives of Jewish and Italian Women in New York, 1870–1924*. Albany: State University of New York Press, 1996.

Gabaccia, Donna R. *From Sicily to Elizabeth Street: Housing and Social Change among Italian Immigrants, 1880–1930*. Albany: State University of New York Press, 1984.

———. *From the Other Side: Women, Gender, and Immigrant Life in the U.S. 1820–1990*. Bloomington: Indiana University Press, 1994.

———. *We Are What We Eat: Ethnic Food and the Making of Americans*. Cambridge, Mass.: Harvard University Press, 1998.

Gandal, Keith. *The Virtues of the Vicious*. New York: Oxford University Press, 1997.

Gardner, Charles W. *The Doctor and the Devil, or Midnight Adventures of Dr. Parkhurst*. New York: Gardner, 1894.

Getz, Lynne M. "Biological Determinism in the Making of Immigration Policy in the 1920s." *International Social Science Review* 70 (1995): 26–33.

Gibbs, Iris, and Alonzo Gibbs. "Moving Day." *Long Island Forum* (June 1973): 105–107.

Gibson, Reverend Otis. *The Chinese in America*. Cincinnati: Hitchcock and Walden, 1877.

Giffen, Allison, and June Hopkins, eds. *Jewish First Wife, Divorced: The Correspondence of Ethel Gross and Harry Hopkins*. Lanham, Md.: Lexington Books, 2002.

Gilfoyle, Timothy J. *City of Eros: New York City, Prostitution, and the Commercialization of Sex, 1790–1920*. New York: W. W. Norton, 1992.

———. "The Moral Origins of Political Surveillance: The Preventative Society in New York City." *American Quarterly* 38 (Fall 1986): 637–652.

Glenn, Evelyn Nakano. *Unequal Freedom: How Race and Gender Shaped Citizenship and Labor*. Cambridge, Mass.: Harvard University Press, 2002.

Glenn, Susan A. *Daughters of the Shtetl: Life and Labor in the Immigrant Generation*. Ithaca, N.Y.: Cornell University Press, 1990.

———. *Female Spectacle: The Theatrical Roots of Modern Feminism*. Cambridge, Mass.: Harvard University Press, 2001.

Gold, Michael. *Jews without Money* (1930), 3rd repr. ed. New York: Carroll and Graf, 1990.

Goldstein, Eric L. *The Price of Whiteness: Jews, Race, and American Identity*. Princeton, N.J.: Princeton University Press, 2006.

Gordon, Lynn D. "Annie Nathan Meyer and Barnard College: Mission and Identity in Women's Higher Education, 1889–1950." *History of Education Quarterly* 26 (Winter 1986): 503–522.

Gottlieb, Agnes Hooper. "Women and Expose: Reform and Housekeeping." In *The Muckrakers: Evangelical Crusaders*, ed. Robert Miraldi, 71–91. Westport, Conn.: Praeger, 2000.

Graham, Stephen. *New York Nights*. New York: George Doran, 1927.

Grant, Madison. *The Passing of the Great Race*. New York: C. Scribner's Sons, 1916.

Guglielmo, Thomas A. *White on Arrival: Italians, Race, Color, and Power in Chicago, 1890–1945.* New York: Oxford University Press, 2003.

Guterl, Matthew Pratt. "After Slavery: Asian Labor, the American South, and the Age of Emancipation." *Journal of World History* 14 (June 2003): 209–241.

———. *The Color of Race in America: 1900–1940.* Cambridge, Mass.: Harvard University Press, 2001.

Habenstein, Robert, and William M Lamers. *The History of American Funeral Directing.* Milwaukee: Bulfin, 1962.

Haddad, John. "The Laundry Man's Got a Knife!" *Chinese America: History and Perspectives* (2001): 31–47.

Hall, Helen. *Unfinished Business in Neighborhood and Nation.* New York: Macmillan, 1971.

Hall, Henry. *America's Successful Men of Affairs: An Encyclopedia of Contemporaneous Biography,* vol. 1. New York: New York Tribune, 1895–1896.

Halter, Marilyn. *Shopping for Identity: The Marketing of Ethnicity.* New York: Schocken Books, 2000.

Handlin, Oscar. *The Uprooted: The Epic Story of the Great Migrations That Made the American People.* Boston: Little, Brown, 1973.

Harney, Robert F., ed. *Gathering Places: Peoples and Neighborhoods of Toronto, 1834–1946.* Toronto: Multicultural History Society of Ontario, 1995.

Harney, Robert F., and J. Vincent Scarpaci, eds. *Little Italies in North America.* Toronto: Multicultural History Society of Ontario, 1981.

Harney, Robert F., and Harold Troper. *Immigrants: A Portrait of the Urban Experience, 1890–1930.* Toronto: Van Nostrand Reinhold, 1975.

Harris, Leon. *Merchant Princes.* New York: Harper and Row, 1979.

Harris, Leslie M. *In the Shadows of Slavery: African Americans in New York City, 1626–1863.* Chicago: University of Chicago Press, 2003.

Hawthorne, Nathaniel. "My Kinsman, Major Molineaux." In *Heath Anthology of American Literature,* vol. 1, ed. Paul Lauter. Lexington, Mass.: D. C. Heath, 1994.

Hewitt, John H. "Mr. Downing and His Oyster House: The Life and Good Works of an African-American Entrepreneur." *New York History* (July 1993): 229–252.

Higbie, Frank Tobias. *Indispensable Outcasts: Hobo Workers and Community in the American Midwest, 1880–1930.* Urbana: University of Illinois Press, 2003.

Higham, John. *Strangers in the Land: Patterns of American Nativism, 1860–1925.* New York: Atheneum, 1970.

Hill, Patricia R. *The World Their Household: The American Woman's Foreign Mission Movement and Cultural Transformation, 1870–1920.* Ann Arbor: University of Michigan Press, 1985.

Hindus, Milton, ed. *The Old East Side: An Anthology.* Philadelphia: Jewish Publication Society of America, 1969.

Hine, Darlene Clark. *Black Women in White: Racial Conflict and Cooperation in the Nursing Profession, 1890–1950*. Bloomington: Indiana University Press, 1989.

————, ed. *Black Women in America: An Historical Encyclopedia,* vol. 2. New York: Carson, 1993.

Hodes, Martha, ed. *Sex, Love, Race: Crossing Boundaries in North American History.* New York: New York University Press, 1999.

Hodges, Graham, "'Desirable Companions and Lovers': Irish and African Americans in the Sixth Ward, 1830–1870." In *The New York Irish,* ed. Ronald H. Bayor and Timothy J. Meagher, 107–124. Baltimore: Johns Hopkins University Press, 1996.

Holder, Calvin B. "The Causes and Composition of West Indian Immigration to New York City, 1900–1952." *Afro-Americans in New York Life and History* (January 1987): 7–27.

Holloway, Karla F. C. *Passed On: African American Mourning Stories.* Durham, N.C.: Duke University Press, 2002.

Hopkins, Charles Howard. *The Rise of the Social Gospel in American Protestantism, 1865–1915.* New Haven, Conn.: Yale University Press, 1940.

Hopkins, June. *Harry Hopkins: Sudden Hero, Brash Reformer.* New York: St. Martin's Press, 1999.

Hurwitz, Samuel J., and Edith F. Hurwitz. *Jamaica: A Historical Portrait.* New York: Praeger, 1971.

Ignatiev, Noel. *How the Irish Became White.* New York: Routledge, 1995.

Jacobson, Matthew Frye. *Whiteness of a Different Color: European Immigrants and the Alchemy of Race.* Cambridge, Mass.: Harvard University Press, 1998.

Joselit, Jenna Weissman. *The Wonders of America: Reinventing Jewish Culture, 1880–1950.* New York: Hill and Wang, 1994.

Katzman, David M. *Seven Days a Week: Women and Domestic Service in Industrializing America.* Urbana: University of Illinois Press, 1981.

Keire, Mara L. "The Committee of Fourteen and Saloon Reform in New York City, 1905–1920." *Business and Economic History* 26 (Winter 1997): 573–583.

————. "The Vice Trust: A Reinterpretation of the White Slavery Scare in the United States, 1907–1917." *Journal of Social History* 35 (Fall 2001): 5–42.

Kellor, Frances A. *Experimental Sociology.* New York: Macmillan, 1901.

Kennedy, Albert J., Kathryn Farra, and Neva Ruth Deardorff. *Social Settlements in New York City: Their Activities, Policies, and Administration.* New York: Columbia University Press, 1935.

Kessler, D. E. "An Evening in Chinatown." *Overland Monthly and Out West Magazine* 49 (May 1907): 445–449.

Kessner, Thomas. *The Golden Door: Italian and Jewish Immigrant Mobility in New York City, 1880–1915.* New York: Oxford University Press, 1977.

Kislingbury, Roger E. *Saloons, Bars, Cigar Stores: Historical Interior Photographs.* Pasadena, Calif.: Waldo and Van Winkle, 1999.

Kisseloff, Jeff. *You Must Remember This: An Oral History of Manhattan from the 1890s to World War II*. New York: Harcourt Brace Jovanovich, 1989.

Kneeland, George J. *Commercialized Prostitution in New York City* (1913), repr. ed. Montclair, N.J.: Patterson Smith, 1969.

Kobrin, Francis. "American Midwifery Controversy: A Crisis of Professionalization." *Bulletin of the History of Medicine* 40 (1966): 350–363.

Konvitz, Milton R. *The Alien and The Asiatic in American Law*. Ithaca, N.Y.: Cornell University Press, 1946.

Krause, Harry P. *The Settlement House Movement in New York City*. New York: Arno Press, 1980.

Kraut, Alan M. *Silent Travelers: Germs, Genes, and the "Immigrant Menace."* New York: Basic Books, 1994.

Kung, S. W. *The Chinese in American Life: Some Aspects of Their History, Status, Problems, and Contributions*. Westport, Conn.: Greenwood Press, 1962.

Kwong, Peter. *Chinatown, N.Y.: Labor and Politics, 1930–1950* (1979), repr. ed. New York: New Press, 2001.

Laderman, Gary. *Rest in Peace: A Cultural History of Death and the Funeral Home in Twentieth Century America*. New York: Oxford University Press, 2003.

Lai, Walton Look. *Indentured Labor, Caribbean Sugar: Chinese and Indian Migrants to the British West Indies, 1838–1918*. Baltimore: Johns Hopkins University Press, 1993.

Landesman, Alter F. *A History of New Lots, Brooklyn*. Port Washington, N.Y.: Kennikat Press, 1977.

Lasch-Quinn, Elizabeth. *Black Neighbors: Race and the Limits of Reform in the American Settlement House Movement, 1890–1945*. Chapel Hill: University of North Carolina Press, 1993.

Leas, Cheryl. *Frommer's New York City, 2002*. New York: Hungry Minds, 2001.

Lee, Erika. *At America's Gates: Chinese Immigration during the Exclusion Era, 1882–1943*. Chapel Hill: University of North Carolina Press, 2003.

Lee, Robert G. *Orientals: Asian Americans in Popular Culture*. Philadelphia: Temple University Press, 1999.

Lee, Rose Hum. *The Chinese in the United States of America*. Hong Kong: Oxford University Press, 1960.

———. "The Decline of Chinatowns in the United States." *American Journal of Sociology* 54 (March 1949): 422–432.

Letwin, Daniel. "Interracial Unionism, Gender, and 'Social Equality' on the Alabama Coalfields, 1878–1908." *Journal of Southern History* 61 (August 1995): 519–554.

Lewis, Earl, and Heidi Ardizzone. *Love on Trial: An American Scandal in Black and White*. New York: W. W. Norton, 2001.

Lewis, Susan Ingalls. "Female Entrepreneurs in Albany, 1840–1885." *Business and Economic History* 21 (1992): 65–73.

Light, Ivan H. *Ethnic Enterprise in America: Business and Welfare among Chinese, Japanese, and Blacks.* Berkeley: University of California Press, 1972.

———. "From Vice Districts to Tourist Attraction: The Moral Career of American Chinatowns." *Pacific Historical Review* 43 (1974): 367–394.

Lin, Jan. *Reconstructing Chinatown: Ethnic Enclave, Global Change.* Minneapolis: University of Minnesota Press, 1998.

Lind, Andrew W. "Adjustment Patterns among the Jamaican Chinese." *Social and Economic Studies* 7 (June 1958): 144–164.

Lippman, Walter. *A Preface to Politics.* New York: Macmillan, 1913.

Liu, Haiming. "Chinese Herbalists in the United States." In *Chinese American Transnationalism*, ed. Sucheng Chang, 136–155. Philadelphia: Temple University Press, 2006.

Liu, Mary Ting Yi. *The Chinatown Trunk Mystery: Murder, Miscegenation, and Other Dangerous Encounters in Turn-of-the-Century New York City.* Princeton, N.J.: Princeton University Press, 2005.

Loewen, James W. *The Mississippi Chinese: Between Black and White.* Cambridge, Mass.: Harvard University Press, 1971.

Lopate, Philip, ed. *Writing New York: A Literary Anthology.* New York: Library of America, 1998.

Lyman, Stanford M. *Chinese Americans.* New York: Random House, 1974.

———. "Marriage and the Family among Chinese Immigrants to America, 1850–1960." *Phylon* 29 (Winter 1968): 321–330.

Lynch, Bernard J. "The Italians of New York." *Catholic World* 67 (April 1888): 67–73.

Mackey, Thomas C. *Pursuing Johns: Criminal Law, Defending Character, and New York City's Committee of Fourteen, 1920–1930.* Columbus: Ohio State University Press, 2005.

Maffi, Mario. *Gateway to the Promised Land: Ethnic Cultures in New York's Lower East Side.* New York: New York University Press, 1995.

Marcuse, Maxwell F. *This Was New York! A Nostalgic Picture of Gotham in the Gaslight Era.* New York: LIM Press, 1969.

Mark, Gregory Yee. "Opium in America and the Chinese." *Chinese America: History and Perspectives* (1997): 61–75.

Markel, Howard. *Quarantine! Eastern European Jewish Immigrants and the New York City Epidemics of 1892.* Baltimore: Johns Hopkins University Press, 1997.

Martyn, W. Carlos. *William E. Dodge: The Christian Merchant.* New York: Funk and Wagnalls, 1894.

May, Ernest R., and John K. Fairbank, eds. *America's China Trade in Historical Perspective: The Chinese and American Performance.* Cambridge, Mass.: Harvard University Press, 1986.

McCabe, James D, Jr. *Lights and Shadows of New York Life; or, Sights and Sensation of the Great City.* Philadelphia: National Publishing, 1872.

———. *New York by Sunlight and Gaslight.* Philadelphia: Douglass Brothers, 1882.

McClellan, Robert. *The Heathen Chinee: A Study of American Attitudes toward China, 1890–1905.* Columbus: Ohio State University Press, 1971.

McDermott, Richard. "The Oldest Building in New York City Knowm to Have Once House a Black-Owned Business." *New York Journal of American History* 66 (2005): 71–75.

McGreevy, John T. *Parish Boundaries: The Catholic Encounter with Race in the Twentieth-Century Urban North.* Chicago: University of Chicago Press, 1996.

McIlwain, Charlton D. *Death in Black and White: Death, Ritual and Family Ecology.* Cresskill, N.J.: Hampton Press, 2003.

McKeown, Adam. *Chinese Migration Networks and Cultural Change: Peru, Chicago, Hawaii, 1900–1936.* Chicago: University of Chicago Press, 2001.

McMahon, A. Michal. *The Making of a Profession: A Century of Electrical Engineering in America.* New York: Institute of Electrical and Electronics Engineering, 1984.

McMahon, Sean. *Social Control and Public Intellect: The Legacy of Edward O. Ross.* New Brunswick, N.J.: Transaction, 1999.

Mele, Christopher, *Selling the Lower East Side: Culture, Real Estate and Resistance in New York City.* Minneapolis: University of Minnesota Press, 2000.

Mendelsohn, Joyce. *The Lower East Side Remembered and Revisited: History and Guide to a Legendary New York Neighborhood.* New York: Lower East Side Press, 2001.

Merwin, Ted. "The Performance of Jewish Ethnicity in Anne Nichols' *Abie's Irish Rose.*" *Journal of American Ethnic History* 20 (Winter 2001): 3–37.

Mezzanno, Michael. "The Progressive Origins of Eugenics Critics: Raymond Pearl, Herbert S. Jennings, and the Defense of Scientific Inquiry." *Journal of the Gilded Age and Progressive Era* 4 (January 2005): 83–98.

Miller, Lawrence G. "Pain, Parturition, and the Profession: Twilight Sleep in America." In *Health Care in America*, ed. Susan Reverby and David Rosner, 19–44. Philadelphia: Temple University Press, 1979.

Miller, Stuart Creighton. *The Unwelcome Immigrant: The American Image of the Chinese, 1785–1882.* Berkeley: University of California Press, 1969.

Mohun, Arwed P. *Steam Laundries: Gender, Technology, and Work in the United States and Great Britain, 1880–1940.* Baltimore: Johns Hopkins University Press, 1999.

Moore, Deborah Dash. "Class and Ethnicity in the Creation of New York City Neighborhoods: 1900–1930." In *Budapest and New York: Studies in Metropolitan Transformation, 1870–1930,* ed. Thomas Bender and Carl Schorske 139–160. New York: Russell Sage Foundation, 1994.

Morantz-Sanchez, Regina Markell. *Sympathy and Science: Women Physicians in American Medicine.* New York: Oxford University Press, 1985.

More, Louise Boland. *Wage Earners' Budgets: A Study of Standards and Costs of Living in New York City.* New York: Henry Holt, 1907.

Morris, Lloyd. *Incredible New York: High Life and Low Life of the Last Hundred Years.* New York: Random House, 1951.

Moss, Frank. *The American Metropolis from Knickerbocker Days to the Present Time: New York City Life in All Its Various Phases,* 3 vols. New York: Peter Fenelon Collier, 1897.

Mott, Frank Luther. *A History of American Magazines,* 3 vols. Cambridge, Mass.: Harvard University Press, 1930.

Mottus, Jane E. *New York Nightingales: The Emergence of the Nursing Profession at Bellevue and New York Hospital, 1850–1920.* Ann Arbor: Research Press, 1981.

Mumford, Kevin J. *Interzones: Black and White Sex Districts in Chicago and New York in the Early Twentieth Century.* New York: Columbia University Press, 1997.

Musser, Charles. "Ethnicity, Role Playing, and American Film Comedy: From Chinese Laundry to Whoopee, 1894–1930." In *Unspeakable Images: Ethnicity and the American Cinema,* ed. Lester Friedman, 39–81. Urbana: University of Illinois Press, 1991.

Musto, David F. *The American Disease: Origins of Narcotic Control.* New York: Oxford University Press, 1987.

The New York Times Guide to New York City. New York: New York Times, 2002.

Ngai, Mae M. *Impossible Subjects: Illegal Aliens and the Making of Modern America.* Princeton, N.J.: Princeton University Press, 2002.

Nicolosi, Ann Marie. "We Do Not Want Our Girls to Marry Foreigners." *NWSA Journal* 13 (Fall 2001): 1–21.

Norris, Frank. "After Strange Gods." *Overland Monthly* 24 (October 1894): 375–379.

Obitz, Shawn. "Tracing Early Chinese Immigration into the U.S.: The Use of INS Documents." *Amerasia Journal* 14 (1988): 39–43.

Odem, Mary E. *Delinquent Daughters: Protecting and Policing Adolescent Female Sexuality in the United States, 1885–1920.* Chapel Hill: University of North Carolina Press, 1995.

Okihiro, Gary Y. *Columbia Reader in Asian American History.* New York: Columbia University Press, 2001.

———. *Margins and Mainstreams: Asians in American History and Cultures.* Seattle: University of Washington Press, 1994.

Ordover, Nancy. *American Eugenics: Race, Queer Anatomy, and the Science of Nationalism.* Minneapolis: University of Minnesota Press, 2003.

Orsi, Robert. "The Religious Boundaries of an Inbetween People: Street *Feste* and the Problem of the Dark-Skinned Other in Italian Harlem, 1920–1990." *American Quarterly* 44 (September 1992): 313–347.

Ostrow, Daniel. *Manhattan's Chinatown.* New York: Arcadia, 2008.

Ovington, Mary White. "The Negro Home in New York." *Charities and the Commons* 15 (7 October 1905): 25–30.

Pascoe, Peggy. "Miscegenation, Law, Court Cases, and Ideologies of 'Race' in Twentieth-Century America." *Journal of American History* (June 1996): 44–69.

———. *Relations of Rescue: The Search for Female Moral Authority in the American West, 1874–1939.* New York: Oxford University Press, 1990.

———. *What Comes Naturally: Miscegenation Law and the Making of Race in America.* New York: Oxford University Press, 2008.

Peck, Gunther. "White Slavery and Whiteness: A Transnational View of the Sources of Working-Class Radicalism and Racism." *Labor: Studies in Working Class History* 1 (Summer 2004): 37–59.

Peffer, George Anthony. "Forbidden Families: Emigration Experiences of Chinese Women under the Page Law." *Journal of American Ethnic History* 6 (Fall 1986): 28–46.

———. "From under the Sojourner's Shadow: A Historiographical Study of Chinese Female Immigration to America, 1852–1882." *Journal of American Ethnic History* 11 (Spring 1992): 41–67.

———. *If They Don't Bring Their Women Here: Chinese Female Immigration before Exclusion.* Urbana: University of Illinois Press, 1999.

Peiss, Kathy. *Cheap Amusements: Working Women and Leisure in Turn-of-the-Century New York.* Philadelphia: Temple University Press, 1986.

Pine, Vanderlyn R. *Caretaker of the Dead: The American Funeral Director.* New York: Irvington Publishers, 1975.

Pitkow, Marlene. "A Temple for Tourists in New York's Chinatown." *Journal of American Culture* 10 (Summer 1987): 107–113.

Pivar, David J. *Purity Crusade: Sexual Morality and Social Control, 1868–1900.* Westport, Conn.: Greenwood Press, 1973.

Plater, Michael A. *African-American Entrepreneurship in Richmond, 1890–1940: The Story of R.C. Scott.* New York: Garland, 1996.

Plunz, Richard. *A History of Housing in New York City: Dwelling Type and Social Change in the American Metropolis.* New York: Columbia University Press, 1990.

Powers, Madelon. *Faces along the Bar: Lore and Order in the Workingman's Saloon, 1870–1920.* Chicago: University of Chicago Press, 1998.

Prell, Riv-Ellen. *Fighting to Become Americans: Jews, Gender, and the Anxiety of Assimilation.* Boston: Beacon, 1999.

Prothero, Stephen. *Purified by Fire: A History of Cremation in America.* Berkeley: University of California Press, 2001.

Quan, Robert Seto. *Lotus among the Magnolias: The Mississippi Chinese.* Jackson: University Press of Mississippi, 1982.

Randall, Mercedes M. *Improper Bostonian: Emily Greene Balch, Nobel Peace Laureate, 1946.* New York: Twayne, 1964.

———, ed. *Beyond Nationalism: The Social Thought of Emily Greene Balch.* New York: Twayne, 1972.

Ravenel, Mazÿck P. *A Half Century of Public Health: Jubilee Historical Volume of the American Health Association.* New York: American Public Health Association, 1921.

Reverby, Susan. *Ordered to Care: The Dilemma of American Nursing, 1850–1945.* Cambridge: Cambridge University Press, 1987.

Richardson, James F. *The New York Police: Colonial Times to 1901.* New York: Oxford University Press, 1970.

Riis, Jacob A. *The Battle with the Slum* (1902), repr. ed. New York: Macmillan, 1969.

———. "The Clearing of Mulberry Bend." *American Reviews of Reviews* 12 (August 1899): 491–499.

———. *How the Other Half Lives: A Study among the Tenements of New York* (1890), repr. ed. New York: Dover, 1971.

———. "Light in Dark Places: A Study of the Better New York." *Century Magazine* 53 (November 1896–April 1897): 247–252.

Ripley, William Z. *Races of Europe: A Sociological Study.* London: Kegan Paul, Tench, Trübner, 1899.

Rischin, Moses. *The Promised City: New York Jews, 1870–1914.* Cambridge, Mass.: Harvard University Press, 1962.

Robert, Dana L. *American Women in Mission: A Social History of Their Thought and Practice.* Macon, Ga.: Mercer University Press, 1996.

Roediger, David. *The Wages of Whiteness: Race and the Making of the American Working Class.* London: Verso, 1991.

Rosen, Ruth. *The Lost Sisterhood: Prostitution in America, 1900–1918.* Baltimore: Johns Hopkins University Press, 1982.

Rundblad, Georgeanne. "Exhuming Women's Premarket Duties in the Care of the Dead." *Gender and Society* 9 (April 1995): 173–192.

Salinger, Sharon V. *Taverns and Drinking in Early America.* Baltimore: Johns Hopkins University Press, 2002.

Salmon, Lucy Maynard. *Domestic Service.* New York: Macmillan, 1897.

Sandmeyer, Elmer Clayton. *The Anti-Chinese Movement in California.* Urbana: University of Illinois Press, 1939.

Sanger, William W. *The History of Prostitution: Its Extent, Causes, and Effects throughout the World.* New York: Harper and Brothers, 1859.

Sante, Luc. *Low Life: Lures and Snares of Old New York.* New York: Farrar, Straus, and Giroux, 1991.

Saunders, Una M. "The Missionary Possibilities of the Women Students of the World." In *Students and the Modern Missionary Crusade: Addresses Delivered before the Fifth International Convention of the Student Voluntary Movement for Foreign Missions, Nashville, Tennessee, February 28–March 4, 1906,* ed. Student Volunteer Movement for Foreign Missions, 75–78. New York: Student Volunteer Movement for Foreign Missions, 1906.

Scherzer, Kenneth A. *The Unbounded Community: Neighborhood Life and Social Structure in New York City, 1830–1875.* Durham, N.C.: Duke University Press, 1992.

Schlesinger, Arthur Meier. *The Rise of the City, 1878–1898*. New York: Macmillan, 1933.

Schwartz, Shepard. "Mate Selection among New York City's Chinese Males, 1931–38." *American Journal of Sociology* 56 (May 1951): 563–568.

Scudder, Vida. *The Church and the Hour: Reflections of a Socialist Churchwoman*. New York: E. P. Dutton, 1917.

Shah, Nayan. *Contagious Divides: Epidemics and Race in San Francisco's Chinatown*. Berkeley: University of California Press, 2001.

Siu, Paul C. P. *The Chinese Laundryman: A Study of Social Isolation*. New York: New York University Press, 1987.

———. "The Isolation of the Chinese Laundryman." In *Contributions to Urban Sociology*, ed. Ernest W. Burgess and Donald Bogue. Chicago: University of Chicago Press, 1944.

Sloat, Warren. *A Battle for the Soul of New York: Tammany Hall, Police Corruption, Vice and Reverent Charles Parkhurst's Crusade against Them, 1892–1895*. New York: Cooper Square, 2002.

Soyer, Daniel. *Jewish Immigrant Associations and American Identity in New York, 1880–1939*. Cambridge, Mass.: Harvard University Press, 1997.

Smith, Daniel Scott. "The Meanings of Family and Household: Change and Continuity in the Mirror of the American Census." *Population and Development Review* 18 (September 1992): 421–456.

Smith, Gene, and Jayne Barry Smith, eds. *The Police Gazette*. New York: Simon and Schuster, 1972.

Smith, John Talbot. *The Catholic Church in New York: A History of the New York Diocese from Its Establishment in 1808 to the Present Time*, vol. 2. New York: Hall and Locke, 1905.

Smith-Pryor, Elizabeth M. *Property Rites: The Rhineland Trial, Passing, and the Protection of Whiteness*. Chapel Hill: University of North Carolina Press, 2009.

Smith-Rosenberg, Carroll. *Disorderly Women: Visions of Gender in Victorian America*. New York: Oxford University Press, 1986.

———. *Religion and the Rise of the American City: The New York City Mission Movement, 1812–1870*. Ithaca, N.Y.: Cornell University Press, 1971.

Soderlund, Gretchen. "Covering Urban Vice: The *New York Times*, 'White Slavery,' and the Construction of Journalistic Knowledge." *Critical Studies in Media Communications* 19 (December 2002): 438–460.

Solomon, Barbara Miller. *In the Company of Educated Women: A History Women and Higher Education in America*. New Haven, Conn.: Yale University Press, 1985.

Spain, Daphne. *How Women Saved the City*. Minneapolis: University of Minnesota Press, 2001.

Spears, Timothy B. *One Hundred Years on the Road: The Traveling Salesman in American Culture*. New Haven, Conn.: Yale University Press, 1995.

Spickard, Paul R. *Japanese Americans: The Formation and Transformation of an Ethnic Group*. New York: Twayne, 1996.

Stansell, Christine. *City of Women: Sex and Class in New York, 1789–1860.* Urbana: University of Illinois Press, 1982.

Steiner, Michael J. *A Study of the Intellectual and Material Culture of Death in Nineteenth Century America.* Lewiston, N.Y.: Edwin Mellen, 2003.

Stelzle, Charles. *Christianity's Storm Center.* New York: Fleming H. Revel, 1907.

———. *Son of the Bowery.* New York: Outlook, 1926.

Stevens, John D. *Sensationalism and the New York Press.* New York: Columbia University Press, 1991.

Stoler, Ann Laura, ed. *Haunted by Empire: Geographies of Intimacy in North American History.* Durham, N.C.: Duke University Press, 2006.

Stover, Charles B. "The Neighborhood Guild in New York." In "Arnold Toynbee," by F. C. Montague. *Johns Hopkins University Studies in Historical and Political Science* 7 (1889): 65–70.

Strong, Douglas M. *They Walked in the Spirit.* Westminster: John Knox Press, 1997.

Sullivan, Mary Louise. *Mother Cabrini: "Italian Immigrant of the Century."* New York: Center for Migration Studies, 1992.

———. "Mother Cabrini: Missionary to Italian Immigrants." *U.S. Catholic Historian* 6 (Fall 1987): 265–279.

Sung, Betty Lee. *Mountain of Gold: The Story of the Chinese in America.* New York: Macmillan, 1967.

Takaki, Ronald T. *A Different Mirror: A History of Multicultural America.* Boston: Little, Brown, 1993.

———. *Iron Cages: Race and Culture in Nineteenth-Century America.* New York: Alfred A. Knopf, 1979.

———. *Strangers from a Different Shore: A History of Asian Americans.* New York: Penguin, 1989.

———, ed. *From Different Shores: Perspectives on Race and Ethnicity in America.* New York: Oxford University Press, 1987.

Tang, Vincente. "Chinese Women Immigrants and the Two-Edged Sword of Habeus Corpus." In *The Chinese American Experience: Papers from the Second National Conference on Chinese American Studies,* ed. Genny Lim, 48–56. San Francisco: Chinese Historical Society of America, 1980.

Taylor, Clarence. *The Black Churches of Brooklyn.* New York: Columbia University Press, 1994.

Taylor, Warren. "The Chinese Quarter of New York." *Munsey's Magazine* 6 (March 1892): 678–682.

Tchen, John Kuo Wei. *New York before Chinatown.* Baltimore: Johns Hopkins University Press, 1999.

———. "New York Chinese: The Nineteenth Century Pre-Chinatown Settlement." *Chinese America: History and Perspectives* (1990): 157–192.

Teng, Jinhua Emma. "Miscegenation and the Critique of Patriarchy in Turn-of-the-Century Fiction." In *Asian American Studies: A Reader,* ed. Jean Yu-Wen

Shen Wu and Min Song, 95–110. New Brunswick, N.J.: Rutgers University Press, 2000.

Thompson's Laws of New York, pt. 2. New York: Edward Thompson, 1939.

Todd, Jesse T., Jr. "Battling Satan in the City: Charles Henry Parkhurst and Municipal Redemption in Gilded Age New York." *American Presbyterians* 71 (Winter 1993): 243–252.

Tolino, John V. "Solving the Italian Problem." *Ecclesiastical Review* (1938): 246–256.

Tomasi, Silvano M. *Piety and Power: The Role of the Italian Parishes in the New York Metropolitan Area, 1880–1930*. New York: Center for Migration Studies, 1975.

———. "Scalabrinians and the Pastoral Care of Immigrants in the United States, 1887–1967." *U.S. Catholic Historian* 6 (1987): 253–264.

Tricarico, Donald. "Influence of the Irish on Italian Communal Adaptation in Greenwich Village." *Journal of Ethnic Studies* 13 (Fall 1985): 127–137.

Trolander, Judith. *Professionalism and Social Change: From the Settlement House Movement to Neighborhood Centers, 1886 to the Present*. New York: Columbia University Press, 1987.

Tsai, Shih-Shan Henry. *The Chinese Experience in America*. Bloomington: Indiana University Press, 1986.

Tuchman, Gaye, and Harry Gene Levine. "New York Jews and Chinese Food: The Social Construction of an Ethnic Pattern." In *The Taste of American Place: A Reader on Regional and Ethnic Foods*, ed. Barbara G. Shortridge and James R. Shortridge, 163–184. New York: Rowman and Littlefield, 1998.

Van Every, Edward. *Sins of New York as "Exposed" by the Police Gazette*. New York: Blom, 1972.

Varacalli, Joseph A., Salvatore Primeggia, Salvatore J. la Gumina, and Donald J. E'Elia, eds. *Models and Images of Catholicism in Italian Americana: Academy and Society*. New York: Forum Italicum, 2002.

Vecoli, Rudolph J. "An Inter-Ethnic Perspective on American Immigration History." *Mid-America* 75 (April–July 1993): 223–235.

Walker, Juliet E. K. *The History of Black Business in America: Capitalism, Race, Entrepreneurship*, vol. 1. Chapel Hill: University of North Carolina Press, 2009.

Walsh, James Joseph. *History of Medicine in New York: Three Centuries of Medical Progress*, vol. 3. New York: National Americana Society, 1919.

Wang, Xinyang. *Surviving the City: The Chinese Immigrant Experience in New York City, 1890–1970*. New York: Rowman and Littlefield, 2001.

Ward, David. *Poverty, Ethnicity, and the American City, 1840–1925: Changing Conceptions of the Slum and the Ghetto*. Cambridge: Cambridge University Press, 1989.

Watson, James L. "The Structure of Chinese Funerary Rites." In *Death Ritual in Late Imperial and Modern China*, ed. James L. Watson and Evelyn S. Rawski, 3–19. Berkeley: University of California Press, 1988.

Weld, Ralph Foster. *Brooklyn Is America*. New York: Columbia University Press, 1950.

Welland, Sasha Su-Ling. *A Thousand Miles of Dreams: The Journeys of Two Chinese Sisters*. New York: Rowman and Littlefield, 2006.

Werblowsky, R. J., and Geoffrey Wisoder, eds. *Oxford Dictionary of the Jewish Religion*. New York: Oxford University Press, 1997.

Whitaker, Jan. *Service and Style: How the American Department Store Fashioned the Middle Class*. New York: St. Martin's Press, 2006.

Wickers, David, and Charlotte Atkins. *Essential New York*. Lincolnwood, Ill.: Passport Books, 1994.

Wilder, Craig Steven. *A Covenant with Color: Race and Social Power in Brooklyn*. New York: Columbia University Press, 2000.

Willensky, Elliot. *When Brooklyn Was the World, 1920–1957*. New York: Harmony Books, 1986.

Williams, Jesse Lynch. *New York Sketches*. New York: C. Scribner's Sons, 1902.

Wilson, Andrew R., ed. *The Chinese in the Caribbean*. Princeton, N.J.: Markus Wiener, 2004.

Wilson, Elizabeth. *Fifty Years of Association Work among Young Women, 1866–1916* (1916), repr. ed. New York: Garland, 1987.

Winch, Julie R. *A Gentleman of Color: The Life of James Forten*. New York: Oxford University Press, 2002.

———. "'A Person of Good Character and Considerable Property': James Forten and the Issue of Race in Philadelphia's Antebellum Business Community." *Business History Review* 75 (Summer 2001): 261–196.

Wong, Bernard. *Chinatown: Economic Adaptation and Ethnic Identity of the Chinese*. New York: Holt, Hart, and Winston, 1982.

———. *A Chinese American Community: Ethnicity and Survival Strategies*. Singapore: Chopman Enterprises, 1979.

Wong Chin Foo. "The Chinese in New York." *Cosmopolitan* 5 (1888): 297–311.

Wong, K. Scott. "Chinatown: Conflicting Images, Contested Terrain." *MELUS* 20 (Spring 1995): 3–14.

Wong, K. Scott, and Sucheng Chan, eds. *Claiming America: Constructing Chinese Amerian Identities during the Exclusion Era*. Philadelphia: Temple University Press, 1998.

Woods, Robert A., and Albert J. Kennedy, eds. *Handbook of Settlements*. New York: Charities Publication Committee, 1911.

Yamin, Rebecca. "Lurid Tales and Homely Stories of New York City's Notorious Five Points." *Historical Archaeology* 32 (1998): 74–85.

———. "New York's Mythic Slum." *Archeology* 50 (March–April 1997): 44–53.

Yee, Shirley J. *Black Women Abolitionists: A Study in Activism, 1828–1860*. Knoxville: University of Tennessee Press, 1992.

Yin, Lee Tom. *The Chinese in Jamaica*, 2nd ed. Kingston, Jamaica: Chung Sun News, 1963.

Yoshihara, Mari. *Embracing the East: White Women and American Orientalism*. New York: Oxford University Press, 2003.

Yu, Henry. *Thinking Orientals: Migration, Contact, and Exoticism in Modern America*. New York: Oxford University Press, 2001.

Yu, Renqiu. *To Save China, to Save Ourselves: The Chinese Hand Laundry Alliance of New York*. Philadelphia: Temple University Press, 1992.

Yung, Judy. *Chinese Women of America: A Pictorial History*. Seattle: University of Washington Press, 1986.

———. *Unbound Feet: A Social History of Chinese Women in San Francisco*. Berkeley: University of California Press, 1995.

Zhou, Min. *Chinatown: The Socioeconomic Potential of an Urban Enclave*. Philadelphia: Temple University Press, 1992.

Index

Page numbers followed by the letter f refer to figures.

Abie's Irish Rose (Anne Nichols), 9–10, 50
Adler, Felix, 49, 112, 142; and the Ethical
    Cultural Movement, 187n58
African Americans and migration from the
    South: migration within New York City,
    45, 186n47; and segregation, 46
African Burial Ground, 86, 88
Anti-prostitution movement (nineteenth
    century), 108–109; and missionaries,
    108; and white slavery, 121–127
Assimilation, 49; and the melting pot
    theory, 152–153; and religion, 170; in
    settlement houses and missions, 138
Autobiography of an Ex-Coloured Man
    (James Weldon Johnson), 63

Baciagalupo, Charles, 95, 97, 98, 101
Baciagalupo, Eugene, 98, 199n80
Baldwin, Ruth (née Bowles), and Com-
    mittee of Fourteen, 130–131, 132,
    205n66
Baldwin, William H., Jr., 112, 117 (*see also*
    Committee of Fifteen); and Tuskegee
    Institute, 130
Banta, Mary E., 212n93; and anti-prostitu-
    tion, 162–163; childhood and education
    of, 162; criticisms of, 148, 164; and

Morningstar Baptist Mission; and True
    Light Mission, 148
Beck, Louis J., 83, 84, 90, 189n13
Bettelheim, Rebekah, 149
Betts, Lillian W., 6
Bird, Sara J.: and the Gospel Settlement,
    109, 147; and undercover activities, 135
Boardman, Annette, 159
Boardman, Clemence, 159, 160, 161
Bowles, Ruth, 130–131, 132, 205n66
Brewster, Mary, 80, 165
Brooklyn Bridge as symbol of connection
    and separation, 46, 47
Brugger, Florence, 164
Buonocore, Frank, 66

Cable Act (1922), 40
Cahan, Abraham, 11–12, 98
Carson, Sarah Libby, 140, 141, 142–143,
    144
Chinatown and Bowery Rescue Settlement
    for Girls, 158, 159–161
Chinese Benevolent Society (CBS), 43–44,
    164
Chinese Consolidated Benevolent
    Association (CCBA), 46, 54, 60, 73,
    189n13; and funerals, 90–91

Chinese Exclusion Act (1882), 40; case files, 55, 56, 71; and citizenship, 46; and labor classifications, 55, 189n13; repeal of (1943), 46, 100

Christodora House, 125f; and assimilationist vision, 140, 145, 146; civic values of, 155–156; criticisms of, 147–148; establishment of, 140–142; evangelical character of, 139, 140, 143–144, 146, 177; and race/ethnic and class relations, 146–147, 153; and radical politics, 154, 155–156

Clara de Hirsch Home for Working Girls, 127–128

Clark, Helen F., 161; and Morning Star Baptist Mission, 162, 163

Cohen, Rose (née Gollup), 12, 22, 165–166

Committee of Fifteen, 75; and coalition building, 113, 115; founding of, 106; leadership of, 112; and neighborhood relations, 116, 119; and The Social Evil, 128

Committee of Fourteen, 106; leadership of, 130–131; methods of, 129–131, 134; objectives of, 128–129; and The Social Evil in New York City: A Study of Law Enforcement (1910), 133

Coppola, Dominick, 66–67, 191n44

Coppola, Louis, 66

Crenshaw, Kimberlé, on intersectionality, 15

Curry, Rev. James B., 147–148; on evangelicalism, 148; on female missionaries, 148

Davenport, Charles B., on eugenics, 106

The Doctor and the Devil (Charles W. Gardner), 109

Eating establishments, 61: Chinese eating establishments, representations of, 62–64; as interracial and interethnic spaces, 64–65

Edson, Dr. Cyrus, 81, 194n10

European Jews: migration of within New York City, 46–47; representations of, 81

Eutemey, Bert V., 29, 42, 43, 44–45, 47, 100

Eutemey, Enos, 42, 43, 44, 45–46; and undertaking business, 46

Eutemey, Louise (née Holmes), 29, 42, 44–45

Foster, George G. (New York by Gas-Light), 107

Funerals: Chinese funerals, descriptions of, 88–90, 197n47; Irish, 96; Jewish, 98–100

Gardener, Charles W., 109–111; The Doctor and the Devil, 109

Gender: and employment patterns, 55, 58; and "Ghetto Girls," 9; and new womanhood, 175

Gollup, Rose, 12, 22, 165–166

Grant, Madison; on immigration, 24, 152; on interethnic mixing, 6; Passing of the Great Race, 6

Gross, Celia (née Rich), 48

Gross, Ethel. See Hopkins, Ethel (née Gross)

Hart, Margaret, 37, 39–40, 47–48, 123f, 189n19

Hawthorne, Nathaniel ("My Kinsman, Major Molineaux"), 107

The History of Prostitution (William W. Sanger), 108

Holmes, Louise, 29, 42, 44–45

Hopkins, Ethel (née Gross): and assimilation, 152–154, 175–176; at Christodora House, 48, 138–140, 149–150, 170; courtship and marriage of, 49, 52, 138; divorce of, 52; and Equal Franchise Society, 150; family and childhood, 48; on intermarriage, 50, 51–52; married life of, 49, 152; and new womanhood, 151; and Women's Political Union, 151

Hopkins, Harry: and career in FDR administration, 51; education and social work career of, 49; on marriage to Ethel Gross, 50, 51, 52; and Midwestern roots, 48–49

Hurley, Johanna, 2–3

Immigration: of Chinese, 33, 37; of European Jews, 48; of Irish, 37; of

Italians, 167; of Jamaicans, 42–43; of Japanese, 34
Intermarriage, 52; between Chinese and Irish, 37; in Jamaica, 43; between Jews and non-Jews, 49–51

Jackson, Anna W., and the Committee of Fifteen, 115
Jacobi, Abraham, 81
Jacobi, Mary (née Putnam), 81
Jacobson, Matthew Fry, on whiteness, 22
Jamaica, Chinese in, 42–44
James, Arthur Curtiss, and Christodora House, 144
James, Harriet: and Christodora House, 144; and civic education, 155, 156
Janney, O. Edward, and American Purity Alliance, 115
Jerome, William Travers, 104, 112
Jewett, Helen, murder of, 107
John Randles Inc., 65–66
Johnson, James Weldon (*Autobiography of an Ex-Coloured Man*), 63
Jones, Alice, 31

Kellor, Frances A., and the Committee of Fourteen, 130, 131–134
Kennedy, William H., 2, 77, 88–89, 91, 179n7, 197n54
Kingsbury, Mary, 130, 131
Kohut, Rebekah (née Bettelheim), and the National Council of Jewish Women, 149

Lathbury, Mary Ann "Artemesia," 161–162, 211n9
Laundries, Chinese, 32, 71–73; Chinese Hand Laundry Alliance, 73
Lexow Committee, 111, 112
Lippman, Walter, on the anti-vice movement, 136
Loeb, Therese, 149, 209n52
Lowell, Carlotta Russell, 117
Lucas, Albert, and evangelicalism, 148

MacColl, Christina I., 139, 140; and activism, 142; background of, 142–143, 207n18; and ecumenicalism, 144–145; and Ethel Gross, 51, 139, 150; and

evangelicalism, 144; and religious conversion, 146, 147; and views of immigrant groups, 146, 154
Matthews, Victoria Earle, 132
Mazet Committee, 111
McKeown, Adam, on Chinese funeral customs, 96
Meyer, Harry, 68, 191n50
Missions and settlement houses: and Chinese immigrants, 158–159; criticisms of, 156, 176; and Jews, 158; as redemptive spaces, 105, 141; and the Second Great Awakening, 157; and Social Gospel, 157–158; and women, 156–157
Molinelli, Joseph, 66–67
Morgan, George W., 112, 115, 117, 119, 120, 122, 127–128
Moskowitz, Max, 118–119
Moss, Frank, 90, 112, 117
Mott Street Poker Club (Alfred T. Trumble), 38–39
Moy, Barbara K., 126f
Moy, Jin Fuey, 82, 158, 159
Moy, Lung Som, 3, 14, 82, 162–163, 176, 194n9
Mumford, Kevin, on interzones, 14
"My Kinsman, Major Molineaux" (Nathaniel Hawthorne), 107

Nathan, Maud, and the Equal Franchise Society, 150
Naughton, James, 91–93, 94–97, 198n56
New York by Gas-Light (George G. Foster), 107
Nichols, Anne (*Abie's Irish Rose*), 9–10, 50
Norr, William (*Stories of Chinatown*), 9–10, 38–39, 122

Page Act (1875), 55, 59, 129, 180n17
Park, Robert E., 7
Parkhurst, Charles H.: and Christodora House, 144; and the City Vigilance League, 109, 136; early life of, 109; vigilante activities of, 109, 110–111, 113
Pascoe, Peggy, on race as indeterminate, 23, 162
Passing of the Great Race (Madison Grant), 6

Proselytizing, conflicts over, 146, 147–149, 166. *See also* Christodora House
Putnam, George Haven, 130
Putnam, Mary, 81

Quan Yick Nam, 120, 204n49

Race: and census inconsistencies, 21, 44; and citizenship and paid labor patterns, 46, 55–60, 82, 93–94; and classification, 22–23; and whiteness, 22–23, 145, 167
Race and ethnic relations: among Catholics, 167–169; racial and ethnic conflicts, 1, 12–13, 37, 73
Randles, Adelaide, 66
Randles, George, 41, 66
Randles, John, 65–66
Randles, Julia, 66
Religious revivalism: and foreign missions, 156–157; and the Second Great Awakening, 157
Restaurants. *See* Eating establishments
Rhinelander, Alice (née Jones), 31
Rhinelander, Leonard (Kip), 31
Rich, Celia, 48
Riis, Jacob A., 61; on Chinese men and white women, 38

Salome of the Tenements (Anzia Yezierska), 152
Saloons as sites of race and ethnic relations, 74–75
Sanger, William W. (*The History of Prostitution*), 108
Satosky, Solomon, 68, 83
Schieffelin, William Jay, and the Committee of Fifteen, 130
Schiff, Jacob H., 149, 209n52; and experiences with anti-Semitism, 149–150
Schiff, Therese (née Loeb), 149, 209n52
Schlansky, Harry Philip, 81–82, 194n13
Scudder, Vida, 144
Seligman, Edwin Robert Anderson, 127
Seligman, Isaac, 130
Sigel, Elsie, murder of, 11, 39, 159
Silverman, Isaac, 104, 118–119
Simkhovitch, Mary (née Kingsbury), and the Committee of Fourteen, 130, 131

Siu, Paul, on isolation and the Chinese as sojourners, 7
Slade, Francis Louis, and the Committee of Fourteen, 130
Slumming as an investigative method, 109, 129, 136
Smith, Charles Edgar, 31
The Social Evil (1902), 128
The Social Evil in New York City: A Study of Law Enforcement (1910), 133
Social Gospel, 49; and missionary work, 160, 175; and urban Progressivism, 143–144
Society for the Prevention of Crime (SPC), 109–110
Sommerfeld, Rose, 127–128
SPC, 109–110
Steele, William C., Jr., 104; report by, 117–118
Stelzle, Charles, 144, 155
Stories of Chinatown (William Norr), 9–10, 38, 122
Strong, Josiah, 144

Thoms, Joseph C., 82, 163
Trumble, Alfred T. (*Mott Street Poker Club*), 38–39

Undertaking: among blacks, 86–88; exclusionary structure of, 93; expansion of undertaking tasks, 92–93, 198n59; as male occupation, 198n63; origins of, 86, 92

Veiller, Lawrence, 102, 106, 130, 205n63
Violence, intra-ethnic, 95

Wah Wing Sang Funeral Corporation, 123f
Wald, Lillian D., 79; and the Committee of Fifteen, 120–121, 127; and the Nurses' Settlement, 80, 165; on settlement work, 141
Washington, Booker T., 130
Wilson, Arthur E., 104, 117, 119, 120
Wirth, Louis, 7
Wong Aloy, 119, 120, 135
Wong Chin Foo, 90
Wong, James, 47, 126f

Wong Jung Que, 17, 37, 38, 41–42, 47, 48, 71, 123f

Wong, Margaret (née Hart), 17, 37, 39–40, 41–42, 47–48, 71, 123f, 189n19

Yezierska, Anzia, 12, 151, 152; *Salome of the Tenements*, 152

Yu, Henry, on interracial marriage and difference, 30

Zangwill, Israel, and the melting pot theory, 12, 152, 180n16

Ziegler, Calvin, 31

Ziegler, Sarah Mildred, 31

Shirley J. Yee teaches in the Department of Gender, Women, and Sexuality Studies at the University of Washington. She is the author of *Black Women Abolitionists: A Study in Activism, 1828–1860.*